Comparative Religion FOR DUMMIES®

by William P. Lazarus and Mark Sullivan

WILEY

Wiley Publishing, Inc.

Comparative Religion For Dummies®

Published by
Wiley Publishing, Inc.
111 River St.
Hoboken, NJ 07030-5774
www.wiley.com

About the Authors

A native of Maine who grew up in northeast Ohio, **William Paul Lazarus** began studying religious history as a child and has never stopped. By age 13, he was teaching Sunday school. After moving to Florida in 1986, he branched out by teaching at various institutions, including Daytona Beach Community College and Stetson University. A professional writer and high school English teacher, he regularly speaks at churches and synagogues around Florida, and had a successful radio show on 1340-AM, WROD, in Daytona Beach. This is his ninth book on various aspects of religious history. He and his wife live in Daytona Beach, Florida.

Mark Sullivan was born in Greenwich Village, Manhattan, and grew up in a traveling, academic family, something like a fantastic traveling circus. He returned to NYC for college, at Columbia University, where he studied Comparative Literature and European Languages. He later attended the Juilliard School of Music for studies in composition.

He has worked in book publishing, in various roles, and as an author, for the past 17 years. His interests include languages, music, swimming, and travel. He lives in Manhattan with his wife, Mariko.

Dedication

Bill's dedication:

This book is dedicated to all the people who encouraged me both professionally and academically from the first time I decided to write and to learn about religious history: my wife, Kathleen; daughter, Maia; my parents; my three brothers, all of whom write and are published, although no one knows where the writing gene came from; and friends like Cynthia Schuster-Eakin, Jon Swebilius, Michael Silverstein, Tom Nimen, and Susan Cerbone.

Mark's dedication:

To my mother, Maureen, and my father, Art, whose love of all things interesting opened my mind from the very beginning of my life. And to my wife, Mariko.

Authors' Acknowledgments

Bill's acknowledgments:

This book could not have been written without the witting efforts of editors and colleagues, and the unwitting efforts of educators like Arthur Tirson, Herbert Mermelstein, and Rabbi Dov Pikelny. They devoted so much effort to helping a young boy learn about faith, even when they realized the knowledge would eventually carry him far away from their beliefs. I couldn't be more grateful for their unselfish — and given my attention span, often heroic — work. I also want to thank Mark Sullivan, who suggested this book and has been unflinchingly encouraging in our collaboration.

Mark's acknowledgments:

Many thanks, first, to Amine Bouchentouf for leading the way at Wiley. His hard work and desire for excellence in his own writing were exemplary.

My appreciation and thanks, also, to Tim Gallan and Vicki Adang for their editorial skills that made this a better book, and to Lindsay Lefevere for getting it all started.

And to my teachers — my parents, Ed Tolk, Edward Said, Michel Riffaterre, Frank Camper, and others — thank you so much for helping me become a better thinker and more appreciative of art and ideas.

To Bill Lazarus, the most industrious writer I know — it was a real pleasure working on this book with you and learning from your prodigious knowledge of these religions.

Finally, to my beloved wife, Mariko, thanks for putting up with "the process" one more time!

Publisher's Acknowledgments

We're proud of this book; please send us your comments through our Dummies online registration form located at www.dummies.com/register/.

Some of the people who helped bring this book to market include the following:

Acquisitions, Editorial, and Media Development

Senior Project Editor: Tim Gallan

Acquisitions Editor: Lindsay Lefevere

Senior Copy Editor: Victoria M. Adang

Editorial Program Coordinator: Erin Calligan Mooney

Technical Editor: Jamsheed K. Choksy

Editorial Manager: Michelle Hacker

Editorial Assistants: David Lutton, Joe Niesen,

Art Coordinator: Alicia B. South

Cover Photo: © Daniela Richardson/ Wiley Publishing, Inc. 2008

Cartoons: Rich Tennant (www.the5thwave.com)

Composition Services

Project Coordinator: Katie Key

Layout and Graphics: Reuben W. Davis, Alissa D. Ellet, Stephanie D. Jumper, Christine Williams, Ronald Terry

Proofreader: Bonnie Mikkelson

Indexer: Potomac Indexing, LLC

Publishing and Editorial for Consumer Dummies

    Diane Graves Steele, Vice President and Publisher, Consumer Dummies

    Joyce Pepple, Acquisitions Director, Consumer Dummies

    Kristin A. Cocks, Product Development Director, Consumer Dummies

    Michael Spring, Vice President and Publisher, Travel

    Kelly Regan, Editorial Director, Travel

Publishing for Technology Dummies

    Andy Cummings, Vice President and Publisher, Dummies Technology/General User

Composition Services

    Gerry Fahey, Vice President of Production Services

    Debbie Stailey, Director of Composition Services

Contents at a Glance

Table of Contents

Chapter 7: The Birth of Islam: The Prophet Submits to Allah 109

Chapter 8: Islam: Submission of the Faithful 125

Introduction

*H*igh school students in Ohio — and maybe elsewhere as well — used to take a course that introduced them to many of the world's religions. In classes filled with children of many beliefs, teachers would talk about how a particular faith developed and how it spread.

Today, when it seems that the faithful in one religion can't resist taking pot-shots at believers in another religion, people may have forgotten how life was in past eras. People of different faiths used to live and work side by side with little concern. At one time, Jews served as advisors and heads of state in Muslim countries. Christians and Jews labored together to build the culture in Catholic Spain. Christians lived in harmony with Muslims in the Middle East.

Less than 1,000 years ago, Catholic Roger II of Sicily relied on Arab scholars and financiers to run his widespread Mediterranean kingdom.

At one time, Jewish and Christian icons were included with the *Ka'baa,* the holiest religious monument in Islam, located in *Mecca,* the holiest city in Islam. Even today, Jerusalem is home to the Dome of the Rock, a sacred Islamic mosque, and the *Wailing Wall,* the last surviving piece of the great Jewish Temple that once existed there.

Visitors to Jerusalem can see religious Jews wrapped in prayer shawls, trudging along ancient streets alongside Muslims and Christians. Overhead, the cry of the Islamic *muezzin,* calling the faithful to prayer, rings out along with the tolling bells of Christian churches. The flag of Israel flutters in the breeze with the Star of David in its center.

Such situations are too rare. Members of the three religions seem to fight more than they pray together. Over time, the three great religions have become separated by seemingly unbridgeable chasms. Actually, they are very much alike.

✔ Judaism, Christianity, and Islam share a common heritage. They each tie their history to a single event and a single person, Abraham, who lived maybe 4,000 years ago.

✔ The three religions all worship the same God and shun the pagan concepts of multiple deities. In Judaism, his name is *Yahweh.* In Islam, the name is *Allah,* which means God. Christians simply call him God.

✔ They have similar holidays. Easter, for example, the holiest day in the Christian calendar, is tied directly to Passover, one of the most significant holidays in Judaism.

✔ Each religion believes Jerusalem is a sacred city.

There are many more links among the three faiths — they share many likenesses and have fewer differences.

But in spite of the similarities between these primary Western faiths, fissures between them continue today. These disputes can be seen in the Roman Catholic pope's apologies for comments he made about Islam, as well as Jewish and Arab fighting over Israel, American battles in Iraq, Iranian insistence that the American president is the "devil," and more acrimonious and violent behavior.

Maybe it's time to review the histories of these religions and use this understanding as a way to create a peaceful path into the future.

About This Book

This book examines and compares the three great religions that believe in the same God. They are among the oldest and most widespread religions on earth. Jews, Christians, and Muslims can be found on almost every continent and in every country.

Each chapter in *Comparative Religion For Dummies* will bring you closer to understanding what each faith's followers believe, how their beliefs compare with their counterparts, and how each religion reached this point in time.

"Dummies" is actually an affectionate term. This is a book for people who don't know about these three great faiths, but want to find out more. All three of these religions encourage education. They can claim most of the world's greatest scholars — some who devoted their lives to helping others understand the world. This book continues that honorable process.

All the topics in these pages, of course, have been extensively researched by many people over the centuries. You can find books that devote thousands of pages to tiny aspects of each religion, as well as whole libraries focused on the founders of each faith. This book gives you an overview, with each chapter standing on its own. You can pick and choose what you want to know. Then when you need additional information, you'll know where to go to find what you're looking for.

Foolish Assumptions

You don't have to be a religious scholar to understand or appreciate this book. We don't assume that you have a background in Judaism, Christianity, or Islam. But if you are familiar with or believe in one of these religions, we think you'll find the comparisons presented in this book to be enlightening. The three religions are more similar than most people realize, and we hope that developing an understanding of the similarities and differences can only improve the current state of affairs in our world.

Conventions Used in This Book

Historians today are moving toward connoting time by using CE (of the common era) and BCE (before the common era.) The old way — BC, meaning "before Christ," and AD, standing for "the year of our Lord" in Latin — was seen as too religious. With so many scholars from so many different faiths working together, no one wanted to offend anyone else's beliefs.

We don't either. However, BC and AD are such a part of our lives and the lives of our readers, we decided to stick to them. We don't want to offend anyone. We're just trying to reduce chances of misunderstanding. We are sure our readers will agree.

A note about translations: Nothing is harder than taking an ancient text and trying to convert it into modern English. It's worse than wrestling pudding. At least, if you do that, everyone agrees that you're talking about pudding. With the ancient documents, particularly those seen as holy, some people even object to the concept of translating.

In Chapter 9, we try to explain why it's so hard to translate the Bible and the Koran, the two principal sacred documents of the three faiths. Nevertheless, they are often the only texts that deal with the oldest portions of religious history, and we relied on the best translations we could find. Other writers may translate the words in a different way, but the gist is the same.

Finally, we use the following conventions to help you understand new words and concepts:

- ✔ We *italicize* all new words and terms that are defined.
- ✔ We **boldface** keywords or the main parts of bulleted lists.
- ✔ We use `monofont` for Web addresses.
- ✔ We've put quick little stories or fun trivia facts in shaded boxes called sidebars. The stuff in these sidebars is interesting, but you don't have to read them to gain an understanding of the topic at hand.

How This Book Is Organized

The book is divided into six parts.

Part I: History Is a Happening Thing

This section introduces the origin of religion and explains the rise of a belief in one God. That's when the curtain opens on Abraham, a nomadic tribesman who is credited with fathering the three faiths. Little is known about him, but historians have uncovered lots of information about his time and beliefs.

The section also explains how all three religions link their history back to Abraham.

Part II: The Development of Judaism, Christianity, and Islam

This part explains how three different religions were nurtured on Abraham's vision. Each developed in a separate environment, endured hardships and setbacks, and then became firmly entrenched in the mind of man.

Chapters 3 and 4 concentrate on Judaism, the oldest of the three religions. The next two chapters, 5 and 6, look at Christianity, which developed directly from Judaism. The third section, Chapters 7 and 8, discuss Islam, which is younger and was born about 600 years after Jesus lived.

You're introduced to beliefs, customs, traditions, and rituals that characterize each faith. In many cases, you see how one belief influenced another or was the source for some idea.

Part III: Shared Aspects of the

In this section, you get the scoop on how members of th
have developed similar approaches to worship and to e:
You discover their sacred texts that serve as a bedrock t
you tour their holy cities.

Part IV: Shared Ideas Among the Faiths

This part focuses on similar religious ideas and concepts that help link the
three religions. They all look to a messenger from God (called a *messiah*),
foresee the day when the world ceases, provide ways to forgive sin, and
propose ideas of what comes after death.

Part V: The Part of Tens

Like all *For Dummies* books, the last few chapters are top-ten lists. This part
lists the main misconceptions about the three religions, our favorite religious
films, and the top ways that the religions have influenced the world.

Part VI: Appendixes

We conclude the book with two appendixes. The first provides a timeline so
you can see when events happened. The second attempts to trace Abraham's
family tree back to Adam, the first man, and ahead to Jesus and Muhammad.

Icons Used in This Book

Information in the book has been highlighted to help you pinpoint exactly
what you need to know.

This icon denotes an important point to keep in mind as you read on. It will
help you understand what follows.

This icon indicates information that reflects some disagreement among
scholars or even within a particular faith.

Where to Go from Here

You don't have to read this book from cover to cover. The chapters can stand alone, so check out the Table of Contents and read whatever topic interests you.

Finally, please let us know what you think about this book. It took a long time to write and produce this book, so we'd love to hear your thoughts. You can write us through the publisher at www.dummies.com. You are also welcome to write the authors at wplazarus@aol.com. We'll try to respond to all legitimate comments.

Part I
History Is a Happening Thing

In this part . . .

Say hello to Abraham, a simple shepherd who moved away from his own country and faith possibly 4,000 years ago. Abraham's quiet announcement of a belief in a single God rocked his own society and still reverberates through the centuries. His revelation inspired three great religions — Judaism, Christianity, and Islam — that now dominate the world.

Those religions developed in the heat and turmoil of the Middle East. Each one centered on the idea of one God, and then diverged in ways of worship. Abraham's genealogy includes two distinct branches that both link and divide Judaism, Christianity, and Islam.

Chapter 1

One God, Three Faiths

In This Chapter

▶ Revealing how religions worked prior to Abraham

▶ Uncovering the origins of monotheism

▶ Discovering how one God led to three religions

In New York City alone, there are 6,500 or so Christian churches, according to the Internet. The Boston area is home to around 6,000 Christian churches. In fact, every American community features many different churches serving Christian residents of various denominations.

When you include buildings for Jews, Unitarian Universalists, Muslims, and other worshippers, our country seems awash in religious structures.

There are so many sects, so many denominations, so many beliefs, that the number of religions seems to multiply daily.

Yet, all of them have an origin. Everybody's religion, whatever anyone believes, started somewhere. In this chapter, we explore some of these starting points and show how they've affected the three major monotheistic religions of today: Judaism, Christianity, and Islam.

Holy Toledo! How Many Gods Are There?

Originally, ancient people believed in magic. Their holy men, called *shamans,* practiced various rituals and had magical sayings that were supposed to heal illnesses, stop storms, grow crops, or change the future.

The people soon realized that these actions and spells didn't work, so they decided that great, distant beings, called *gods,* watched over all aspects of life and controlled everything. These deities could only be reached through rituals and prayer. The ancient people developed thousands of gods, each of whom was responsible for some aspect of human life.

Religion was born. Religion began as a way for people to understand lightning, thunder, good or bad fortune, birth, death, and all the other events in their lives.

Religion quickly became an integral part of life. For example, Egyptians, who originated one of the earliest civilizations, began to create rituals to "guarantee" that the Nile River flooded on time every year. When the Nile flooded, it brought rich, fertilizing soil to their farmland. Without it, they would starve. The Egyptians developed calendars based on the stars so they would know exactly when their gods would send the floods.

Not that far away from Egypt, Babylonians built large pyramid-like structures to their gods and invented a style of writing to record the amount of grain and beer that worshippers donated to their temples.

Every early religion worshipped many deities. Scientists call that belief *polytheism,* which means "many gods." Still, some people began to believe that there was only one God who controlled everything.

The religions that believe in one God practice *monotheism* — the opposite of polytheism — which comes from the Greek for "one god."

Monotheism Develops

Monotheists have never been the majority of humans. Even today, roughly half of all humans accept the idea that there is only one God. But the followers of one God belong to two of the world's largest religions, Christianity and Islam. They developed their faith by building on ideas generated by an older religion, Judaism. Table 1-1 shows how the number of believers in each monotheistic faith compares to the others.

Table 1-1	Largest Monotheistic Faiths
Religion	*Members*
Christianity	2.1 billion
Islam	1.3 billion
Judaism	14 million
Baha'i	7 million
Unitarian Universalist	800,000

Ancient gods get a new life

Although few people today worship the ancient gods, their names live on in our everyday lives. Here are a few examples:

- Wednesday is named for Wodin, the chief god of the Norwegians.

- Thursday is named for Thor, another Norse god. He carried a big hammer, and when he threw it, it made a loud noise humans called thunder.

- Saturday is named for Saturn, a Roman god of agriculture.

- March is named for Mars, the Roman god of war.

- June is named for Juno, the chief Roman goddess.

There are many more: All the planets are named for Roman gods. Neptune, covered by a blue methane haze, got its name, for example, because Neptune was the Roman god of the deep blue sea.

Many companies today have taken symbols from ancient religions and use them in their logos. For example, the winged feet featured in the Goodyear Tire & Rubber Co. logo comes from the shoes worn by Mercury, the swift messenger of the Roman gods.

Egypt tries the one-god concept

Historians think the first people to be monotheists were the Egyptians, although their belief didn't last long. Egyptians developed several important gods, including one named Ptah. He was once the chief deity of a city, but eventually became the main god of the country. The other gods were seen as manifestations of Ptah. All people had to do was pray to Ptah, regardless of other gods.

Later, after the god Amon had replaced Ptah in the Egyptian belief system, an Egyptian leader (called *pharaoh*) named Amonhotep IV became tired of having his rule interfered with by priests. So, he changed his name to Ikhnaton around 1300 BC and declared that the god Aton was the only god.

Ikhnaton is the first person known in history to have declared that his god was the only god. In many ways, he had no choice.

- If he suffered a defeat in a war, or if there was a natural disaster, people in his country would say that another god was stronger than Aton. If there were no other gods, Ikhnaton wouldn't face that problem.

- If something did go wrong, Aton could be called on to reverse the situation. If there were other gods, and the problem disappeared, Ikhnaton would have faced competition from the priests of the rival god. Having only one god prevented that.

- ✔ Egyptians thought that Ikhnaton was the living embodiment of god. It was far easier for him to perform the proper rituals and observe holidays for one deity than for a multitude.

- ✔ Ikhnaton destroyed the power of the priests of Amon, while creating a priesthood of Aton that was totally beholden to him.

- ✔ Human nature tends to narrow down the list of gods anyway. Even the Romans, who had multiple gods, often combined them, paring down the total.

Ikhnaton's religion was the first-known true monotheism and occurred about 1,300 years before Jesus. The belief in Aton was recorded in pictures on temple walls and in letters. Ikhnaton's reign today is best known for the magnificent bust of his beautiful wife, Nefertiti, which is considered the finest statue to survive from ancient Egypt.

Ikhnaton ruled for a handful of years, and his religion died with him. Only when ancient letters from his reign were dug up in the 1900s did we know how much confusion he caused.

Sigmund Freud, who developed psychology in the late 1800s, suggested that the priests of Ikhnaton may have taken their dying faith to the slaves, helping generate Judaism. Later scholars don't think that happened. For starters, the Jews worshipped a God named Yahweh, not Aton.

Yahweh steps down from the mount

One group of people who lived in the middle of all these religious ideas was called *Semites*. Semites are credited with developing modern monotheism.

Most non-Egyptian residents of the ancient Near East were Semites. Several times, they invaded Egypt and conquered the land. At other times, they built great empires. The Babylonians, the Assyrians, and the Israelites were all Semites.

The first famous Semite who promoted monotheism was a man we know as Abram, who would later have his name changed to Abraham. He would identify his God as Yahweh.

Yahweh means "I am that I am" or "I was what I was." Yahweh was originally viewed as a mountain deity who appeared in thunder and lighting. His "still, small voice" was heard by those who believed in him and who listened to him (1 Kings: 19:2).

Yahweh's commands and directions were eventually written down in books that were collected in what we call the Bible.

When did Abraham live?

One famous historian, American archaeologist William Albright, suggested Abraham was born about 4,000 years ago. Albright based that dating on contracts that Abram signed with the Hittites and the Philistines, people who lived in neighboring countries. Those contracts are mentioned in the Bible.

Today, historians believe the biblical contracts resemble contracts from around 900 BC rather than the older ones Albright cited.

Unfortunately, the Philistines and Hittites aren't around to ask. The Philistines probably showed up in Israel about 3,200 years ago. The Hittites, who lived in what is now Turkey, were really important 3,400 years ago. Both disappeared from history before the first books of the Bible were written down around the sixth century BC.

Today, historians have no idea when Abraham lived, but 4,000 years ago is a convenient place to start (which is what we decided to do for the timeline in Appendix A). People then didn't have a universal calendar like we do, so dates are difficult to figure out.

Following Abraham's Lead: Judaism

The children of Abraham believed in Yahweh, but they weren't true monotheists for centuries. They had other gods. We see that fact in people's names, which contained the names of other deities. For example, an ancient Israelite prince's name included the name of the Canaanite fertility god, Baal, and so on.

Some of the names endure today: Dani*el*, Nathani*el*, and Rach*el*, among others, contain the name of the bull god of the Canaanites, *El*. Later, followers of Yahweh borrowed that name and gave it to their God. In time, Yahweh was known by many names.

Josiah and his faith: The beginnings of Judaism

Eventually, all the other gods disappeared in the Jewish land. In the seventh century BC, the followers of Yahweh lived in the small country of Judah and were threatened by armies from Babylonia. The Judean priests then claimed to have found a book that reported the history of the people and how God didn't accept other gods. The king of Judah, Josiah, was so moved that he ordered the other religious symbols stored in the temple to be destroyed.

From that time on, monotheism was the only belief of these people, whom we know today as Jews.

Their name was derived from the country, Judah, which was once the name of a mountainous region around their capital city, Jerusalem. The people living there were known as Judahites. When the Judahites became the largest tribe, their name evolved into the name of their religion, Judaism.

Josiah really felt that by worshipping one god, he and his people would be protected against the Babylonians. In those days, a people's deity was responsible for shielding his people against the wrath of other gods. If the enemy conquered, that meant the losers had a weaker god, so they gladly accepted the stronger deity as their own.

That's what happened after the ten tribes north of Judah had banded together under the name of Israel. When they were conquered by the Assyrians around 722 BC, they adopted the Assyrian gods and disappeared from history. We know them as the *Ten Lost Tribes*. They probably accepted the Assyrians gods when their deity failed to shield them.

The priests of Judah had other ideas. They said that, win or lose, Yahweh was god. The priests made several important decisions that helped guarantee that their religion would survive:

- ✔ **They said there were no other gods.** Other monotheists accepted the existence of different gods, but said their god was watching over them. *Jews simply argued there were no other gods.* In a way, they had no choice. If they accepted the existence of other gods, and their country was conquered, their people would believe the other gods were stronger. Eliminating other gods, as Ikhnaton had done in Egypt (see the earlier section, "Egypt tries the one-god concept"), erased that threat to their belief.

- ✔ **The priests banned images of God.** Previously, people always made idols to represent their deities. Jews did not. Their God was invisible and would always be with them. Ironically, perhaps because of this ban, few Jews have ever excelled in the visual arts.

- ✔ **The priests insisted that their God was not responsible for just the Jews, he was universal.** Previously, deities were assigned different countries as their "portion." With no other gods, Yahweh was responsible for everyone.

God becomes universal

The Bible contains a book, dated to the sixth century BC, that tells us when the Jews decided Yahweh was God, wherever they lived.

The prophet Jonah, in the text that bears his name, was ordered by God to go to Nineveh to preach to the people there. Nineveh was the capital of Assyria, so the people Jonah was to talk to were the members of the ten conquered Israeli tribes now living in their conqueror's land. Jonah didn't want to go, so God sent a "great fish" (today we believe it was a whale) to swallow him and deposit him on Assyrian soil. Jonah reluctantly preached to the people, and, to his amazement, his audience listened. (Check out Jonah 1:15–4:2 for the story of Jonah's ordeal.)

This is the first recorded incident where God is seen as universal; that is, not limited by any borders, nor even by the condition of his believers.

God provides protection and an identity

The idea of a universal God shielded the Jews from adopting rival religions when they were conquered. The Babylonians were the first to enslave the Jews. After Josiah was killed fighting the Egyptians, the Babylonians had little trouble taking Jerusalem in 597 BC. The Jews, like the Israelites in the north, were required to leave their homeland.

However, they carried the idea of monotheism with them. As a result, they weren't tempted to follow the Babylonian gods. When the Persians defeated the Babylonians about 60 years later, the Jews were free to return home. They were convinced that God had acted on their behalf. Monotheism was now firmly entrenched.

Jews were the only monotheists then, but they soon had company. For more on the history and practices of Judaism, see Chapters 3 and 4.

The many meanings of "Semite"

The name *Semite* is derived from a story in the Bible about a great flood. In the story, Noah, his three sons, and their families escape the rising water by building a large boat (better known in the story as an *ark*) and filling it with animals. Everyone else in world drowned, so everyone living now must be related to Noah's family.

One of his sons was called Shem. All the people supposedly related to him today are still known as "Semites."

Scholars who study language eventually used the term *Semitic* to refer to anyone who speaks Hebrew, Arabic, and related tongues. Today, Semite means Jewish to most people. This is the main usage, versus a general term for a group of people who created a civilization in and around the ancient Middle East.

Christianity: Crossing in a New Direction

Jesus and his new religion, Christianity, arrived about 600 years after the Jews became total monotheists. By then, the Jews had escaped control by the Babylonians, Persians, and Greeks, only to be overtaken by the newest world power, the Romans.

Some Jews saw the Roman conquest as a decision by God to punish the Jews for failure to follow his laws. They looked for someone to lead them back into God's good graces.

In time, they saw Jesus as that person, the *Messiah,* or anointed king. Born in Galilee, the northern part of the Roman state of Judea, Jesus was crucified on a cross around AD 30. That cross became a symbol of a new religion, which took its name from the Greek word for "messiah," *Christ.*

Paul finds a way to link beliefs

Christians argued that they had replaced the Jews as God's "chosen people." They also were sure that the world was coming to an end and that only people who followed Jesus's teaching would be taken into heaven (see Chapter 14).

That message was spread by a man we know as Paul. Like Abraham, though, we don't know what he looked like, but he left behind letters written to small congregations he founded around the Roman Empire.

Paul's letters, known by their Greek name, *epistles,* were combined with four biographies (called *Gospels*) of Jesus to create another Bible, called the *New Testament.*

Eventually, Christians combined the Jewish Bible, what they called the *Old Testament,* with their book to create a single sacred text. Jews don't recognize the New Testament because they don't believe Jesus is the Messiah or that God shifted his protection from them to Christians.

The Christian message spreads through the empire

The second great monotheistic religion took a while to win acceptance. The Romans hated the Christians, because, among other reasons, they refused to worship the emperor like a god.

Dodging arrest, Paul traveled widely and was able to reach many people. He and his companions spoke at Jewish religious houses (called *synagogues*) and convinced many people to follow Jesus. He taught monotheism, but said God sent Jesus to lead people to the truth.

Then in AD 70, the Romans who were fighting Jewish rebels destroyed the Temple (see Chapter 10), the central religious site of ancient Jews. To many people, this was proof that God had deserted the Jews. Paul was dead by then, but his message now took on new urgency. Christianity began to grow. Roman emperors fought against Christianity before Constantine embraced it. By the end of the fourth century, it had become the only legal religion of the empire.

The second great monotheistic religion was in place. It is also the second religion (after the first, Buddhism) that would attempt to become a world religion. We cover the history and practices of Christianity in more detail in Chapters 5 and 6.

Islam: Submitting to God

In the desert land southwest of Judah, another religion began to develop in the seventh century AD. Eventually, it would become the third large monotheistic faith, and the third attempt (after Buddhism and Christianity) at a world religion spanning the globe.

Its founder was Muhammad, a herder who listened to the stories of Jewish and Christian travelers. He lived in Mecca, a crossroads city in the desert far south of Jerusalem. Nearby was a stream that local residents insisted had been visited by Abraham. Mecca also housed the most sacred object in the region. Called the *Ka'baa,* it was a stone believed to have come from heaven (for more on the Ka'baa, see Chapter 7).

Around his 40th birthday, Muhammad began to tell his relatives that the angel Gabriel had visited him and called on him to become a prophet of God. In his language, the word God was pronounced *Allah.*

Muhammad called this new monotheistic religion *Islam,* which means "submission." The name is derived from the Arabic word for peace, *salaam.* Members of the new faith are called *Muslims,* which means "he who submits."

Muhammad said that Ishmael, Abraham's oldest son, was the father of the Arabs. Jews claim they descend from Isaac, Abraham's second son. Therein lies the split between the two religions, traced back to a favored son.

Islam started slowly, like Christianity, but surged in strength in only a few years when Muhammad and his small band surprised and routed a bigger, more seasoned army of Meccans. The next hundred years after Muhammad lived saw Islam spread with amazing rapidity, reaching faraway borders.

Convinced by the victory that Muhammad's deity was stronger than their pagan gods, many Arabs flocked to Muhammad's banner. The third of the great monotheistic religions had taken its place under the sun. Chapters 7 and 8 cover the history and practices of Islam.

Chapter 2

Following Abraham's Path

Abraham is an appropriate guide into religious history for anyone. He is the forefather of three great monotheistic faiths. Today, the three faiths touch lives worldwide. Together, about 40 percent of all humanity worships the same God

Since the seventh century, however, members of the religions have continued to battle for the minds and hearts of mankind. This often open warfare has resulted in virtually nonstop crusades, massacres, terrorism, and death, right up to the present.

Yet, at the core of each religion stands the same man, Abraham, a simple Chaldean who was inspired to greatness and sired a gigantic family tree. (You can see just how big Abraham's family tree is in Appendix B.) This chapter looks at what is known about the patriarch and how Judaism, Christianity, and Islam are tied to him.

What We Do and Don't Know about the Historic Abraham

Because all three religions claim Abraham as their patriarch, it would be nice to know something about him. Unfortunately, few records have survived. He does appear in the Bible, which contains the history of the Jewish people and covers an estimated 1,000 years of history. The stories there are all that remain of Abraham's extraordinary life.

The name "Abraham" does appear in other ancient texts, but they only indicate it is a relatively common name. None of the citations could refer to our Abraham. They appear in the wrong time period or cite specific people unrelated to any account of the biblical Abraham.

Still, historians can make some educated guesses about Abraham and what he may have looked like based on various images of Semites that were carved into rocks and left in the ground.

In Abraham's day around 1900 BC, men wore thick, braided beards, so he would have sported one of those. And he would have been dressed in a robe. Pants wouldn't come along for another 1,500 or so years.

He lived during a great time for his region. A powerful king named Hammurabi had finally ousted the Elamites, who had conquered the area a few hundred years earlier. Hammurabi (or as he is also known, Amraphel) founded a new capital in a city he named Babylon, which means "Gate of God." He then renamed the area Chaldea, where Abraham would live.

But was Abraham real? Good question. Historians today are divided on whether the tales about Abraham are mythology. The problem is a lack of archeological records. For example, in one biblical account, Abraham leads an army against a coalition of seven kings. None of the names of the kings has ever been uncovered in any ancient document from that region.

In the secular view, however, Judaism had to begin somewhere, and someone had to believe that God had spoken to him. Why not call that person Abraham?

Taking a tour of Father Abraham's neighborhood

Abraham lived in Ur in the southern part of Chaldea. (Today, that land is part of Iraq.) Ur was located southeast of the city of Babylon. As best as archeologists and historians can piece it together, the Sumerians, who lived farther to the valley's south, founded the country of Babylonia. Eventually, Babylon gave its name to the whole area.

No one actually put down a wooden stake and surveyed the land. Boundaries were kind of irregular. Real estate in those days usually only had a definitive border if it was along a river, and most property lines were described simply as "we live over here" and "they live over there."

Chaldea, a southern region of Babylonia, was located on rich delta land created by the deposits of the two great rivers of the area, the Euphrates and Tigris. At the time, this region of the Middle East wasn't crowded. Populations are hard to estimate, but there probably weren't more than a few million people alive worldwide then.

Ur is long gone, but it was quite a place in its time. People left stories about visiting Ur, making it seem like a kind of Las Vegas of the ancient world. Today, it's just rubble, but you can imagine what a thriving city looked like:

- Stone houses.
- Lots of tents for the many nomadic tribesmen making brief stops on their endless journeys.
- A palace or two for any royalty.
- A mansion for the governor.
- Unpaved, rocky streets.
- Plenty of roaming dogs and pigs, as well as herdsmen with sheep.
- Carts pulled by small, overburdened donkeys and horses. Camels would not be tamed until much later.
- Open-air food markets where a shopper could pick through figs, dates, pomegranates, and grains like wheat, barley and rye.
- Here and there would have been impressive temples. One or two would have been shaped like a layered triangle, called a *ziggurat,* with stones laid on top of each other so a priest could climb to the top.

Following the laws of Abraham's time

Babylonian history is complex, with many kings coming and going. Abraham would have had to be very careful not to get crushed in the onslaught of various armies.

A stone tablet records that King Sargon of Akkad destroyed Babylon about 4,350 years ago, and put the city under new management. Then Hammurabi came along. The king decided to clean up so many years of misrule by writing down laws for the land. He called the laws the *Chaldean laws,* also known as the Code of Hammurabi. Abraham, then, grew up under Hammurabi's laws.

This was the first time a king had written down the laws so all of his subjects would know them. This system meant the local priests and judges could not change the rules at will. In the past, different people in power created their own rules and regulations. The king's laws superseded all of that.

From the Code, we get the Judeo-Christian biblical statement "an eye for an eye" without crediting the source. That phrase had become so much a part of the language by the time it was written into the Bible that its origins had been forgotten.

Speaking Abraham's language

Abraham would have spoken Babylonian, as well as *Aramaic* (from Aram). Aramaic was a group of languages, really, and contained many dialects. Old Aramaic is long gone, but it remains the language of half of the *Talmud* — the record of rabbinic discussions pertaining to Jewish history, customs, ethics, and law.

No one remembers the country of Aram anymore, but at one time, it was very important to business (today the area is called Syria). It sat in between Chaldea and the rich and ancient land of Egypt. Everyone who wanted to be a successful businessman in those days had to learn Aramaic, just as corporate leaders worldwide these days have to learn English. Just a handful of people speak Aramaic today, making the language endangered.

Practicing religion before Abraham came on the scene

Before Abraham came along, people believed in many gods. They had a god of fertility; a god responsible for storm, for rain, and for many other aspects of life. The names varied according to the region: Baal, Thoth, Ishtar, Elul, Isis, and many more.

Stone images, or *idols,* of the gods who Ur residents worshipped were everywhere. You could buy small ones from the idol shops on the street. Large idols stood at some city gates, outside rich people's houses, and, of course, at the different temples around town.

Most idols were made of clay, baked and painted or enameled. Having an idol was a reminder of and a sign of respect for the god it represented, much like some people have crosses or menorahs on display in their homes or offices today. It was also a public display that showed how the owner of a big idol might be a little bit more religious than the guy who had a smaller idol outside his doorstep.

People knew the idol wasn't a god, but figured that having the god's image around couldn't hurt. After all, these deities sometimes did some pretty awful things, like send terrible storms, fires, or invasions. You wanted to be on their good sides.

Of course, an idol was due the same respect as the god it represented. That meant sacrifices. Babylonian gods demanded and received lots of sacrifices. In fact, ancient records about beer were actually made by priests keeping track of donations and sacrifices.

The priests spoke for the gods. They told everyone the rules. How did the priests know the rules? They received the word directly from the gods in divine inspiration, or they read holy scrolls and interpreted the texts. Typically, the priests worked for the king, and the king was granted his right to rule from the gods. Kings were usually related to the gods somehow, as a son of a god or as the human manifestation of a god on earth. This was a pretty cozy situation.

Abraham's Early Years

Abraham would have known all about the gods. His father, named Terach, made idols, the stone and/or wood representations of the various gods. No one knows for sure that idol carving was Terach's occupation, of course, because no one has ever found an idol with any trademark from the manufacturer. Still, old Jewish stories claim that Terach produced idols in his shop.

Under normal conditions, Abraham would have stayed in Ur and, eventually, taken over his father's business.

There were many reasons for a young man to stick around Ur. Ur was a big, prosperous city, even when Abraham lived there. It had been bigger and greater hundreds of years earlier when its reputation was pretty wild, but Ur would have been more than a country outpost 4,000 years ago.

It wasn't Babylon, of course, the capital a few hundred miles to the northwest. Abraham may have dreamed of going there, like young people today dream of living in New York, Los Angeles, or some other major city. People didn't travel much in those days, but an adventurous young man like

Abraham would have had no trouble getting wherever he wanted to go. The whole region was linked by canals and waterways. Some provided water to crops; others carried travelers around the bustling metropolis.

If Abraham was a homebody and not inclined to float off anywhere, he might have dreamed of taking over his dad's business. Or he might have wanted to own land and have his own flock of sheep. Maybe he considered becoming a salesman and setting up deals with companies in Aram or in Egypt.

In some ways, it really doesn't matter what Abraham thought, because his future changed right along with his dreams. Urged on by a divine voice, he left Ur. He left his father. He left his idols.

There's a lovely Jewish story that, before leaving home, Abraham smashed his father's idols.

One day when Abraham (then called Abram) was left alone to mind the store, he took a hammer and walloped all the idols except the largest one. He placed the hammer in the hand of that giant idol. When his father returned and asked what happened, Abraham said, "The idols got into a fight, and the big one smashed all the other ones."

"Don't be ridiculous," his father said. "These idols have no life or power. They can't do anything."

"Then why do you worship them? They have eyes but see not," Abraham told his father. "They have ears and hear not."

With that, Abraham rejected the faith of his father, his grandfather, and all the Chaldeans who preceded him.

The Beginnings of Judaism

Abraham is called "the first Jew." However, Abraham wasn't a Jew. He lived long before there were Jews. Instead, according to Jewish Scripture, God spoke to Abraham and promised him that if he obeyed the will of God, he would become the "father of many nations." So Abraham rejected idolatry and obeyed the one God.

However, Abraham didn't exactly become the father of nations. Instead, he became the father of Western religions. Three faiths trace their origins to him. He is their patriarch. Muslims consider Abraham the first *monotheist* (a person who believes there is only one God), and therefore the first Muslim who "submitted to the one, true God."

Agreeing to the covenant

Abraham rejected everything in his own culture. Instead, he chose to believe in a God who later identified himself as Yahweh and made Abraham an offer: If Abraham would leave his home and his family, then God would make him a great nation and bless him.

Abraham accepted this offer, and the *b'rit* (covenant) between God and his descendants, who became known as Jews, was established. (Genesis 12 in the Old Testament tells the full story.)

The idea of a b'rit is fundamental to Judaism. Jews believe they have a special contract with God, which involves rights and obligations on both sides. In the biblical book of Exodus, God revealed the law, and the entire nation responded, "Everything that the Lord has spoken, we will do" (Exodus 24:7). According to Jewish tradition, every Jewish soul that would ever be born was present at that moment and agreed.

By that same tradition, Abraham was subjected to ten tests of faith to prove his worthiness for this covenant. Leaving his home was one of these trials.

Before Abraham was called by God, he was known to his family and friends as Abram, which means "My father is Ram," a reference to a pagan god. But just as God was changing other things in Abraham's life, he changed his name, too:

> "Neither shall thy name any more be called Abram, but thy name shall be Abraham; for a father of many nations have I made thee." —Genesis 17:5

Historians can only guess what the changing name meant. Perhaps the wanderer's new name symbolized his new relationship with God. The "H" in Hebrew is the symbol of life. Perhaps that's what the additional letter meant.

Isaac's close call demonstrates Abraham's love for God

Judaism traces its lineage through Abraham's youngest child, Isaac. He was the only legitimate (no: Ishmael was legitimate, too: Jews just don't accept him; Isaac was the only son of Sarah; that is the distinction bill) son of Abraham and his wife, Sarah, who could carry on the family name.

Isaac the risen god?

Some scholars note that Isaac vanishes from the sacred text for a while after the attempted sacrifice. He doesn't return until much later and then only duplicates his father's activities. It's as if the authors didn't know anything else about Isaac.

Some scholars argue that Isaac actually was sacrificed, and the story was changed later when Jews banned human sacrifice. That claim is supported by the existence of an idol found by archaeologists identified as "the great Isaac."

Could Isaac have been a risen god, as existed in almost every other ancient culture in the Middle East except Judaism? Ancient religions invariably had a god who died and was reborn as a way of symbolizing the conquest of death by true believers. This idea eventually will seep into Christianity.

Judaism, however, only has one God. As a result, there is no risen god. Historians have suggested that Isaac was a risen god incorporated into early Judaism, and then shed after the faith became truly monotheistic in the seventh century BC.

Isaac is involved in one of the most crucial stories in Jewish literature. God tells Abraham to take Isaac to the top of Mount Moriah and sacrifice him. Abraham and Isaac go to the mountain where Abraham places his son on an altar and ties him up. Just as Abraham is about to stab Isaac, God stops the sacrifice and substitutes a ram instead. (See Chapter 22 in the biblical book of Genesis for all the details.)

The story is heralded as demonstrating pure obedience to God, even to the point where Abraham was willing to kill his child. Followers of Judaism, Islam, and Christianity are expected to demonstrate the same sort of obedience and do whatever God asks of them.

Following the family tree

Isaac's son, Jacob, was renamed Israel and is considered the father of the 12 tribes of Israel. Judah, the sire of the Jews, was one of the tribal leaders.

The tribes accepted Abraham's vision and followed his God. They produced the earliest literature collected in the Bible and continue to be faithful to God, who first called Abraham from his father's shop perhaps four millennia ago.

The followers of Abraham called themselves "the chosen people," a designation that meant not that they were special, but that they were designated by God to carry his message to the rest of the world.

Here is the list of Jacob's 12 sons. Most of these men became a patriarch to the 12 tribes of Israel:

- ✔ Reuben
- ✔ Simeon
- ✔ Gad
- ✔ Dan
- ✔ Asher
- ✔ Judah
- ✔ Levi
- ✔ Issachar
- ✔ Zebulun
- ✔ Naphtali
- ✔ Joseph
- ✔ Benjamin

The list of the 12 tribes of Israel varies from the list of Jacob's 12 sons because his son Joseph was given land in the name of his two sons, Ephraim and Manassas. The tribe of Levi was given responsibility for the religion but not accorded any land. Today's Jews identify themselves with the tribes of Judah and Benjamin.

In Islam, Ishmael Finds a New Way

Islam, which is the youngest of the three monotheistic faiths, traces its roots to Abraham's other son, Ishmael.

According to the Bible, when Sarah, Abraham's wife and then known as Sarai, could not conceive a child, she allowed her handmaiden, Hagar, to sleep with Abraham so her husband would have an heir.

> "Now Sarai, Abram's wife, had borne him no children. But she had an Egyptian maidservant named Hagar; so she said to Abram, 'The Lord has kept me from having children. Go, sleep with my maidservant; perhaps I can build a family through her.' Abram agreed to what Sarai said. So after Abram had been living in Canaan ten years, Sarai his wife took her Egyptian maidservant Hagar and gave her to her husband to be his wife. He slept with Hagar, and she conceived. . . . So Hagar bore Abram a son, and Abram gave the name Ishmael to the son she had borne. Abram was eighty-six years old when Hagar bore him Ishmael." —Genesis 16:1–4

Sarah wasn't exactly happy when she found out that Hagar was carrying Abraham's baby (yes, even though it was her idea), and forced the pregnant Hagar to run away.

> "The angel of the Lord found Hagar near a spring in the desert. And he said, 'Hagar, servant of Sarai, where have you come from, and where are you going?'
>
> "'I'm running away from my mistress Sarai,' she answered.
>
> "Then the angel of the Lord told her, 'Go back to your mistress and submit to her.' The angel added, 'I will so increase your descendants that they will be too numerous to count.'" —Genesis 16:7–10

Ishmael then disappears from Jewish history; his death, at age 137, is his only other mention in the Bible. However, Muhammad, the Meccan prophet who proclaimed a monotheistic religion that became Islam, had a different view. He said that the angel Gabriel told him that Arabs are directly related to Ishmael. That also reflects the Jewish view that Ishmael is the father of the Arabs.

In addition, according to Muhammad, Abraham and his son rebuilt the sacred shrine in Mecca called the Ka'baa, which had been first erected by Adam.

Islam has no other stories about Ishmael, but continually lists him as one of the early prophets of their faith prior to the last, and greatest, prophet, Muhammad.

Muhammad introduced a new faith, called Islam, to the people of the Middle East in the late sixth century. Islam was centered around Abraham's God, whom Muhammad called Allah. Muhammad thought Jewish residents of his area would accept this new faith, but they rejected Muhammad's teachings. So he focused on his Arab brethren. Chapter 7 explains Muhammad's background and his role in founding Islam.

Jesus Joins the Genealogy

Between the time of Judaism and Islam's founding, a religion called Christianity developed with direct links to Abraham.

Two of the authors who told the story of Jesus, the founder of the faith, listed him as being a direct descendant of Abraham. They left us genealogies tracing Jesus back to Abraham.

In the opening chapter of Matthew, we read,

> "The book of the generation of Jesus Christ, the son of David, the son of Abraham. Abraham begat Isaac; and Isaac begat Jacob; and Jacob begat Judas and his brethren." —Matthew 1:1–2

After many, many begats, we reach Jesus in verse 16:

> "And Jacob begat Joseph, the husband of Mary, of whom was born Jesus, who is called Christ." —Matthew 1:16

Jesus's complete genealogy as recorded by Matthew is included in Appendix B.

Luke, the other author, details Jesus's family heritage in Chapter 3 of his account and goes back toward Abraham:

> "And Jesus himself began to be about thirty years of age, being (as was supposed) the son of Joseph, which was the son of Heli, . . . which was the son of Jacob, which was the son of Isaac, which was the son of Abraham . . ." —Luke 3:23, 34

The evangelist continues on, recounting the generations to Adam.

Christianity is based on a belief that Abraham's God sent his only son, Jesus, to earth as an atoning sacrifice for the sin of disobedience caused by Adam, the first man. Adam disobeyed God by eating from the tree of knowledge, and as a consequence, God thrust Adam and his wife, Eve, out of paradise, the Garden of Eden. Adam's sin was so great that only a great sacrifice would make up for it.

Christians believe that God sent Jesus to earth where he was crucified to pay for all sins, and then he rose from the dead. Christians see Jesus's resurrection as God's promise of eternal life for those who put their faith in him. Chapter 5 explains Christianity's roots.

Three Faiths: One Founder

Judaism, Christianity and Islam continue to bring their messages to mankind. Each links its existence back to one man, Abraham, a simple herdsmen who, one day, rejected the culture of his fathers to follow a new path and who beckons us to follow him yet today.

Part II
The Development of Judaism, Christianity, and Islam

The 5th Wave　By Rich Tennant

"I'm listening to a golden oldie. Recitations of the Koran."

In this part . . .

Although Judaism, Christianity, and Islam are siblings, they belong to a feisty family and were born in very different times. All three almost died at birth, but each one endured hardships and setbacks before becoming firmly entrenched in the mind of man.

We start with Judaism, the oldest monotheistic religion. Filled with great kings and prophets, it has generated concepts that have influenced human thinking for generations. At the same time, societal pressures changed the faith.

Originally an offspring of Judaism, Christianity quickly developed into a robust faith that became the largest single religion in the world. Christianity, like Judaism, generated a variety of holidays and rituals to worship God.

Linked to Abraham and the wellspring of traditions, Islam found its own path to a deep, abiding faith. Led by the Prophet Muhammad, the religion of the desert created a faith that touches all aspects of Muslim life.

Chapter 3

Judaism: Oy Vey, What a History!

During a recent trip to New York, Bill and his friend Tom were walking down a Manhattan side street when they noticed an old synagogue under repair. New York is dotted with these old buildings that have been refurbished after hundreds of years of use.

Tom wondered if the old synagogue was still in use. He asked an elderly man standing nearby who clearly belonged to a group of religious Jews called *Hasidic.* The man wore a black hat, had a beard and unruly sideburns, and fringes poked out from under his coat in accordance with biblical law.

The man asked if they were Jewish. Bill had been raised in a Jewish family, but Tom hadn't. That didn't matter. In seconds, they were wearing a skullcap *(kepot)* and prayer shawl (*tallit;* see Chapter 4 for more on these clothing items), and were standing in a small chapel inside a nondescript brick building.

A very young man, maybe 12, was leading prayers to honor his late father. To be a valid service, the congregation needed ten adult Jewish males (called a *minyan*). With Tom and Bill present, the magic number was reached.

When the memorial portion of the service ended, they were invited to stay for the regular Friday night Sabbath service. They declined and never did find out if the old synagogue was being used. But they did have a chance to observe one of the oldest forms of worship still functioning anywhere in the world.

In this chapter, you find out more about how Judaism started and has endured for close to 4,000 years.

What's in a name?

Names used in the Bible for Jewish leaders and for God have various origins.

✔ The original name for Jews, *Hebrew,* is of unknown origin. It is thought to translate "from across the river," a reference to people who crossed the Euphrates River, which waters the land around Babylon. Abraham would have had to ford the Euphrates and its sister waterway, the Tigris, when he left Ur.

✔ The name *Israel* was given to Jacob, Abraham's grandson. It's believed to mean "he who strives with God." The reference is to a story in the Bible where Jacob wrestled all night with an angel of God. (You can read the whole story in Genesis 32:22–32.)

Eventually, Israel replaced Hebrew, and the Jewish people became known as *Israelites.*

✔ The familiar words *Jew* and *Judaism* are derived from the name of the most powerful of the 12 tribes of Israelites, Judah.

✔ Another name that rings in Jewish history is *Moses.* His name is not Hebrew for "lifted from the water," as the Bible says, but rather is a perfectly good Egyptian name.

It exists in Raa<u>mses</u>, the supposed Pharaoh of the era, and in Thut<u>mose</u>, a great Pharaoh of another era. *Moses* means "son of." Raamses means "son of Ra," the Egyptian word for spirit. Thutmose means "son of Thoth," the god of wisdom.

✔ The Jewish name for God is *Yahweh,* which is really just four vowels. At one time, no one but the Jewish high priest was allowed to pronounce the name, and he could only utter it on one day of the year. Early documents can be dated by whether the divine name appears in them. His name appears in some ancient documents.

Some scholars conjectured that the Israelites got the name Yahweh from the sound wind makes when it whips across the tops of mountains. After all, Yahweh was depicted as a mountain god.

Because symbols and other names were eventually used to represent God's name in holy texts, translators ended up with *Jehovah* in English. That was just an effort to make sense of symbols used to represent the name of God in print.

From Abraham, Judaism Takes the Long Road

You are so used to the idea that there is one God that you may not be aware that religions based on this idea had to struggle to survive. That was particularly true for Judaism, the oldest of the three great monotheistic faiths.

When Abraham decided to follow a god named Yahweh about three millennia ago, he didn't think anyone else would join him. He didn't preach to anyone. His children adopted their father's belief, but no neighbors did. (See Chapter 2 for the story of how Abraham came to be the father of the faiths.)

Abraham didn't develop any rules for his new religion either. The laws and customs that comprise Judaism today developed over centuries, finally becoming recognizable to modern eyes around the sixth century BC.

Initially, the people who became Jews were called *Hebrews*. They claimed Abraham as their father and lived as shepherds around the area now known as Israel.

The dates for early Jewish history are tentative, simply because time has erased many of the landmarks that would help locate people and places. Worse, many cities were destroyed or now exist under different names.

Like father, like son: The leaders after Abraham

After Abraham died, Jewish history shifts its focus to his son Isaac's family. Jacob, Isaac's youngest son, took center stage, and he was followed by Joseph, Jacob's second-youngest son, who rose to be second in command in Egypt.

Egyptian historians have insisted that Joseph never reached any position of authority within the government. The Egyptians detested and feared the Semites, which is a term used to describe people who spoke a related language, like the Hebrew of the Jews. They weren't likely to let a Semite like Joseph become one of their primary rulers. Their dislike was understandable. At one point, Semitic raiders, known to the Egyptians as *Hyksos* (foreign conquerors), overthrew the native pharaoh and ruled the country between about 1750 and 1550 BC.

Given the native Egyptians' animosity toward Semites, some scholars have proposed that Joseph could have reached power during the time of the Hyksos.

Over the river and through the desert, to Pharaoh's land we go

According to the Bible, Joseph was his father's favorite and was given a special colorful coat to reflect that feeling. His brothers were jealous and sold Joseph into slavery. After a series of adventures, he finally came to the attention of the ruler of Egypt, the Pharaoh. Joseph reached his high office among the Egyptians by interpreting a dream that frightened Pharaoh, predicting a terrible seven-year famine throughout the land. The Bible reports that when famine struck the region, Jacob and his sons were forced to seek food in Egypt where Joseph was overseeing food storage and distribution. The Bible says the family then settled in Egypt at the invitation of Pharaoh, who extended the offer because he respected Joseph and wanted to help him reunite with his family. (Tim Rice and Andrew Lloyd Webber wrote a hugely popular Broadway musical back in the 1960s called *Joseph and The Amazing Technicolor Dreamcoat.*)

The purpose of the story may be to explain how the Jews ended up in Egypt. Many Jewish customs and rituals seem to have an Egyptian tinge (see Chapter 4 for more on Jewish holidays and practices). Historically, Egypt was the dominant nation in the region. Many of its ideas would have naturally filtered into surrounding cultures, especially when carried along by powerful armies. No one had to live in Egypt to adopt them. That's why some historians argue that the Jews never actually settled in Egypt.

Moses, Receiver of God's Laws

After the Jews had made Egypt their home for many, years, a new leader arose among them to lead the Jews to the *Promised Land,* today known as Israel. Someone who could lead the Jews out of Egypt was needed because the Israelites didn't enjoy their stay in their adopted homeland.

After Joseph died, a new pharaoh of Egypt came to power and didn't know how Joseph had helped save the Egyptians from starvation and death. The new pharaoh enslaved the newcomers. The Israelites were forced to build cities, and they became embittered by the experience that lasted, according to accounts written much later, about 400 years. They thought God had forgotten them, and they prayed for rescue.

Eventually God responded. He sent Moses, the son of slave parents. Raised in the palace, according to the biblical account in the book of Exodus, Moses didn't know his parentage until he killed a vicious overseer and fled into the desert after discovering the truth.

In the arid land of Midian, he had a face-to-face meeting with God before a bush that was on fire yet remained unscathed by the flames. God ordered Moses to return to Egypt. There he confronted the pharaoh and demanded the slaves be set free.

Relying on plagues and walls of water to escape slavery

Armed with a staff that reverted to a snake upon command and performed miracles, Moses succeeded in freeing his countrymen from captivity with the help of God, who sent ten consecutive plagues:

- ✔ The Nile River turned to blood
- ✔ Frogs
- ✔ Lice
- ✔ Flies
- ✔ Sick animals
- ✔ Boils
- ✔ Hail
- ✔ Locust
- ✔ Darkness
- ✔ Death of the firstborn

The Jews remember the plagues every year during the Passover holiday, which commemorates the Exodus of the Jews from Egypt. (See Chapter 4 for more about Passover.)

The plagues convince pharaoh to allow the Jews to leave Egypt. However, he changes his mind and chases them to the Sea of Reeds — some people mistranslate the words as the Red Sea. The Suez Canal now sits where the Sea of Reeds once was. Moses parted the waves so the Jews could cross, and the following Egyptians drowned in the returning waters.

A song that Miriam, Moses's sister, reportedly sang as the Israelites rejoiced on the opposite bank of the waterway is still repeated in Jewish houses of worship around the world. Its age adds authenticity to the account, although archaeology has found no evidence for an actual exodus.

In the biblical account, after Moses and the Jews left Egypt, they spent 40 years wandering through the Sinai Desert before they reached the Promised Land (Israel).

Counting on the Ten Commandments

During the Jews' long trek through the desert, God called Moses up to Mount Sinai for a little chat. There, according to the biblical text, Moses accepted the Ten Commandments from God. They have been the guiding moral precepts for Western society ever since. The commandments, as written in the biblical book of Exodus, Chapter 20, go like this:

1. You shall have no other gods before Me.
2. You shall not make for yourself a carved image.
3. You shall not take the name of the Lord your God in vain.
4. Remember the Sabbath to keep it holy.
5. Honor your father and your mother.
6. You shall not murder.
7. You shall not commit adultery.
8. You shall not steal.
9. You shall not bear false witness against your neighbor.
10. You shall not covet.

Joshua takes control

Moses died overlooking the land that the residents then called Canaan after turning over his leadership to Joshua. Moses was not allowed into Israel because he had disobeyed God, according to the Bible. The text says he banged a rock to bring forth water instead of letting God's word suffice.

Joshua, who had been Moses's assistant, guided the Israelites in their conquest of Canaan, a land described as flowing with milk and honey. He parted the water of the Jordan River so the people could pass, directed attacks on major cities, and then distributed the captured land among the 12 tribes of Israel (Chapter 2 has more details about the tribes).

In the biblical account included in the book of Joshua, the escaped slaves overwhelm major Canaanite cities and take control of the land. However, historical findings to date don't support that tale.

No evidence of an invasion of the land has ever been found. The conquest should be easy to prove. Every cultural group produced its own ceramic pots with a unique design. Canaanite ceramics then should be different from the ones produced by the former Hebrew slaves. Unfortunately, ceramics found by archaeologists are unchanged for centuries.

Moreover, some cities supposedly destroyed by Joshua and his army — like Jericho and Ai — were already in ruins during the era when Joshua must have lived.

The debate is not settled, and supporters of the account continue to dig for evidence.

This issue is significant because Jewish claims for Israel date from God's promise to Abraham and continual Jewish occupation of the land after the Exodus. The lack of a conquest would create a shadow over Jewish claims.

The Days of the Judges

After the Exodus from Egypt, the Israelites lived in Canaan and adopted the gods of other residents there, including deities like Moloch who demanded human sacrifice. Their leaders in those confusing days were called *judges,* individuals who arose when trouble threatened and would save their people.

Judges were colorful people who did all sorts of things to help get rid of foreign conquerors. One of them was Samson, who, like a sun god, lost his power when his hair (rays of the sun) was shorn by a devious mistress. He was strong and eventually destroyed a temple filled with enemies.

Another was Gideon, who may have been a real king and whose name has been borrowed in modern times by earnest folks who pass out Bibles world-wide. Gideon led an army to rout enemies of his people.

The last judge was named Samuel. Unhappy with continual invasions by enemies, the people pressed him to find someone to rule over and protect them. He finally agreed after warning them that a king would raise taxes and use their young men in his army.

The Time of Kings

Samuel first chose a tall man named Saul to be king. Saul had lots of problems, both with rebellious followers and with his own mental health. His favorite son, Jonathan, even supported a fella named David, who played musical instruments for Saul and would succeed him as king one day.

Eventually Jonathan and Saul were killed by the Philistines, the chief enemy of the Jews at the time. David seized the throne but is credited with the immortal lament: "How the mighty have fallen."

David starts a dynasty

David had played many roles before becoming king. He even fought on behalf of the Philistines before seizing the throne after Saul died. Just to be safe, David also killed virtually all of Saul's relatives.

David is considered Israel's greatest king. His descendants were expected to rule the land. That's why Jews, in later times, looked to David's family for a new anointed king (or a *messiah*) to arise to throw off foreign control. Jesus was thought to be of the line of David.

David had a successful reign. He subdued enemies along Israel's border, captured Jerusalem and made it his capital, and brought back the holy carrying case (called an *ark*) of the Lord.

David was also the first king to be guided by *prophets,* holy men who told the people what God wanted of them.

Solomon rules wisely

King David was succeeded by his son, Solomon. He built the holiest building in Jewish history, the Temple (see Chapter 10). God was supposed to live there.

Solomon had many wives, reportedly entertained visiting monarchs like the Queen of Sheba, and lived lavishly. He imported wood and materials from around the known world and became famous for his wisdom.

Splitting into two kingdoms

The Jewish kingdom did not endure, but split into two parts after Solomon died: Israel in the north; Judah in the south.

Israel had a series of kings, while Judah was led by David's descendants. Neither land was strong enough to defend itself long against the huge empires that began to appear on the horizon.

Who were the prophets?

Jews recognize major and minor prophets. The distinction isn't a reflection on what the individual said, but how much of his writings survived the passage of time.

Major prophets are:

- Isaiah
- Jeremiah
- Ezekiel

Minor prophets include:

- Amos
- Habakkuk
- Haggai
- Hosea
- Joel
- Malachi
- Micah
- Nahum
- Obadiah
- Zechariah
- Zephaniah

Getting Conquered: The Jews Find Themselves in Hot Water

Abraham probably thought he had bought himself a pack of trouble when he loaded up his ox cart and headed east from Ur into the unknown wilderness (see Chapter 2). Actually, he had it easy compared to hisdescendants who have been conquered and attacked by many different countries and people ever since they moved into Canaan perhaps 3,000 years ago.

The list of conquerors includes:

- Assyrians, a tribe located in what is now Syria, who swept over Israel. The residents were forced to leave, becoming the *Ten Lost Tribes.*
- Babylonians, who captured Judah and sent its residents into captivity.
- Persians, who let the Jews return home about 60 years after the Babylonians drove them away.
- Greeks, led by Alexander the Great.
- Syrians, who succeeded the Greeks after Alexander's kingdom shattered.
- Romans, who created an enormous empire throughout Europe, northern Africa, and the eastern portion of Asia.

What happened to the Israelites?

Historians speculated for years about the fate of Israelites after they were overwhelmed by the Assyrians around 723 BC. Writers as late as the 1800s thought the Native Americans were descendants of the missing tribes. Today, by using chemical markers in blood, scientists have traced the last descendants of those Israelites to a tribe living in South Africa.

Monotheism arrives

From Moses to the time of the Babylonians in the sixth century BC, the Israelites weren't *monotheists* (people who worship only one god). They believed that their God was supreme, but they recognized the existence of other gods and worshipped them.

Jewish teachers, called prophets, continually called on believers to put their faith totally in God, who, they said, would protect his people from foreign invaders.

In those days, people accepted whichever god seemed the strongest. Conquerors had no trouble imposing their religious beliefs. After all, the winner's god definitely had to be stronger than the god of the losing side.

Besides, no one wanted to be wrong. Why not keep all the gods happy, just in case one of them actually had some power? As a result, a famous prophet, Jeremiah, in the sixth seventh century BC complained that God was using the Babylonians to punish the Jews for maintaining the snake god of Moses and other idols in the Temple. Soon after, King Josiah ordered all the foreign idols destroyed.

As a result of prophets, the old idols were banished in the seventh century BC, and Jews became true monotheists. Never again would they turn to another deity, even after their land was finally conquered by the Babylonians late in the sixth century BC.

Living under foreign rule

Conquerors, typically on their way to Egypt, besieged tiny Judah and dominated the landscape. As a result, Jewish leaders were forced to write down their history so their traditions wouldn't die out. Eventually, many of those writings would be collected into a book today known as the Bible (see Chapter 9).

At the same time, guided by prophets, Jews began to see themselves as a nation of priests instructed by God to carry his message to the world. They created laws to isolate themselves from others, banning intermarriage, for example. They wanted to remain pure and to avoid violating rules that could lead to problems. They saw the various conquests as divine punishment for their own misbehavior, and they studied the holy texts to figure out exactly what they must do to avoid more punishment.

The Babylonian invasion was enough. That meant they must live in the Holy Land, which is another name for Israel. Jews who chose not to were (and are) said to be living in *diaspora,* which comes from the Greek and means "to sow" or "to scatter." The belief is that they have chosen temporary living quarters elsewhere and will eventually join other Jews in Israel.

Jews did manage to shake free of conquerors briefly from about 142 BC to 63 BC. Then until 1948, Israel remained under foreign control.

While the Romans ruled Israel, Christianity developed (see Chapter 5). As this new faith grew stronger, Jews fought three wars against the Romans and lost them all. Still, the Romans didn't hate the Jews.

They teased them about taking a day off every week and didn't understand their dietary restrictions (see Chapter 4 for details on these practices). But the Romans actually catered to such religious convictions. Food normally distributed to the poor on Saturdays went to impoverished Jews on Sunday. Roman emperors were clearly aware of Jewish laws.

Even when Emperor Caligula ordered his statue placed in the Temple around AD 40 to the outrage of the Jews, the Roman regional officer in Judea delayed long enough to avoid offending the Jewish residents, even at the risk of his own life. The officer's decision was vindicated when the emperor was assassinated. The demand for a statue died with him.

Christianity's Emergence Puts the Jews on the Defensive (Yet Again)

The Romans' live-and-let-live attitude toward the Jews changed with the advent of Christianity. In an effort to hold back views believed to be contrary to the fledgling church, leaders of the new faith developed rules to control and eliminate what they saw as heresies. The new Christians were particularly upset that Jews didn't accept Jesus. Many did, of course, but others refused to abandon their religious views.

In time, Christianity grew much bigger than Judaism. Christians began to attack Jews, accusing them of killing Jesus.

Jewish persecution (called *anti-Semitism*) has lasted 2,000 years and has occurred in many forms:

- ✔ Christian church leaders eventually passed laws restricting where Jews could live and work. Ironically, many of the laws were based on restrictions that Jews originally used against their non-Jewish neighbors.

- ✔ Jews were often sent to isolated living areas called *ghettoes*.

- ✔ They were attacked in murderous raids called *pogroms*. Crusaders heading to the Middle East often massacred Jews as they passed through cities and villages en route.

- ✔ If Jews were allowed to live in a country, they were required to take hated jobs, like money lending or tax collecting. Those responsibilities didn't endear them to anyone. Because they were outside the church, Jews could charge interest on loans, whereas Christians weren't allowed to collect interest. However, after the businesses were established, Jews often would be ordered out and their goods and money confiscated.

- ✔ For many centuries, Jews were invited into European countries to help develop the commercial part of society. After they succeeded, they were forced to depart and leave everything behind.

- ✔ At one point, all Jews were ordered out of Spain and banned from living in most European countries. The English statesman Oliver Cromwell let Jews return to England in the 1600s because he was convinced the world wouldn't end until Jews were found in every country.

- ✔ During the 1930s and 1940s, an estimated 6 million Jews were killed by German Nazis as part of the Holocaust.

Jews endured all these persecutions because, when one area closed to them, another might be available. As a result, at one time, Spain was a haven. Then Poland took over. No place stayed open for long. America was the first region that permitted them religious freedom, and that wasn't until the 1600s.

How Jews Have Influenced Society

The extended persecutions greatly affected the Jews. In some ways, the pain and agony gave birth to aspects of the Jewish character that changed the world.

Jews still constitute a tiny fraction of the world's population, but they have contributed to education, science, and even humor and popular culture in surprising numbers.

Emphasizing education

Isolated and separated from society, Jews turned to their holy books. Tevya, the main character in the beloved Broadway musical *Fiddler on the Roof,* wishes he were rich so he could "study the holy books with the learned men seven hours every day . . . That would be the sweetest thing of all."

The emphasis on education and acquiring knowledge to understand God's commands meant Jews became very scholarly.

Because of the desire to read and understand God's laws, Jews continue to populate the academic world in numbers far beyond their meager population. Jews today comprise approximately 0.25 percent of all people in the world and 2 percent of the U.S. population. Yet, as of 2007:

- ✔ At least 173 Jews and people of half-Jewish ancestry have received the Nobel Prize, accounting for 23 percent of all individual recipients worldwide since 1901. More than 37 percent of American Nobel Prize winners have been Jewish.

- ✔ In research fields like chemistry, economics, medicine, and physics, 27 percent of all winners worldwide have been Jewish. Almost 40 percent of the American winners in those categories have been Jewish.

- ✔ The largest percentage of Jewish Nobel Prize winners has been in economics. In this category, 55 percent of the U.S. recipients have been Jewish.

Jews are not necessarily smarter than other groups of people. But because they were powerless and unable to muster up an army to defend themselves throughout much of their history, they relied on their intelligence to survive. They rewarded those among them who were smarter and, as a result, created an ethnic trait that has remade the world in many ways.

The three major thinkers who had the greatest impact worldwide in the last 150 years were all Jewish:

- ✔ Albert Einstein in science and math

- ✔ Sigmund Freud in medicine and psychology

- ✔ Karl Marx in social behavior and government

None of them was particularly religious, but all of them are products of a culture that stressed the importance of knowledge.

Inventing languages

Jews created their own languages for everyday life. For centuries, Jews had adopted the language of whatever land they called home. Their holy book was written principally in Hebrew, but the language of the day was typically Russian or Polish, spoken in the Eastern European homes where the vast majority of Jews lived after 1492.

In an effort to communicate without interference from authorities, Jews developed secret tongues.

- ✔ In Spain, the language was called *Ladino*.
- ✔ In Germany and, later, Russia, the language was *Yiddish*.

Both languages shared a common trait. They sounded like the native tongue, but the words were written with Hebrew letters. As a result, if an administrator could read Hebrew, he would find himself trying to translate an unfamiliar word.

Ladino barely survived when the Jews were tossed out of Spain in 1492, but Yiddish thrived on stage and in media, even in the United States. Yiddish theater started in Russia and moved to London before shifting to New York in the late 1800s. Yiddish newspapers once reached millions of readers.

Eventually, Yiddish words slid gracefully into English, enriching the language. Familiar terms like *schlep, nosh, kibitz, oy vey,* and others were born in Yiddish, which began to die out when persecutions finally stopped after World War II.

Today, the language is reportedly being revived. Historians are scrambling to record the last Yiddish speakers and to preserve old newspapers. However, the language lives on in our everyday words, a constant reminder of how the *tsuris* (sorrow) of yesterday can evolve into the *naches* (joy) of today.

Jewish humor: The joke's on everyone

Jewish humor is distinctive and has swept the world. All cultures have certain traits we associate with their comical way of appreciating the world. Jews, however, stand out. Locked in ghettos and forgotten for centuries, they developed new ways of laughing at the world.

In many ways, laughter was their only weapon.

Meeting a couple of Jewish characters

Jews didn't just tell jokes. They developed stock characters whose foibles were familiar to their audiences. They include:

- The **schlemiel,** who trips and falls while carrying a tray of food. (If a mistake's gonna happen, he'll be the one to make it.)
- The **schlimazel,** the poor sap who the food lands on. (Bad luck has a way of finding this person.)
- A **shnorer,** who is always begging for money.
- The **comic emcee,** who keeps the entertainment moving by cracking jokes. Sometimes he insults the members of the audience.

In one classic joke, a wealthy man declines to give his usual gift to a shnorer. The shnorer complains. The wealthy man explains that times are hard and money tight. The aggressive shnorer replies, "You have troubles, so I should suffer?"

These stereotypes are familiar to us because Jews carried them with them onto the stage and into movies.

Strutting on stage and screen

Entertainment became a key aspect of Jewish life. In Russian *shtetls* (small isolated villages), the Purim holiday became a time when Jews could lampoon Christians (Chapter 4 has more details on this holiday). Jews developed skits that are now a mainstay in entertainment.

They came up with the comedian who misspoke constantly, the nutty professor, and others. Jewish humor remains distinctive, carrying on a tradition more than a thousand years old.

The list of great Jewish comedians seems almost endless. They have starred in movies and been the leading performers on multiple radio and television shows.

Here's a sampling, starting with older performers: Jack Benny, Milton Berle, George Burns, Jerry Lewis, the Marx brothers, Sid Caesar, Henny Youngman, Don Rickles, Alan King, Jack E. Leonard, and Rodney Dangerfield. Today's Jewish comics include Adam Sandler, Ben Stiller, Billy Crystal, Jerry Seinfeld, and many more.

Jewish humor in the Bible

The Old Testament contains many examples of humor that became distinctively Jewish.

In the story of Esther, for example, the king asks Haman, his evil prime minister, how someone should be properly honored. Thinking he is the person to be praised, Haman suggests that a dignitary lead the individual through the city on a horse, shouting the reason for the king's benevolence. The king agrees and orders Haman to lead Mordecai, Haman's bitter enemy, around on the horse.

In Judges, we are told about a king who was killed by a Jewish judge, but the king's guards didn't respond because they confused the smell caused by the wound with the usual odor from the king's toilet.

Jewish humor is invariably this dark, vivid, and sarcastic.

Fulfilling their dreams in America

Perhaps the greatest gift Jews gave their new land was the ideas encapsulated in the American Dream, which wasn't necessarily a white, Anglo-Saxon Protestant concept:

- ✔ The right to be left alone. (Protestants rejected this idea completely.)

- ✔ The ability to achieve success on one's own merit. (Again, Protestants assigned success to God.)

- ✔ The chance to own a house and to raise a family without government interference (This idea was brought by Jews; it was not the American ideal before Jews came here.)

All those hopes developed in ghettos, where Jews were hounded by authorities and forced into the military. They weren't allowed to buy homes or to live in peace. They were limited by their religion in choices of jobs and careers, and scorned and abused by people of different faiths.

Dominating the silver screen

Welcomed to America by the Statue of Liberty, which bears a poem written by a Jewish poet, the Jewish immigrants found a way to express themselves in literature and the movies.

Jews did not create the movies, but they dominated the early years of cinema. Jews like Harry Cohn, the Warner brothers, Sam Goldwyn, and Louis Meyer transformed a bedraggled art form, once shown as a signal for patrons to leave a live performance, into the most significant cultural powerhouse of our time. The Oscars, awards these men bestowed to add importance to this scorned medium, have become one of the most appreciated prizes in any field.

In keeping with the desire to boost education (see the earlier section "Emphasizing education"), the movie moguls reproduced great literature on screen in hopes of educating the masses. As a result, some of this country's greatest writers, artists, designers, and musicians worked for the movies.

Hollywood was a dream, but it was also the image of what Jews wished the world was like. The idea of a little man standing up and succeeding against all odds, a standard theme of American life, was born in the desperation of Abraham's distant relatives. In time, Americans accepted that vision as their own.

Flying the Blue and White Banner of Israel

While Jews were developing their own identity in this country, they also gained a homeland.

For centuries, many Jews wanted to go to Palestine, the name given to what had been Israel. However, that was very difficult. In the late 1800s, wealthy Jews began to buy up land in Palestine and welcomed Jews to settle it. However, that only increased anger between the new settlers and the long-term residents, the Arabs.

As a result, moving to Palestine grew harder in the 20th century. England, which controlled the Holy Land after World War I, was caught between the demands of the Arab herdsmen and the newly arrived Jewish settlers. Small bands representing each interest blew up buildings and each other in desperate efforts to get the English to turn the land over to Jewish or Arab control.

Eventually England, which had been battered physically and financially during World War II, turned the matter over to the United Nations.

In April 1948, in perhaps the most dramatic single political event in the history of the United Nations, the General Assembly overwhelming voted to divide Palestine into two units:

- ✔ Jordan, to house Arabs
- ✔ Israel, to serve as a Jewish homeland

For the first time since 63 BC, the Jews had regained control of the Holy Land.

Over the last 60 years the Jews have had to beat back Arab armies determined to destroy this new country. Today, Israel boasts one of the most powerful military forces in the world and is an independent nation.

In some ways, Jews have returned to the position that began with Abraham: a powerful leader with the strength, courage, and a belief in God strong enough to withstand any challenge.

Chapter 4

Judaism Finds God in Everything

*O*ne summer when Bill was growing up, a Jewish neighbor of his announced that he wanted to become a *cantor,* a person who sings Hebrew prayers at Jewish services. To reach that goal, he had to learn Hebrew. So he decided he was going to talk to his friends, including Bill, only in that ancient language. For the entire summer, he shouted during baseball games, chatted on the way home, and otherwise shot the breeze speaking only Hebrew. Nobody understood a word he said, but by the end of the summer, he was fluent in Hebrew and on his way to learning the liturgy.

His single-minded determination reminds us of the intensity that Judaism requires in a believer's life and behavior. Each Jew wants to follow the laws so he fulfills God's commandments and, at the same time, doesn't evoke divine anger. Over the centuries, Jewish sages have developed a list of 614 *mitzvoth* (good deeds) that a devout Jew should try to accomplish in his lifetime.

Not all will become cantors, but the distinct practices and aspects of the faith serve to make Jews completely committed to the God of Abraham. In this chapter, you find out just what those symbols, rituals, and holidays are that define Judaism.

A Little of This, A Little of That

Judaism has been something like a sponge, quickly absorbing new ideas from surrounding cultures and then transforming them to meet the needs of Jews. Egyptians, Babylonians, Greeks, and other long-forgotten ancient people provided concepts that Jewish leaders transformed into today's rituals and holidays. As a result, the religion has developed a singular set of beliefs that has allowed it to endure for thousands of years.

The basic tenet of the faith is that there is one God who is intricately involved in daily life. His presence remains the one truth first revealed by Abraham, and the underlying basis of Judaism today. Jews believe that God rescued their ancestors from Egyptian captivity, "choosing" them to carry his word to the rest of the world. That's why they are called the *chosen people*. Although now divided into multiple sects, they are steadfast in the belief that God created man and entrusted Jews to tell mankind of his presence and his requirements for proper behavior.

They celebrate God with daily prayers of thanks, many of which are taken directly from a collection of ancient texts called the Bible. The prayers are placed on the walls of homes and recited during religious services.

Their enduring faith in a single God allowed Jews to reject the pagan beliefs of powerful cultures, like the Greeks and Romans, and to survive centuries of persecution and hatred in the Christian era. Today, that faith links them in an unbroken line back to Abraham, the man credited with first heeding God's call. (See Chapter 2 for more on Abraham's life and descendants.)

Maintaining Daily Practice

Jewish sages have developed a variety of rituals over the years designed to remind believers of God's presence in their lives. You might leave a note on the refrigerator or tie a string around a finger to remember something. Jews do similar things. Leather straps wrapped around the arms of devout Jews, for example, are shaped into Hebrew letters to reflect religious messages. Even a children's game is played with a top that bears Hebrew letters. They are the initials for "A great miracle happened there" and are meant to remind participants (who are often more focused on winning chocolate) of the Jewish victory over the Syrians almost 2,200 years ago. With such a long history, Jews can link every religious activity to some historical event or ritual.

Let us pray

Jews consider prayer the most important daily ritual. They believe they are on earth to praise God. As a result, their prayers, some of which are thousands of years old, are typically designed for that purpose. Even the *Kaddish,* a mournful sounding prayer said at funerals and during the portion of services to remember the departed, only praises God and has no mention of death.

Jews do pray for the rain in the proper season, for good health, and for the safety of loved ones. Like Christians and Muslims, they have prayers when they wake up, prayers when it's time for a little shut-eye, prayers during weddings, and prayers for new seasons, new moons, and other special events. Jews have a prayer over bread, over wine, and for just about every other kind of food.

Unlike other religions, however, Jews don't have prayers for personal property. In World War II, U.S. General George Patton asked a Christian padre to write a prayer for good weather so the Allied pilots could see to provide protection for the soldiers on the ground. He couldn't have asked a rabbi for a prayer like that.

The Shema

The most important Jewish prayer is known by its first word in Hebrew, *Shema.* That means "hear." The full prayer in English is: "Hear, oh, Israel, the Lord, our God, the Lord is one." This prayer is considered the watchword of the Jewish faith and reflects the belief begun by Abraham that there is only one God.

The prayer adds, "These words which I command this day shall be in thy heart . . . and upon the doorposts of thy house." So observant Jews place the prayer in a box called a *mezuzah* and nail it by their front door. Over the years, Jews began to decorate mezuzahs, and they have become works of art in themselves.

The Shema shows up somewhere else, too. Orthodox Jews wear *tefillin,* which is a long leather strap with a tiny box connected to each end. A Jew slips a copy of the Shema in each of the boxes and wears the tefillin during prayer, with one box dangling between his eyes and the other in the left hand. The leather strap winds around the worshipper's left arm. Why? Because the Shema requests that its words be kept in the "forefront of thy eyes" and near the heart. The left arm is closest to the heart. (Find out more about special prayer garb in the upcoming section, "Exploring the worship wardrobe.")

No kneeling please, but you can rock away

REMEMBER

You won't find Jews kneeling down to say the Shema, no matter how important the prayer is. In fact, you won't find kneeling benches in a synagogue, unlike churches. Traditionally, Jews don't believe in bowing to man or God. They don't bow in a synagogue in case someone might think they're bowing toward the rabbi.

A story in the Bible tells of a man named Mordecai who gets into serious trouble because he declines to bow to the Persian Prime Minister Haman. Haman threatens to kill all the Jews because of Mordecai's faux pas. Of course, Haman loses in the end. (You can read the details of Mordecai's predicament in the book of Esther in the Bible.)

Many Jews tend to rock back and forth during prayer in a kind of meditation. Jews call it *davening* and say it allows them to gain a mystical connection with their inner feelings. To an outsider, davening creates an image in a synagogue of a misguided chorus line. Christian services tend to be highly organized with everyone on the same page. In orthodox Jewish services, members of the congregation rock back and forth while murmuring their own prayers from the prayer book. No one seems to be doing the same thing, except for an occasional "amen" when a prayer is completed.

Exploring the worship wardrobe

Jews have developed special clothes for prayers. One difference between sects of Judaism is how much ritualistic clothing is required. The most liberal Jews, called *Reform,* dress in standard clothes for religious services. They don't wear the religious get-up. Other Jews, whether praying at home or in a synagogue, typically put on a prayer shawl and a skullcap.

The prayer shawl, called a *tallis* or *tallit,* is a thin cloth that goes around a man's shoulders and can stretch to the waist. Orthodox Jews use the tallis to cover their heads when praying. Because Judaism is a male religion founded and run by men, women (with the exception of female rabbis) don't have to worry about wearing a tallis.

The corners of the tallis always feature tassels (called *zizit*), like the ones on a mortar board at graduation. That's because the Bible contains an order that clothing must have tassels or fringe. Because clothing these days doesn't come with that ol' time frizzy styling, the shawl itself contains fringe and fulfills the law. No one knows anymore why the Bible contains such a demand, but, as with many laws, precedent is sacred.

Devout Jews wear a tallis under their regular clothes. The fringes poking out under the coat fulfill the biblical injunction without messing up a nice suit.

The skullcap, called a *kepot* or *yarmulke,* also has a very old history. In ancient times, people carefully covered their heads when entering a sacred building or shrine. Veils worn by religious women in Catholic Masses carry on that tradition. However, in time, people started removing their hats to indicate their devotion. Jews retained the old tradition, though, and now they place skullcaps by the entrance to the synagogue's sanctuary so male Jews can cover their heads during services. More orthodox Jews never remove their skullcaps, which have become works of art.

The skullcaps may also be linked to the power invested in hair. Orthodox women shave their heads to eliminate hair, which could lure men away from their religious studies. They wear wigs instead. (Sometimes these wigs are quite beautiful, which may cause problems anyway.)

Keeping kosher

Jews got a lot more than prayers from the Bible that also served up menu options. These requirements were organized in the Talmud and are collected under the heading *kosher,* meaning ritually prepared. Some foods that are commonplace in restaurants, like ribs, shrimp, and oysters, can't be eaten by Jews; other foods are perfectly acceptable. (Chapter 11 in the biblical book Leviticus and Chapter 14 in Deuteronomy outline the Jewish dietary habits.)

Acceptable foods:

- ✔ Jews can eat any animal that has cloven hooves and chews its cud. So sheep, cattle, goats, deer, and bison are kosher.
- ✔ Jews can dine on chicken, geese, ducks, and turkeys. Some people avoid turkey, however, because it's not mentioned specifically in the Torah.
- ✔ Anything in the water with fins and scales is okay.

Forbidden foods:

- ✔ The rules bar dining on camel, rock badger, rabbit, and pig.
- ✔ All the prohibited fowl are birds of prey or scavengers.
- ✔ Sharks are out. So are shellfish such as lobsters, oysters, shrimp, clams, and crabs.
- ✔ Don't even think of grabbing a handful of chocolate-covered termites. Of the "winged swarming things," only a couple are specifically permitted. However, the great sages had to put on their thinking caps for this rule. Even 2,000 years ago, they had no idea what insects the biblical text referred to. To avoid breaking the law, they forbade eating any insect.
- ✔ Rodents, reptiles, and amphibians are all no-nos.

Kosher rules changed Judaism

The kosher laws help explain why Jews split into sects. In the 1700s, all Jews were orthodox and followed biblical rules, like the kosher laws. However, Jews who came to this country sometimes settled in tiny, rural communities. They found it impossible there to find a kosher butcher or to hunt up enough appropriate food. As a result, far-sighted rabbis suggested that some laws didn't need to be followed in the modern world. That led to the Reform and Conservative movements. Jews in those sects rarely keep kosher.

Kosher laws also are linked to animal rights. The Bible orders Jews to kill animals with the least amount of suffering. They also were banned from eating blood. Jews combined the two requirements by killing animals by slitting their throats. The animals bled to death with minimal suffering. In time, sages added other laws to reduce animals' suffering. In ancient times, when hungry people would simply slice meat off a living animal, kosher rules represented a major step against cruelty to animals.

 Jews also can't eat milk, eggs, fat, or organs from banned animals. That can create some problems. For example, rennet, an enzyme used to harden cheese, usually is derived from non-kosher animals. That makes kosher hard cheese difficult to find.

No one is really sure why some animals were considered worth eating and others were not. Modern scholars believe there were religious reasons behind the rules. Say a nearby pagan tribe worshipped crabs. To prevent Jews from falling into the error, their leaders banned the animal from the dinner plate. The rules may also have been designed to keep Jews ritually pure. Kosher laws definitely serve as a reminder. Any Jew who follows the rules can't forget her religion.

Kosher laws affect more than the dinner plate.

- ✔ Animals destined for the dinner table must be killed in accordance with Jewish law. That means all blood must be drained from the meat or broiled out of it before it is eaten.

- ✔ Fruits and vegetables are permitted, but must be inspected for bugs.

- ✔ Meat can't be eaten with dairy products. At home, a Jewish family that keeps kosher has two sets of dishes: one for food with milk elements; one for food with meat. There are two sets of silverware and utensils, too. That way, there's no danger the wrong foods can meet.

  This rule outlaws cheeseburgers, chili with cheese, meat tacos with cheese and a whole bunch of other delectables.

- ✔ Grape products (jelly, juice, wine) made by non-Jews may not be eaten.

To be sure no kosher laws were violated, even by accident, Jewish sages eventually clarified some of the rules to indicate precisely how long after eating meat a person could also dine on cheese; how dishes can be cleaned to eliminate possible contamination; and so on.

Today, it's easy to find kosher food in a grocery store. Just look for a U. Manufacturers can't use a K because that initial is used for kilogram. To be labeled kosher, the food item can't contain anything that's banned or has come into contact with a forbidden item. A rabbi must supervise the manufacturing process to assure that there's no contamination.

Remembering the Sabbath

The one holiday followed by Jews and Christians alike is called *Sabbath.* That's a day of the week dedicated to God. It's the day of rest; no work and no play — just rest. No holiday is more identified with the Jews than this day of rest. To the Greeks and Romans, the Sabbath was proof that the Jews were crazy. Who took a day off? And *every* week, too? They probably shuddered to think slaves might pick up that routine.

Yet, the day is honored with its own commandment: "Remember the Sabbath and keep it holy." The Bible gives two reasons for Sabbath:

- ✔ In Genesis, God rests on the seventh day after creation.
- ✔ In Deuteronomy 5, the Sabbath is tied to the *Exodus* when the Jews hurried out of Egypt ahead of the Egyptian army. Jews are supposed to use the Sabbath to remember this important event and to thank God for his help.

The two explanations imply an earlier meaning. In the ancient Babylonian account of creation, historians found several similar concepts. All of them, including Sabbath, are derived from the Babylonian word meaning "to cease." In the Babylonian story, called the *Enuma Elish,* the gods destroy mankind and then cease working on the seventh day.

Also, in Babylonia, the last day of the week was dedicated to Sin, the moon goddess whose name lives on in the word "Sinai." The Babylonians considered it an unlucky day, like we might think of Friday the 13th. Jews probably reversed the idea to give it a nicer meaning. After all, living in Babylon they would see the day commemorated no matter what they did.

Jews still chose the last day of the week, Saturday, for their day of rest. Early Christians held their Sabbath prayers on Saturday and Sunday, before shifting to Sunday only.

Because the Jewish day begins at sundown, religious Jews start their prayers Friday night and end their worship at sundown the next day. Many go to religious services or pray at home.

Don't flip that switch!

How does someone avoid working on the Sabbath? Better yet, what's work? Early Jewish sages spent a long time on both questions. Some of their rules were translated in American culture as *blue laws,* which prohibited stores from opening on a Sunday. Those laws finally were erased after World War II.

Although Reform and even Conservative Jews today don't follow the "no work on Saturdays" rule, Orthodox Jews won't work on Sabbath to this day. Many won't even drive cars on the Sabbath. As a result, devout Jews often live near their synagogues so they can walk to services. Visitors touring Jerusalem by car today are warned to avoid the very religious section because Jews there will stone cars for violating the Sabbath.

Really pious Jews won't cook or turn on lights on the Sabbath because the smallest action of flipping a light switch is considered "work." Instead, they may hire a non-Jew to flip on a switch. Clever! That's not the only ingenious way Orthodox Jews avoid work. Elevator call and floor buttons are also off limits for Orthodox Jews on the Sabbath. Imagine living on the 50th floor of a high-rise building. Walking up several dozen flights of stairs hardly seems like less work than pushing an elevator button. In high-rise buildings inhabited by stricter Jews, an elevator often is kept running all day, and it simply stops on every other floor. Residents need only walk up or down one level to catch a ride, and they never have to push a button. These very observant Jews have therefore exercised no intention and done no work by pushing the button to go up, and they are absolved from breaking a rule. An interesting — and sneaky — solution!

Observing Jewish Holidays

Jewish holidays developed in rhythm with the seasons. Born in a farming culture, Judaism built on that environment for spring and fall holidays, but also drew on significant events to fill the calendar with festivities and remembrances.

High Holy Days: Rosh Hashana and Yom Kippur

The two most important religious holidays on the Jewish calendar are *Rosh Hashana* and *Yom Kippur,* which are ten days apart in late September or early October. Rosh Hashanah, which is the Jewish New Year and means "head of the year," kicks off the annual cycle of prayer and religious thought called *Days of Awe* or *High Holy Days.* Yom Kippur, also called the *Day of Atonement,* ends the holidays. Even nonreligious Jews crowd synagogues during these times.

Why eight-day holidays?

Jewish holidays are of varied length. Originally, many were seven days long — especially those related to planting and harvesting. That's because of the astrological link to the sun, moon, and five visible planets.

The actual date for the holiday to start was announced by sages in the holy Temple, based on their computations. However, when the Temple was destroyed in 70 AD, Jewish leaders feared that Jews now scattered would not begin the holiday on the correct day. So they added one day to every holiday except the Sabbath.

So the spring planting holiday became eight days long. A later holiday, like Hanukkah, also became eight days long.

The old candelabra, which was the symbol of Judaism, also went from seven candles to eight.

Although Rosh Hashana marks the beginning of another year, the holiday doesn't resemble anything like the huge celebrations held around the world on December 31. Jews don't set off fireworks or gather for big parties with noisemakers and balloons. Instead, they go to synagogues to thank God for whatever happened the previous year and to look forward to a better new year.

Yom Kippur is even more solemn. Religious Jews don't even eat all day, cleansing their bodies while asking God to forgive their sins. For Catholics, this would be like a one-day confession that takes care of the whole year. Jews pray that God will enter them in the Book of Life for another year. They are also required to ask other people they may have wronged for forgiveness.

On both Rosh Hashana and Yom Kippur, children are expected to take off from school, and devout Jews don't work. This can cause problems in the secular world. In the 1960s, Los Angeles Dodgers pitcher Sandy Koufax, who is Jewish, kicked off a furor by refusing to pitch on Yom Kippur, despite a tight pennant race. Other Jewish athletes have faced similar dilemmas, as have religious Christians and Muslims on their most important holidays.

Passover: Recalling the great escape

This eight-day spring holiday is directly linked to the most significant event in Jewish history: the Exodus from Egypt led by Moses (flip to Chapter 3 for more on this event). In fact, Passover is probably the oldest, continually celebrated holiday on earth. However, it originally had nothing to do with Jews or Egypt.

Party like it's 5769!

When to celebrate a holiday can be tricky business. The Jewish calendar was developed centuries ago and, like all ancient calendars, was based on the moon. People could see the moon change, while the darn sun seemed to stay the same. So they marked the passing of time by the arrival of the new moon. However, a lunar calendar is shorter than one based on the sun. The moon runs through its cycle in about 28 days. The solar calendar averages 30 days a month. Regardless, the Earth needs 365.25 days to complete one circuit around the sun in a year. The lunar calendar, however, falls short of that requirement. To make up the missing days, Jews add a month (Adar 11) to the calendar seven times every 19 years.

That's why Jewish holidays can occur in different months in the English calendar. The only Christian holiday that moves around the calendar is Easter because it's tied to the Jewish holiday of Passover (see Chapter 6). Also, because of the lunar calendar, Jewish holidays run from sundown to sundown.

Using the Bible, Jewish sages decided that the world began about 5,769 years ago. That corresponds to 2008 in our English calendar.

Centuries before Abraham, Middle Eastern shepherds used to sacrifice a lamb to their deities every spring. Then as Judaism began to develop, the annual shepherds' lamb roast was combined with an otherwise unknown holiday for dry bread and adapted to the Jews' miraculous escape from Egypt. That took place around the eighth century BC. Passover has been an important Jewish holiday ever since.

Passover simply wouldn't be a Jewish holiday if it didn't involve food restrictions and special rituals:

- Religious Jews carefully clean their houses before the start of the holiday to be sure no unacceptable foods are still around when Passover starts.

- During the holiday, Jews often use a different set of dishes to prevent contact with the wrong food.

- The menu is limited. Jewish sages noted that the fleeing slaves wouldn't have had time to cook properly or gather up vegetables difficult to harvest. So they banned potatoes and carrots, among other foods, that have to be dug up.

- No bread is allowed because there wouldn't have been time to bake. According to the story in Exodus, Jews had to flee Egypt in a rush, what with the Egyptians chasing them and Moses parting the Red Sea. Therefore, they had no time to wait around for their morning dough to rise, or *leaven*. Instead, they simply packed it up and carried it out, pronto. As a result, the hot sun baked this unleavened dough into crackers called *matzoh*. Jews eat matzoh during Passover to remind themselves of their ancestors' escape from the Egyptians. Matzoh can be crumbled into cereal, mixed with eggs, toasted, or used like breading.

The Seder's sad past

Today, the Seder is simply a large meal when the Passover story is retold amid friends and family. In the Middle Ages, however, the festival dinner was tainted by serious charges leveled by Christians. Jews were accused of needing fresh blood to make matzoh for Passover and killing young Christian children to get it.

However, Jewish law bans the presence of blood at meals. Kosher laws require the use of salt to drain blood from meat. Blood was seen as the life force and not to be eaten. Despite that, many Jews were killed by Christians convinced that the vicious libel was true.

The Seder is also linked to Christianity. In the Gospels, Jesus is said to have attended a Passover Seder before his trial and crucifixion. He is described raising one of the four required glasses of wine as a symbol of his coming sacrifice.

Christianity added to the interpretation by seeing Jesus as the "Lamb of God" and likening his death in the spring to the sacrifice of the *paschal lamb* (the lamb slain and eaten at Passover by the ancient Jews).

The holiday includes prayer and a family gathering, called a *Seder,* where the story of the Exodus is retold. Seders are held the first, second, and last days of the holiday. Symbols of the Exodus are placed on a large Seder plate. Items include a bone to signify the sacrifice of a lamb; an egg, which symbolizes spring; a sprig of parsley, also a symbol of spring; horseradish, which reflects the tears that the slaves shed before they were rescued; a concoction of apples, walnuts, wine, and cinnamon, which resembles the mortar used by slaves to build Egyptian buildings; and several pieces of matzoh.

Each participant at the Seder also drinks four cups of wine. An additional cup is left out for Elijah, the biblical prophet whose return is expected to introduce a golden age of peace.

One piece of matzoh is hidden for children to find later for a reward. The meal can't end until the *afikomen* (dessert) is found, ransomed, and eaten. Many families have stories of sitting around the Seder table for long hours while children haggle with whoever is running the Seder.

Planting and harvesting holidays

Spring planting and fall harvest holidays are normal for many religions. People once lived by the rhythm of the changing seasons. As a result, holidays built around sowing and reaping took on special significance in ancient times. Jews have two such holidays, now both eight days long.

- ✔ The spring holiday is called **Shavuot** and marks spring planting. The tail end of Shavuot is called *Shemini Atzeret*, when the Jews remember when Moses received the Torah from God. The final day of Shemini Atzeret is called *Simchas Torah*.

- ✔ The fall holiday, **Sukkot,** once required Jews to live in small huts for seven days along with samples of grains being harvested. Devout Jews still build little huts, called *sukkoths*, behind their homes during Sukkot and decorate them with fruits.

Purim: A great reason to party

The early spring holiday of Purim isn't that important religiously, but has remained extremely popular. Jews dress up in costumes, put on saucy plays, and shake loud noisemakers. It's even permissible to get drunk on Purim.

The holiday supposedly began as a way of recalling a supposed Jewish victory over the mammoth Persian army. In a biblical book that bears her name, Esther rescues the Jewish people after Haman, the evil Persian prime minister, gets the king to approve an order allowing the Persian troops to kill all the Jews. Esther persuades the king to arm the Jews, who then defeat the Persian army. Haman and his sons eventually are hung on gallows meant for the Jews.

The entire episode is a moral tale, not an historical one. *Purim* means "lots," as in "odds," rather than a place to park cars. However, the holiday started out as a pagan event that Jewish leaders branded with a new meaning. Jewish children liked the festival so much that Jewish leaders figured they were better off adopting the holiday and creating some kind of Jewish tie rather than trying to fight it. Jews in the Middle Ages shifted the emphasis of Purim from Persia to celebrating a hoped-for defeat of Christians who harassed them. Even though that meaning has been lost, the festivities roll on today.

Hanukkah: In praise of victory and light

You've probably heard of this holiday because it's celebrated around Christmas in December with candles and gift giving. The holiday, however, has nothing to do with Jesus. It commemorates when Jewish troops retook the Temple from the Syrians in 165 BC.

Hanukkah means "redemption," because the Jews were able to clean the Temple and return it to its holy ritualistic standard. The Syrians had allowed the place to be used as a pig sty and deliberately desecrated the building.

The origin of the sukkoths remains unknown

Jewish sages and historians have come up with three different explanations for the makeshift shelters known as sukkoths, built by Jews during the fall holiday of Sukkot.

One idea is that the little structures actually reflect the temporary, movable housing the Jews used when they left Egypt under Moses's leadership. On the other hand, the huts may replicate shelters that Jewish shepherds used while tending the sheep well before Egypt came into the picture.

A third possible origin comes from even farther back. To prove a young man was adult, many ancient people used to set up small huts some distance from a village. The youngster would have to live there and fend for himself for a designated time. After the interval passed, the boy was now a man and welcomed back into his tribe.

Most non-Jews have heard the story that Hanukkah lasts eight days because a small amount of holy oil found in the Temple burned far longer than expected. That tale comes from the Talmud, however, and probably was written years after Jews retook the Temple.

Actually, the soldiers were so busy fighting that they didn't have time to celebrate Sukkot, now an eight-day harvest holiday. So they celebrated it when the Temple was recaptured. The next year, Hanukkah was devoted totally to the big win.

Today, Hanukkah is typically celebrated with songs and fried potato cakes called latkes. Jews light candles on a menorah each night and say several holiday-related prayers. In many homes, Hanukkah includes gifts given to children as a substitute for Christmas gifts.

Jews also have a Hanukkah game, which involves a spinning four-sided top called a dreidel. Participants create a pot with antes — typically with chocolate coins. Each side of the top contains a different Hebrew letter. Depending on which letter turns up when the top stops, the spinner may win the pot, half the pot, nothing, or have to match the pot.

Other holidays

The Jewish calendar is dotted with at least 36 Jewish holidays every year. They highlight biblical stories and special events in the long Jewish history. Most are commemorated with brief ceremonies or prayers. They include:

- **Tu B'Shevat,** which is a festival to honor trees. The first known environmental holiday, it takes place in January or February.

- **Tisha B'av** remembers the Temple. The first one was destroyed by the Babylonians. The second one fell to the Romans about 600 years later. Ironically, both temples seem to have been destroyed on the same day of the year, near the end of summer.

- **Yom HaShoah,** which honors those killed during World War II in the Holocaust. Held a week after Passover, this holiday recalls the nearly 6 million Jews massacred by the Germans. It is marked with prayers and candlelight ceremonies.

Understanding Jewish Rituals

Jews have developed a variety of rituals over the centuries for special occasions such as birth, marriage, and achieving adult status. These rites of passage exist in every religion and culture, but those that characterize Judaism are designed to fulfill biblical commands or to acknowledge the presence of God in daily life.

Circumcision: No getting around it

Circumcision remains the one aspect of Judaism that has endured since the beginning of the faith. To Jews, a circumcision is a joyous event, a *bris,* and usually conducted by someone trained for the procedure, called a *moyel.* In the ritual, the foreskin on the tip of the penis is removed in accordance to biblical commands. Prayers accompany the brief operation.

In the Bible, God orders Abraham to initiate the procedure. Moses is almost ambushed by God for not circumcising his son. His wife, Zipporah, rescues Moses by performing an abrupt operation on her son (Exodus 4:25). Moses apparently did not require circumcision while the Jews wandered the desert for 40 years, but Joshua reinstituted the practice (Joshua 5:2–10).

The idea itself predates Judaism. The operation began in Egypt or even earlier, possibly to reduce pleasure in sexual relations. It may also have developed to replace human sacrifice. This way, only an unnecessary portion of the body was dedicated to a deity, not the whole person. That's why females were circumcised as well, losing their clitoris in what today is considered mutilation, but is still practiced in some Muslim sects.

Cultures throughout time have looked at the ancient ritual in different ways:

- Greeks and Romans disagreed completely with the procedure. The Romans actually passed several laws banning circumcision, although they did not require Jews to stop. Greeks would not allow it. Jewish athletes actually underwent a procedure to sew on the missing foreskin so they could compete in Greek athletic competitions, which were conducted in the nude!

- Early Christians objected, too. At the Council of Jerusalem (Acts 15), they joined the Romans in prohibiting the ritual. Paul, the leading missionary, actually separated groups into circumcised and uncircumcised. He told parents not to circumcise their kids (Acts 21:25) and warned his assistant, Timothy, about the "circumcision group." (Titus:1:10–16)

- Americans didn't mind as much. The practice became very widespread in this country about 1870. It was seen as a way to prevent self-stimulation, then considered a horrible activity with dire consequences for practitioners. Americans carried the surgical procedure with them around the world. For example, Koreans began to circumcise their children after being introduced to American culture during the Korean War.

- The practice peaked internationally in 1971 after a series of medical reports found no medical evidence to support the operation. However, the American Academy of Pediatrics issued a report that year rejecting circumcision. The number of procedures has declined slowly ever since. That may change. More recent studies, published in 2007, found that wives of circumcised men have fewer health problems associated with childbirth.

Circumcision remains the one sure link between Jews of every generation back to the hallowed patriarchs like Abraham, Isaac, and Jacob. It's not an insignificant "slice of life."

Bar mitzvah: All grown up in God's eyes

The one Jewish rite of passage most familiar to non-Jews may be the *bar mitzvah,* which marks the moment when a Jewish boy becomes accepted as an adult in the religious community. In the ceremony, a teenage boy (or girl in a *bat mitzvah*) reads from the Torah and, often, leads the service. When the ceremony is completed, the youngster is considered a full-fledged member of the congregation.

Most people think it's an ancient custom, but a bar mitzvah is a surprisingly new ritual. Christians developed confirmation as a way to mark entry into adulthood, but Jews had no similar event for centuries. A boy was viewed as a man when he was capable of reading directly from the sacred texts. That could be any time. Religion was man's work; women need not concern themselves.

To counter Christianity, in the 12th century, Jewish leaders developed the bar mitzvah ("son of a good deed"). In the early 1900s, a rabbi with only daughters came up with a bat mitzvah ("daughter of a good deed") and guided his girls through the event.

By the 1960s, bat mitzvahs and bar mitzvahs had become standard in the Jewish community. They remain a significant part of Jewish life and are commemorated with parties after the ceremony. Those affairs can be lavish with huge dances and endless presents. The "good deed" these days may refer to property given as a gift.

Mazel tov! Celebrating a Jewish wedding

Jewish weddings follow precise ritualistic rules. The ritual begins when the bride and groom sign a legal document, called a *get,* (ketubah) in front of their rabbi. This document has been very important for millennia. It is a legal contract focusing on divorce. Should the groom die before the nuptials, his fiancé actually was banned under Jewish law from getting married again.

The bride and groom then gather under a canopy, called a *chuppah,* to recite their vows. The chuppah is a remnant from the ancient days when the bridal couple — in what usually was an arranged marriage — met in groom's room or tent. In fact, in those days, two ceremonies took place, one for betrothal, followed as long as a year later by the wedding. Talk about long engagements! At the conclusion of the betrothal period, the community escorted the bride to a room (the chuppah), where the bride and groom consummated the marriage.

These days, the chuppah is just a canopy, and the honeymoon is a private occasion without onlookers to verify the bride's virginity or the groom's virility.

In the final part of the wedding ceremony, the groom breaks a glass by stepping on it. The broken glass has been linked to the memory of the destroyed Temple, or is seen as a reminder that a little sadness accompanies even the greatest happiness. The glass originally was thrown against a wall, as though at a drunken party. In Germany, at one time, the glass was broken on a stone set against the north wall of the synagogue. Supposedly, evil spirits would be scared away by the noise. The breaking of the glass could even represent the end of a wife's virginity. Or, as one wit noted, it's the last time the groom gets to put his foot down.

The truth is that no one knows how the idea originated, but it's likely to have something to do with evil spirits. They were always spoilsports, and people continually came up with dramatic plans to counter them.

Another important aspect of a Jewish wedding is the "get" *kebutah*. It, too, is a legal document, but it is designed to shield the bride by spelling out her legal rights. The document has been turned into a canvas for artists. Because Jews are banned from making graven images, Jewish artists have decorated everything from legal documents to ornaments.

Understanding Jewish Symbols

From candelabras to six-pointed stars, Jews have developed various symbols throughout their long history. The images decorate flags and homes, and are worn on jewelry as constant reminders of a proud heritage.

The menorah

The *menorah,* a seven-pronged candelabra, has served as a symbol of Judaism for centuries. One is shown in Figure 4-1. It appears in many ancient documents and inscriptions. Today, most Jewish homes have a menorah, which is put out on holidays or placed in the window during Hanukkah.

Figure 4-1:
Menorahs are typically seen during Hanukkah.

The usual menorah today has nine prongs: eight for the candles, and one for the candle used to light the others.

The menorah appears throughout history. Here are a few examples:

✔ According to the Bible, Solomon's Temple featured ten golden menorahs: five along the northern wall and five along the southern wall. Another menorah sat in the courtyard. They vanished when the Babylonians razed the Temple.

✔ The Second Temple had only one menorah, which Syrian king Antiochus appropriated in the second century BC. When Jewish troops retook the Temple from the Syrians in 165 BC, they added a menorah to replace the stolen one.

✔ General Titus recorded the image of the menorah on the arch he built in Rome to commemorate his victory over the Jews and the destruction of the Temple in AD 70. The arch still stands in Rome. His design, however, does not match the biblical description. Titus's menorah features an octagonal base. The Bible says the Temple's menorah stood on three legs, shaped, perhaps, like lion's paws. The artist who incised the menorah into stone may not have seen it. We can't check. The artifacts taken from the Temple are thought to have been carried off when the Vandals sacked Rome in the first part of the fifth century.

Jewish scholars who have looked at the menorah and its seven candleholders have suggested its design was inspired by a plant. More likely, it's an astrological device representing the five visible planets and the sun and the moon. That would also explain the persistent use of the number seven throughout the Bible, something vegetation would not reflect.

The ark

Every synagogue features a large container placed against the eastern wall to hold the sacred scrolls. It's called an ark, mirroring the wooden box that once carried God around. The word comes up in three stories in the Bible. The great ship of Noah in the flood; the basket that carried baby Moses in the Nile; and the container holding the stone representing God were all called arks. (In Chapter 10, you find detailed information about the sacred Jewish scrolls.)

Arks can look very different depending on the synagogue, but all are made of wood. They typically are located on the back of the altar and can feature huge doors or look like small boxes.

The ark is of Egyptian origin. They, too, carried around gods in similar containers.

The Jewish star

Today, many Jews like to wear jewelry with the six-pointed Jewish star on it (see Figure 4-2). The star became prominent in the Middle Ages as various rulers searched for ways to identify Jews among their people. England's Edward I forced Jews in the 13th century "to wear a piece of yellow taffeta shaped like the Ten Commandments. French Jews of the 14th century were required to wear circular yellow badges, and Pope Paul IV in the 16th century had Jewish men wear yellow hats and women yellow kerchiefs," according to an historical report.

Finally, one of the kings hit upon a six-side star and required his Jewish residents to don it. No one knows who actually began the concept, but the idea spread quickly. In time, the six-pointed star became exclusively connected to Jews.

In the 1890s, Theodore Herzl, the founder of Zionism (the movement to bring Jews back to Palestine), used the star on the masthead of his journal *Die Welt*. The Nazis naturally thought the star was a Jewish image and required all German Jews to wear one. Today, the star, known in Hebrew as *Magen David*, is in the center of the Israeli flag. Despite its name, King David probably never saw one. Still, the star does appear in ornamentation on walls dating as far back as the sixth century BC.

The six-pointed star was simply another image to be worn by Jews until it became idealized as a symbol of Judaism. Jewish boxers have even had the star sewn on their trunks.

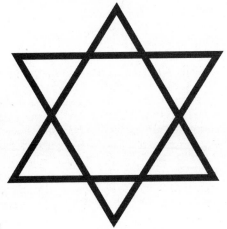

Figure 4-2:
The six-pointed star is a prominent symbol of Judaism.

Chapter 5

Jesus and the Origins of Christianity

· ·

In This Chapter

▶ Getting to know Jesus

▶ Understanding how Christianity developed

▶ Seeing how the Christian world split apart

▶ Appreciating the role Christianity has played in the world

· ·

Bill's daughter was enrolled in an Episcopal school in Daytona Beach, Florida, when she was 4 years old. She enjoyed classes, and every day she would tell her parents what she had learned.

One day she reported that her class had been introduced to Jesus. Tell us about him, her parents suggested.

"He was a Jewish carpenter from Florida," she explained.

Jesus has been asked to fill many roles in the lives of his followers since he died about 2,000 years ago, but this one may have been a first. This chapter looks at how Jesus inspired Christianity, other cultures' reactions to this new religion, and the divisions within the faith.

Jesus's Life and Death

Jesus, the founder of Christianity, has been the subject of many stories and books. He may have been the most important person to live in the last 2,000 years.

Jesus left no portrait

Just like no one knows what Abraham looked like, we don't know what Jesus looked like either. However, we can guess. Jesus would have been short — diets in those days had little protein, limiting growth. He would have been dressed in a fringed robe and, as any Jew of his day, worn a skullcap. He would have had a dark beard and long hair because religious figures dedicated to God didn't shave or cut their hair.

Many attempts have been made to construct an image of Jesus by using the descriptions of other Jews living in that era. Because we have yet to uncover a portrait — and probably never will, given the Jewish ban on graven images — every generation has created its own vision of Jesus. Some have been borrowed from other cultures.

The Romans envisioned a "good shepherd," whose gentle gaze and long hair has given rise to similar images of Jesus. A statute of the Egyptian goddess Isis with her son Horus was once mistaken for Mary and Jesus, and widely imitated.

A remarkable birth

Abraham, as mentioned in Chapter 2, enters the religion scene as a full-fledged adult. Stories of his childhood never survived. Jesus, in contrast, arrives as a beautiful baby, asleep in a manger. His entire life is played out in the pages of the Bible's New Testament. As with the Old Testament, multiple versions of many stories appear in the sacred text, giving us a distinct view of how Jesus was seen by different people in the first century.

For example, two of the four Gospels (the word *Gospel* means "good news") in the Bible include stories about Jesus's birth. In Luke, Jesus's parents, Mary and Joseph, trek to Bethlehem to comply with the demands of a Roman census. There, Jesus is born in a stable with shepherds to welcome him. He then is taken to the Temple for the traditional baby-naming ceremony and circumcision. In Matthew's account about the birth, Jesus is born in Bethlehem, and three kings guided by a star bring him gifts. Then he is rushed off to Egypt because King Herod is imitating the Egyptian pharaoh of old and trying to kill all the newborn males. The two stories form the basis of Christmas, the Christian celebration of Jesus's birth.

The Gospels of Mark and John don't include birth stories, and Jesus is presumed to have been born in the obscure village of Nazareth in Galilee.

In another example, the first three Gospels insist Jesus comes from the line of David, while in the fourth, the Gospel of John, a townsperson asks how Jesus could be the Messiah if he isn't related to David. John suggests Jesus is about 50 when he begins to preach; the other three think he is about 30. The age is significant: In Jewish teaching, a man doesn't become wise enough to really understand Scripture until he turns 30.

Still, two millennia later, we can develop a basic understanding of this extraordinary individual, who is believed by more than 2 billion people to be God who came to Earth.

The few historical records of Jesus's life

Our history of Jesus is confined to the information contained in the Bible's New Testament.

Roman and Jewish historians of the era when Jesus lived did not mention Jesus in any significant way. Here are the only mentions of Jesus or Christians in historical records that have been found. Any reference to Christians helps us pinpoint when Jesus might have lived.

- Cornelius Tacitus (AD 55–120) said Christians were blamed for the fire that destroyed Rome in AD 64. "Nero looked around for a scapegoat, and inflicted the most fiendish tortures on a group of persons already hated by the people for their crimes. This was the sect known as Christians." That only shows that Christians were living in Rome then.

- Lucian, a second-century Greek satirist, wrote, "The Christians, you know, worship a man to this day — the distinguished personage who introduced their novel rites, and was crucified on that account." His text is so late that he must have gotten his information from practicing Christians.

- Pliny the Younger, Roman governor of Bithynia in Asia Minor around AD 112, wrote a letter to Emperor Trajan asking for advice for dealing with Christians: "I have never participated in trials of Christians. I therefore do not know what offenses it is the practice to punish or investigate, and to what extent." Emperor Trajan replied, "They are not to be sought out; if they are denounced and proved guilty, they are to be punished."

The men were concerned because Christians did not worship Roman gods. To the Romans, that failure could cause the god to be angry and punish them. Christians were harassed and sometimes killed for their stubborn opposition to the pagan faith.

This letter exchange only proves that the Christians were involved in regular worship services at this time and had drawn the attention of Roman officials. It doesn't help us pinpoint any facts about Jesus. Recently, several historians argued that the letters may be forgeries anyway.

✔ Emperor Hadrian (AD 117–138), in a letter to Minucius Fundanus, the Asian proconsul: "If, therefore, the provincials can clearly evince their charges against the Christians, so as to answer before the tribunal, let them pursue this course only, but not by mere petitions, and mere outcries against the Christians. . . ."

✔ Gaius Suetonius Tranquillas, chief secretary of Emperor Hadrian, has two references to Christians in his books, which appeared around AD 117–138. In his account of Emperor Claudius's reign, he wrote, "As the Jews were making constant disturbance at the instigation of Chrestus, he expelled them from Rome." Later, writing about Emperor Nero, he noted, "Punishment by Nero was inflicted on the Christians, a class of men given to a new and mischievous superstition." Both are very late in Christian history and are vague. "Chrestus," means "Good" and is not necessarily a reference to Jesus.

✔ Josephus (AD 37–100?), a Jewish historian of the era, wrote the following: "About this time there lived Jesus, a wise man, if indeed one ought to call him a man. For he was one who performed surprising deeds and was a teacher of such people as accept the truth gladly. He won over many Jews and many of the Greeks. He was the Messiah. And when, upon the accusation of the principal men among us, Pilate had condemned him to a cross, those who had first come to love him did not cease. He appeared to them spending a third day restored to life, for the prophets of God had foretold these things and a thousand other marvels about him. And the tribe of the Christians, so called after him, has still to this day not disappeared."

The most controversial of all citations, it was not mentioned by Church fathers for another 300 years after Josephus died and must be an addition written into his text. Christians, for example, were not called by that name in Josephus's lifetime.

Preaching and teaching God's word

As an adult in Galilee (a region that lies to the north of Jerusalem), Jesus began to preach, speaking out for social justice and expressing love for all mankind.

He called on his followers to prepare for the coming end of the world and the arrival of a kingdom of God filled with peace. Scholars have identified what they believe is the essence of Jesus's teachings:

✔ God loves you and is with you.

✔ Love one another.

✔ Every person has immense value.

✔ The kingdom of God has come to earth.

✔ Believers will face final judgment in heaven or hell.

✔ God forgives those who ask.

As a result of Jesus's messages, some of his followers thought Jesus was the promised leader sent by God, a person known as the *Messiah* (see Chapter 13 for more about this concept). The Gospel accounts of Jesus are unclear whether Jesus himself claimed that role. In some places, he seems to. In others, he seems to avoid a direct answer. Later, his followers were sure Jesus was that special person.

His status was affirmed to believers by miracles he was credited with, including raising a man from the dead and turning water into wine. These miracles parallel accounts in the Jewish Bible where they are performed by prophets like Elijah. Historians today argue that the miracle accounts are later additions to the Jesus saga.

Jesus's claims stir the pot and create controversy

Despite his calls for peace and love, Jesus wasn't especially appreciated by the people of his day.

✔ **Romans didn't like Jesus or anyone who preached about a new kingdom.** After all, they were quite happy with the current kingdom, which was led by their emperor. They thought their emperor was a god and worshipped him. As a result, they attempted to kill anyone who suggested that someone else was God.

✔ **Jewish authorities couldn't have been pleased with Jesus either.** They were trying to accommodate the Romans and avoid bloodshed. They thought Yahweh would step in on their behalf eventually and oust the Romans anyway. Jesus's message of a coming end of the world could only heighten unrest, which is the last thing they wanted.

✔ **Jews who wanted to live in peace with the Romans rejected Jesus, too.** They didn't want the Romans attacking them because of Jesus's insistence on a kingdom of God.

✔ **Militant Jews rejected Jesus's call for peace.** Some Jews had decided not to wait for Yahweh to return to set the Romans straight, so they formed guerilla units that harassed Roman troops. They thought God would help them defeat their enemies and spurned any idea of peace.

A date with the cross

With so many opponents, Jesus had little chance to be heard or to survive. According to Christian reports, Jesus was eventually arrested and tried for treason by the Romans for claiming to be or being proclaimed as the king of the Jews.

The Romans then crucified Jesus; crucifixion was an excruciating manner of death in which a victim was nailed to a cross and left to die. Jesus was buried, but, according to his followers, arose in three days to reappear to his disciples. (You can read the accounts of Jesus's death and resurrection in Matthew 27–28; Mark 15–16; Luke 23–24; and John 19–20.)

Jesus's disciples (and Christians to this day) believed that Jesusconquered death and, if they followed his teachings and believed in him, they, too, could be saved from death.

No one knows exactly when Jesus died. The conflict in biblical dates has created problems in developing a chronology for Jesus. As historians found when trying to estimate when Abraham and his descendants actually lived, the problems of locating Jesus in known history are difficult. We would be helped by archaeological data or accounts left by other historians. Unfortunately, little has survived.

Many historians use 33 AD as the date of Jesus's death, even if it conflicts with aspects of his life story. For example, Passover that year did not fall on a weekend, but Jesus was supposedly crucified on Friday at the start of the Passover holiday.

In the first years after Jesus's death, few people knew about him. No writers or historians of the era wrote about him, except for one disputed paragraph in the book by Josephus, the Jewish historian of the first century AD.

As Christians note today, it's remarkable that a man who attracted so little attention in his era has become the center of the world's largest religion. They see God's hand in that situation.

The First Believers

The earliest followers of Jesus may have been called *Nazarenes.* The term comes from the Old Testament and was used in connection with two important figures there: Samson and Samuel. Samson was a judge who helped the Jews fight off the Philistines. Samuel was a judge and a prophet, linking the eras of judges and prophets together.

The tie between Samson and Samuel was the hair. Both were Nazarenes, a Jewish sect that developed around the concept of holy men completely absorbed in God. They vowed never to shave or cut their hair or nails, leaving their bodies as God created them.

Early Christians may have followed those guidelines because they copied the name. Some argue that the Nazarenes got their name because Jesus supposedly lived in the city of Nazareth.

No trace of historic Nazareth has ever been found. A city in Israel today that bears that name may or may not be the same one. Nazareth may have been a tiny suburb of a larger city, but evidence of its presence is scant until several hundred years after Jesus died.

What the early followers believed

The first Nazarenes lived in Jerusalem and continued to be faithful Jews. Later, they would be called *Ebionites* (meaning "poor ones"), a derisive reference to their communal living and the sharing of their minimal possessions. They viewed themselves as a reform movement within Judaism. They saw Jesus as a prophet and *sage* (a wise Jewish man who studied Scripture; see Chapter 11 for more on these folks).

They gathered together for worship and brought animals for ritual sacrifice at the Temple. They observed the Jewish holy days, circumcised their male children, followed kosher dietary laws, and practiced the teachings of Jesus as they interpreted them. These Jews truly believed Jesus had warned them about an onrushing end of the world.

The idea that the world was about to end has enjoyed a lot of support throughout history, predating Jesus, but the belief was very current in his day, as it is in modern times.

The ongoing religious turmoil, wars, and philosophical differences during the years that the Romans ruled the Jews led to a widespread conviction that God would punish the world with some kind of mass destruction.

A leader chosen by God was to herald the end of the world, an event known as *Armageddon.* After all, the concept of a final end was so overwhelming that it needed a divine being, a *messiah,* to bring it about. The early followers of Jesus believed he was the person destined to rule the new world that would arise when the old one was destroyed. See Chapter 14 for details on the end of the world idea.

But, given the believers' small numbers and isolated position in a tiny country on the eastern rim of the Roman Empire, how would anyone else find out about Jesus and his message?

The first missionary of Jesus

Paul took on that task of spreading Jesus's message. In letters (or *epistles*) preserved in the sacred texts, Paul said he was native of the city of Tarsus, in what is now Turkey. He claimed to have first persecuted the fledgling Nazarene sect, and then joined it and traveled throughout the Roman Empire to form small colonies of believers.

Paul believed that Jesus was sent by God in preparation for the coming end of the world. Paul began writing no earlier than AD 39, at least 30 years before the Gospel of Mark, the oldest book in the New Testament, was written. Some historians put the date of Paul's first letters as late as AD 50.

Paul's goal was to reach as many people as possible so that, when the end came, they could be saved. History was not his touchstone; philosophy was.

Paul may not have intended to start a new religion, but his approach opened the door to many people who felt stymied by Jewish laws but wanted to be part of the "Chosen People."

Just as Jesus had in his day, Paul faced many obstacles, too.

- ✔ **He was not well liked within the Nazarene community.** They were the first followers of Jesus, after all, and he was a late arrival. They were downright vicious in their criticism of him.

  In the surviving *Heresies by Epiphanius,* the Ebionites testified that "Paul had no Pharisaic background or training; he was the son of Gentiles, converted to Judaism in Tarsus, came to Jerusalem when an adult, and attached himself to the High Priest as a henchman. Disappointed in his hopes of advancement, he broke with the High Priest and sought fame by founding a new religion."

- ✔ **He had never met or even seen Jesus.** That put him at a disadvantage with the original followers of Jesus who did know him and his teachings. Some of the ideas Paul expressed conflicted with what the early Christians were teaching. For example, Church leaders wanted followers to follow Jewish laws, but Paul did not.

- ✔ **Paul's ideas about what Jesus taught and meant differed from the Nazarenes' beliefs.** The Nazarenes followed Jewish laws, for example, while Paul thought belief in Jesus without following the laws was enough to guarantee a place in heaven.

- ✔ **Paul said he suffered from some kind of infirmity.** Some historians today think he meant epilepsy.

Eventually, Paul was taken into Roman custody after a disagreement with the Nazarene leaders, taken to Rome, and, at least according to legends, executed there. Nevertheless, his strenuous efforts to share Jesus's message with the world led to the rise of Christianity.

A New Religion Grows

In spite of Paul's best attempts to reform Judaism through belief in Jesus — or, maybe, because of them — Jesus became the central figure amid a wide array of religious ideas. His followers were still mainly Jewish, but that wouldn't last long.

Many Jews were drawn to Jesus's call for peace and love. They had grown up with a militaristic deity. Jesus reflected a God who preferred peaceful coexistence. Others, called *God-fearers,* appreciated the fact that they didn't have to be circumcised to become a member of the "Chosen People."

Many pagans were attracted to the morality and ethics exhibited by Jesus's followers. Pagan philosophers noted how members of the early Christian community took care of each other; they wished their own religious communities were as loving.

Still, for at least the first decades after Jesus, followers continued to worship in synagogues and in the Temple. They read the same holy texts and followed the same religious practices as other Jews.

The only exception was observing the Sabbath. The early Christians started their Sabbath on Friday night with the rest of the Jewish population, but extended the holiday through Sunday (see Chapter 6). That may have been because Jesus rose from the dead on a Sunday.

The destruction of the Temple fuels growth

The Christian movement remained part of Judaism until AD 70, when the Temple in Jerusalem was destroyed by the Romans. To the Jews, the Temple was God's home. Its loss signified his unhappiness with them. To Christians, the end of the Temple implied that God had fled the Jews and that they were the new "Chosen People."

People whom Paul had converted and those living in colonies around the Mediterranean now constituted the bulk of the faith. They no longer had to contend with the Nazarenes.

The Nazarenes, who made their homes in Jerusalem, probably didn't survive the civil war against the Romans or the destruction of the city in AD 70. Jewish historian Josephus described a desperate group of Jews who made a suicidal charge against the Roman soldiers as the Temple burned. Some historians believe that group to be the Nazarenes.

Christians separate from Judaism

Over time, friction arose between mainstream Jews and the followers of Jesus. For starters, Jews firmly believed that any mistake on their part could cause the wrath of God to descend on them, as had happened in the past. No one wanted to go through Babylonian captivity again.

Moreover, Roman control of their land implied that God was already unhappy. How would he react to believers among them who now worshipped a dead messiah? No prophetic statements had prepared Jews for a messiah who died before achieving the expected goal of ruling over an independent Jewish theocracy.

As beliefs about Jesus solidified, some believers began to argue that Jesus was God incarnate, an idea that Jews rejected. To them, God was a spirit who would never become a man.

Finally, around AD 90, Jewish religious leaders began to insert into the regular services a prayer that condemned those who taught something contrary to traditional Jewish views. Followers of Jesus knew the prayer was meant for them. They responded by creating their own meeting places for religious services.

In time, they had a separate religion and a new name. *Christ* is the Greek word for "messiah." Greek was the language of the new religion; so, its followers became known as Christians.

The number of Christians began to grow rapidly and quickly eclipsed Judaism. Jews banned *proselytizing* (an attempt to convert someone to a religion), which had helped build their population to such heights, in fear that Christians were spying on them. Jews still do not recruit converts today.

Christian practices: It's no mystery

Christianity seemed to be part of a large group of beliefs once called *mystery religions*. They were all very different, but shared some common ideas.

> ✔ **They all had secret rituals to allow a follower closer contact with a deity.** *Communion,* the central Christian ritual of eating bread and wine in remembrance of Jesus, is one such ritual (see Chapter 6).

✔ **They contained an annual cycle in which life is renewed each spring and dies each fall.** Followers of the mystery cults found deep symbolic significance in the natural processes of growth, death, decay, and rebirth.

✔ **They included a myth in which the deity either returned to life after death or else triumphed over his enemies.** Implicit in the myth was the theme of redemption from everything earthly and temporal.

✔ **They were primarily concerned with the emotional life of their followers.** The cults used many different means to affect the emotions and imaginations of their followers and to invoke a "union with the god:" processions, fasting, communion, a play, acts of purification, blazing lights, and esoteric liturgies.

One of the biggest differences between Christianity and the other mystery religions was that the mystery religions didn't emphasize following specific beliefs. The Christian faith recognizes only one legitimate path to God and salvation, Jesus Christ. The other mystery religions were not so straight-laced, so members commonly traipsed from one cult to another.

In addition, other ideas began to circulate around the followers of Jesus, which apparently set off a wave of explanations for his life and death.

Perhaps the largest group that took an interest in the fledgling faith was the *Gnostics,* a philosophical and religious movement with roots in pre-Christian times.

Gnostics claimed that Jesus carried a message from heaven that allowed them to acquire *gnosis,* or inner knowledge. This gnosis was identified as the spark of divine thought that had been obscured by ignorance.

Christian leaders belittled Gnostics and their followers as heretics. By the sixth century, Christianity succeeded in overcoming the Gnostic movement. The only group to have survived into modern times is the Mandaean sect of Iraq and Iran. It has fewer than 15,000 members.

The big time arrives: Legitimacy in the Roman Empire

Christians fought for centuries against many faiths that developed around Jesus. After Gnosticism was defeated, the new religion took on other pagan faiths that abounded in the Roman Empire.

A brief attempt under the Roman Emperor Julian late in the fourth century to revive pagan faiths failed after he was slain in battle.

With Julian's death, Abraham's sole survivors consisted of a handful of Jews. The swelling multitudes of Christians were now in control of the Empire. To any onlooker, that would have been a strange scenario, considering how hard the Romans originally fought to suppress the faith.

Early Christians faced persecution because they refused to worship the Roman emperor. Many were killed in terrible ordeals and tortured, including being attacked by wild animals in Roman spectacles. The persecutions continued off and on for several hundred years. Some of the early records that mention Christians are from regional governors writing their emperors for advice in how to deal with Christians.

The outright persecutions ended in the beginning of the fourth century when Emperor Constantine, whose mother was Christian, legalized the faith. About 70 years later, Christianity was declared the only legal religion in the Roman Empire.

Nicene council sets the belief

As Christianity grew in members and power, the religion developed a solid philosophical base. Emperor Constantine invited some 250 to 318 church leaders from countries around the Mediterranean to meet in Nicea in 325 to resolve their differences.

More than religion was involved. Early Christians adopted the Roman view that the gods were responsible for the country's stability. If a debate raged, and no one knew who or what was the correct belief, then the country was in grave peril. The issue of what constituted the true belief was debated widely:

> "If you ask a man for change for a piece of silver, he tells you which way the son differs from the father; and if you ask for a loaf of bread, you get a reply that the son is inferior to the father," wrote Gregory, Bishop of Nyssa, after visiting Constantinople, the capital of the Roman Empire in the fourth century. "If you ask if your bath is ready, you are solemnly told the son is made out of nothing."

At the Nicean meeting, after much debate, the Church fathers approved the concept that God the Father, Jesus, and the Holy Spirit formed a single divinity. This is commonly known as the *Holy Trinity*.

The momentous work of shaping the Christian church would continue in future councils (also known as *synods*). Leading bishops met on a pretty regular basis through the fourth century. In time, they became known as Catholics, from the Latin word for "universal." When the religion split, the western side took the Name Roman Catholic; the eastern have, Greek Orthodox. See below and Chapter 6 for more information about the different Christian denominations.

Over that time, the bishops decided

- ✔ The correct days to celebrate the birth of Jesus, Christmas; and his death, Easter
- ✔ The calendar we use today, including the familiar AD and BC
- ✔ Church structure, which was based on the Roman government
- ✔ Procedures to become a priest and the rules that govern the priesthood

The delegates to Nicea in 325 approved a statement that binds all believers together. The *Nicene Creed* is still dutifully recited by the Roman Catholic faithful throughout the world during Mass. Here's the traditional version of the prayer:

We (I) believe in one God, the Father Almighty, maker of heaven and earth, and of all things visible and invisible.

And in one Lord Jesus Christ, the only begotten Son of God, and born of the Father before all ages. (God of God) light of light, true God of true God. Begotten not made, consubstantial to the Father, by whom all things were made. Who for us men and for our salvation came down from heaven. And was incarnate of the Holy Ghost and of the Virgin Mary and was made man; was crucified also for us under Pontius Pilate, suffered and was buried; and the third day rose again according to the Scriptures. And ascended into heaven, sits at the right hand of the Father, and shall come again with glory to judge the living and the dead, of whose Kingdom there shall be no end.

And (I believe) in the Holy Ghost, the Lord and Giver of life, who proceeds from the Father (and the Son), who together with the Father and the Son is to be adored and glorified, who spoke by the Prophets. And one holy, catholic, and apostolic Church. We (I) confess one baptism for the remission of sins. And we (I) look for the resurrection of the dead and the life of the world to come. Amen.

The Greeks split while the Romans grow in influence

There were still disagreements between the eastern half of the Roman Empire and the western portion. In the fourth century, Emperor Constantine had created the division by moving his capital from Rome to Constantinople in what is now Turkey.

Holy body parts multiplied like the loaves and fishes

When the Arabs claimed they had the cross upon which Jesus died in their possession, Christians weren't worried: There were enough *relics* to go around. Many people had grown disgusted with the selling of saintly relics, which led to the multiplication of body parts and endless frauds.

The Archbishop of Mainz, for example, supposedly owned "a fair piece of Moses's left horn (based on a biblical mistranslation), a whole pound of the wind that blew for Elijah in the cave of Mount Horeb, and two feathers and an egg of the Holy Ghost." By the mid-1500s, 56 fingers of Saint Peter the Dominican dotted European churches, along with 26 heads of Saint Juliene, 309 bodies of Saint George, 12 heads of Saint John the Baptist, and 70 veils of the Virgin Mary, not to mention many tears and footprints of Jesus.

The Greek half of the church eventually split away over the question of whether Jesus was "like" or "as" God. The two factions still disagree. Greek Orthodox Christians have their own leader today, called a *patriarch,* and do not obey the *pope,* the leader of the Roman Catholics. Occasional attempts at reconciliation have failed, especially after the Turkish armies overwhelmed Constantinople in the 1400s.

The Western world watched the great city fall, ending the last remnant of the Roman Empire. Constantinople's name was changed to Istanbul, and the Christian faith once based there was scattered.

The Roman Catholic Church had similar problems. Various marauding tribes conquered Rome, but the Church leaders took over for the departed Roman authorities and built their own political and social organization. As a result, the Church dominated society. Spreading out rapidly, Church missionaries converted pagan groups and retained the faith of millions until the religion splintered in the 1500s.

It's Hard to Keep Everyone Happy

The Church leaders knew people weren't happy, but they were surprised when the faith fell apart.

Rumblings against the powerful Roman Catholic Church had radiated through Europe for centuries. Small cults, designed to purify the faith, rose and fell, or cowered in distant mountains after soldiers sent by the pope massacred everyone in sight.

The Church couldn't maintain a united front, making it vulnerable to reformers. During one sorry episode, the pope fled Rome for Avignon, France, and then returned. At one time, three popes were in power simultaneously.

The first Pope John XXXIII was charged with a long list of crimes, including murder and rape. He may have been guilty of most of them.

For a brief period, the Church-led Crusades reconquered the Holy Land. That lasted less than 200 years. Eventually, the Arabs, under Saladin, held off English king Richard the Lionhearted, and Jerusalem once again was under Muslim rule. The Arabs seized reported remnants of the cross that once bore Jesus.

Martin Luther spells out his displeasure

Despite the discord, the Church survived and thrived. Then in 1517, it met its match when confronted by Martin Luther, a solemn Catholic monk.

Luther was upset after John Tetzel, a salesman sent by the Vatican to market indulgences, showed up in Wittenberg where Luther was teaching. *Indulgences* supposedly allowed people to rapidly pass through *purgatory,* a kind of unpleasant way station en route to heaven. People bought them for dead relatives. Many people objected to them, including Luther.

Convinced that the Church had lapsed into heresy, Luther decided to mimic Abraham and metaphorically smash the idols. On Halloween, Luther wrote down his complaints in Latin, creating 95 theses attacking the pope and Church practices, and nailed them to a church door that was used for public announcements.

His complaints eventually circled Europe, aided by the invention of the printing press just 60 years earlier.

Instead of being burned for his behavior, Luther was protected by German princes who were upset that the Church controlled a vast percentage of the Germanic land and siphoned off too much of the local proceeds. With Luther, they had a new religious leader to follow.

Luther's goal was to purify the Church, but, like many reformers before and after him, he ended up creating a new faith that opposed the old one.

Luther was very courageous. Called to answer charges of heresy in 1521, Luther marched bravely, like Daniel, into the lion's den of angry cardinals. Expected to apologize and denounce his own writing, Luther said, "Unless I am convinced by proofs from Scriptures or by plain and clear reasons and arguments, I can and will not retract, for it is neither safe nor wise to do anything against conscience. Here I stand. I can do no other. God help me. Amen."

Protestants reform, the Church counterreforms, and fighting ensues

Luther and his German princes soon had plenty of company as countries around Europe picked sides in what became known as the *Protestant Reformation*.

The name *Protestant* comes from the fact the participants were "protesting" against the Roman Catholic Church.

The Church did not accept this new *schism* (or split) quietly, creating a "counter reformation." The movement led to the founding of new religious orders, the cleansing of existing ones, and elimination of many of the abuses that had led to the creation of new Christian sects.

France and Spain stayed with the old beliefs of the Catholic Church. The Netherlands and, eventually, England did not. They didn't necessarily become Lutheran either. Luther's bold stance encouraged other theologians to offer their individualized views on God, Jesus, and salvation.

Some of the new leaders, like John Calvin, Ulrich Zwingli, and John Knox, were far more radical than Luther. They attracted followers, too. Soon, the religious conflict sawed Western society in half. No magician could unite the Catholic and Protestant portions.

Christians didn't see Muslims as their worst enemies any more; their Satan lay within their own ranks. As a result, from the 1520s to 1648, the two sides of Christianity fought with undisguised ferocity.

The Catholic Church created an order of priests called Jesuits to teach the faith, convert nonbelievers, and oppose Protestants. Today, the Jesuits are revered for scholarly and missionary pursuits, but in the early days of that order, they aided the Catholic Church's Inquisition. The Inquisition allowed priests to ask accused people whether or not they really believed in Christianity. The Jesuits were seeking people who claimed to be faithful but really were not or who taught ideas opposed to traditional Catholic teachings. Those who didn't were often turned over to the civic authorities to be burned.

English sailors reported horror stories of comrades captured by Catholic (mostly Spanish) forces and burned at the stake or sent to galleys as slaves. No cruelty on either side was considered sufficient when trying to protect the sainted Prince of Peace from desecration.

Meanwhile, both halves of Christianity fought for control, sparking explorations of the world as well as scientific investigations aimed at discovering God's intentions.

The religious conflicts led to the first "modern" war when Charles VIII of France led his troops across the Alps toward Italy with an eye on conquering the country. From that point on, Europe rang with the clash of weapons as Catholics fought Protestants and each other. Popes even led troops into battle.

The toll was incredible: Germany and Austria together lost 8.5 million people; Bohemia's population dropped from 3 million to 800,000. In Bohemia, a German state, 29,000 of the existing 35,000 villages were deserted. Starvation killed many of the noncombatants.

The rise of science in a Christian world

For centuries, people relied on faith to understand the world. Eventually, scholars began to develop ways to investigate the world. Science expanded rapidly, starting in the late Middle Ages. From Holland came the telescope. Through it, Dutch scientist Anton van Leeuwenhoek revealed far more about the heavens than anyone reading Genesis ever could discover.

Although such men of genius as Galileo, Harvey, Newton, Bacon, and Pascal also lived at this time, science often was the subject of fierce criticism. Many of the findings — such as Galileo's discovery of moons around Jupiter, meaning earth's moon is not unique as religious folks thought — seemed to contradict faith. Religion, caught in the backwash of scientific advances, fought to avoid being drowned. Scholars abruptly shifted the earth outside the center of the universe. Other long-held ideas collapsed, too. Evolution provided an answer for how mankind emerged. Space explorations discovered new worlds.

When critics' efforts failed to hold back the scientific tide, science was probed to support religious views. In 1650, the Reverend James Ussher, archbishop of Armagh, issued his famous study in which he "calculated" that the world was created in 4004 BC. Dr. John Lightfoot, vice chancellor of the University of Cambridge, added to those findings that life began at 9 a.m., October 23, of that year. Ussher's views became thought of as inspired as the Bible itself.

The end result of all that turmoil was the development of many Christian sects. Not until the 20th century did science find the tools to date ancient materials and demonstrate that the world was billions of years old.

Today, the Church endorses scientific exploration. As a result, Christians lead the way in many fields of study.

Conflict revives Armageddon ideas

Caught up in the turmoil between Protestants and Catholics and between science and religion, many people looked to the heavens. They were sure the world was going to end.

Predictions rolled from newly coined prophets like silver dollars moving through a stamping machine. The continued delay of the *Parousia* (the re-appearance of Jesus) naturally heightened speculation.

Christians scoured the Bible for clues. Because the canonical book of Revelation mentioned a 1,000-year reign (Revelation 20:5), *chiliasts* (from the Greek for "one thousand") believed the end of the first millennium would bring about the end of the current age.

In the 16th century, with the Western world horrified and sickened by the carnage from the religious wars, the concept of Jesus's return to earth enjoyed a rebirth of interest, beginning in England. Quakerism, for example, owes its beginning to chiliastic thought. They initiated a new wave of new predictions of Armageddon.

The Jehovah Witnesses, Seventh-day Adventists, Church of Jesus Christ of Latter-day Saints, and several other Christian sects were all founded in the 1800s, at least in part on the basis of (obviously inaccurate) forecasts of an immediate end of the world.

Christianity Today

Christianity has moved easily into modern times and is the largest single religion on Earth. Christian concepts remain ingrained in world culture, from art and music to literature and film.

Even modern wars take on religious connotations. World War I, which was between European states with United States joining the side of England and France, was called a "crusade," drawing on the memory of the religious crusades from hundreds of years ago. In the same way, the allied attacks on Iraq and Afghanistan in this century have been called a "crusade." Muslims in those countries describe it in the same words used by their counterparts when Christians invaded the Middle East starting in the 11th century.

Christians create immortal works

In its 2,000-year history, Christianity has enriched our lives enormously. As Dr. Jaroslav Pelikan, one of this country's foremost religious historians, discovered in his research, if Christianity were removed from Western civilization, little would be left.

He's right. What would the world be like without music like Handel's *Messiah,* the artwork like Michelangelo's ceiling of the Sistine Chapel, the warmth of Christmas, or the philosophical insights of a Roger Bacon, Thomas More, or C.S. Lewis? Our seasons revolve around Christian ideas; our lives are infused with Christian icons like Jesus, Mary, Peter, Paul, and James, who are integral to our lives and literature.

The Roman Catholic Church, the largest single Christian denomination, has changed to accommodate new ideas. For example, religious services were once held only in Latin. Reforms approved in 1963 allowed churches to use the native language instead. At the same time, some saints thought to be mythical were eliminated from the calendar, among other reforms. In the process, several denominations that were once combatants have made peace. The Catholic Church has been working with the Anglican and Lutheran churches.

Meanwhile, Christian missionaries still fan out across the world to bring the message of Jesus to more people. That has led to occasional conflicts in Islamic countries. See Chapter 18 for details.

Christian holidays are followed worldwide, even in countries with small or no Christian population. Christian themes radiate through political debates. In many ways, Christianity has evolved into the world's religion.

Chapter 6

Christian Beliefs and Practices

• •

In This Chapter

▶ Christian holidays: More than a reason to party

▶ Summing up holy sites

▶ Putting faith into practice through rituals

▶ Looking at symbols

▶ Trying to count up the various denominations

• •

*B*ill's grandfather-in-law belonged to a liberal Scottish Christian group with fewer than ten members. He founded the sect and brought it to this country. His three children joined Protestant sects. When Grandfather Bambeck died, his miniature Scottish-born faith disappeared.

Grandfather could have become a great patriarch if his ideas had intrigued enough followers, or one really important and influential follower — like Constantine the Great, who supported Christianity way back in the fourth century and made the religion powerful. That's how a small cult develops into a sect and, finally, into a great religion. Christianity and Islam began that way, starting tiny with a handful of people gathered around Jesus or Mohammad, and then slowly expanding by attracting new followers.

Christianity, both then and today, consists of various cults and sects. Many of these groups developed because people read the New Testament faithfully. They discovered new ways to appreciate Jesus through rituals, holidays, and symbols. Above all, they tried to live according to his teachings. They serve to remind us how vibrant the faith is and how important Jesus is to each new generation of believers.

This chapter examines the Christian holidays, rituals, symbols, and sects that define the world's largest religion.

The First Noel: Christmas and the Roots of Christianity

Every year, Christians celebrate the birth of their founder. Biblical accounts vary, but most Christians believe Jesus was born in the city of Bethlehem in a barn outside an inn. Angels came to visit him, as did wise men or kings bearing gifts. The resulting holiday features seasonal songs called *carols,* as well as religious services, decorations, parties, and other holiday events.

To a somber church father living some 1,800 years ago, today's hoopla around this holy day would be stunning. Christmas wasn't even celebrated with any known festivities for at least 200 years after Jesus was born. Even the term *Christmas,* so familiar to us, was unknown then. The word comes from two Old English words *Cristes moesse,* meaning "the mass or festival of Christ." The suffix *–mas* is derived from the closing Latin words of a religious service: *Ite missa est,* meaning "it is ended."

Because Christianity didn't develop in a vacuum, much of what we take to be Christian started in another culture and was adopted and modified by believers. Christmas is no exception. Many aspects of the festive occasion have antecedents reaching back deep into history.

Santa himself was born in Dutch stories about Saint Nicholas, who brought little children gifts on December 6. When the English conquered the Dutch city of New Amsterdam and changed its name to New York, English children saw their new Dutch friends get gifts and pestered their parents for the same thing. Because the English Christians didn't believe in saints, the closest holiday for which they could give gifts was Christmas. Saint Nicholas's name was *anglicized* (changed to English) to Santa Claus, and he began to deliver presents to good little English children on December 25. In time, he became the internationally recognized symbol of Christmas.

Aspects of today's festivities extend beyond the mandatory red costumes and fake beards of Santa. Christmas add-ons include everything from mistletoe, poinsettias, boughs of holly, eggnog, and fruitcakes to lights, decorations, trees trimmed with ornaments and other decorations, holiday-themed clothing, greeting cards, and, of course, carols.

To some Christians, the secular activities have detracted from the religious aspects. To remember the holy season, many Christians display a *nativity scene* (also called a *crèche*). Figurines of Mary, Joseph, baby Jesus, the three wise men, shepherds, and animals are often set up on church lawns and in private homes. The nativity scene was developed in the Middle Ages to help explain the story of Christ's birth to illiterate parishioners. The most popular holiday carols, like "Silent Night" and "Hark! The Herald Angels Sing," reflect the deep feeling Christians have for this sacred day. For many Christians, Christmas is a day for prayer, meditation, and somber reflection on the life and words of Christ.

Some people use *Xmas* as an abbreviation. Actually, the *X* is the Greek letter *chi,* which is the first letter of the word *Christ.* As a result, *Xmas* is actually appropriate usage, despite occasional objections from religious purists.

Why a holiday for the Nativity?

Christmas doesn't show up on the list of Christian festivals described by early Church fathers. Origen, the most prolific writer among the early Church hierarchy, didn't like the idea of a birthday party at all. He noted that the birthdays of Moses, Abraham, and other prophets didn't warrant a single slice of cake. In the holy texts, he added scornfully, only sinners celebrate their birthdays.

Arnobius, another great leader of that day, satirically commented on the "birthday of the gods." He felt that celebrating Jesus's birthday would equate Jesus with the Roman emperors, whom pagans thought of as gods, rather than with God, the Father. After all, Roman emperors enjoyed annual feasts on their birthdays.

However, opposition faded as Christianity began to grow. The new faith smacked into other religions, like those believing in a god named Mithra, which celebrated the birthday of its founder. Roman holidays, such as the Saturnalia, also seemed a lot more fun with parties and special events.

Finally, in the third century, leaders of the Church decided that a day dedicated to the birth of Jesus would help retain and attract members. By that time, many smaller churches had already begun to hold annual celebrations.

Why December?

When the Church finally decided to have a holiday to mark Jesus's nativity, the question was when to celebrate it. In AD 200, when the holiday finally earned an official mention in the Church, the big day was May 20. Religious leaders thought the ninth month of their calendar corresponded to the ninth month of the calendar at the time when Jesus lived.

Other dates suggested for Jesus's birthday included April 19 and April 20. March 28 earned a vote because that was the day, supposedly, when the sun was created. (A later study found that Christ's birthday has been earnestly placed on virtually every day of the year, with each claim supported by ample evidence or wise conjecture.)

The issue was debated well into the fourth century. Finally, most Church fathers agreed to observe the birth of Christ on December 25. As a result, Christmas is celebrated then, but in Hispanic countries, the big day is January 6, when the traveling Magi supposedly arrived in Bethlehem to worship baby Jesus.

So the decision to place Christmas on December 25 was political, not religious. Church leaders opted for December for several reasons:

- **They wanted to counter a variety of holidays.** Every year, the Romans celebrated a huge December event called the *Saturnalia,* a wild affair in which slaves and masters could switch roles. In addition, the Romans marched around with evergreen boughs and gave gifts.

  Christians also wanted to overshadow the holiday that celebrated the December birthday of Mithra, the Zoroastrian god of truth and light. Roman soldiers had adopted Mithra, so he was a formidable foe to the new Christian religion.

- **Pagan holidays marked the beginning of winter and, with it, the death of the sun god.** He died on December 22 and was reborn on December 25. The rebirth concept dovetailed with the Jesus story.

Note that Christmas is more than a single day. Christians use the weeks before Christmas to prepare themselves spiritually to celebrate Christ's birth. After Christmas, they remember special events that took place shortly after Jesus was born. The Christmas season includes

- **Advent,** which marks the start of the Church calendar and spans the four weeks leading up to Christmas. Advent, which means "coming," refers both to the birth of Jesus and his promised return to judge all mankind. Customs vary throughout Christianity, but believers see this holiday as a time to prepare for Jesus.

  Scripture readings for Advent reflect this emphasis with selections focusing on themes of accountability faith, judgment on sin, and the hope of eternal life. To Christians, Advent signifies Jesus's presence in this world, requiring a focus on ethics and appropriate behavior.

  Specific colors are linked to each of the four weeks of Advent, including blue and purple. At one time, Christians fasted on Saint Martin's Day during Advent and also handed out gifts. The gift portion was later transferred to Christmas. Wreaths and candles are also part of the celebration.

✔ The **Feast of the Immaculate Conception,** celebrated during Advent on December 8. The day commemorates Mary, Jesus's mother, who herself is believed to have been born without sin.

✔ **Twelfth Night,** which marks the last day of the holiday on January 5. Many of the holiday traditions, such as the wassail drink and fruitcakes, actually began with this holiday. It once marked the end of an ancient pagan holiday that began with Halloween, but became absorbed into Christianity. In some countries, Twelfth Night was the last day Christmas decorations could be left up and marked the beginning of festivals leading up to Easter. At one time, baptisms were conducted on this day, but the holiday has lost much of its religious significance.

✔ **Epiphany,** which is January 6. Epiphany grew out of Hanukkah, the Jewish festival of lights (see Chapter 4). Epiphany marks the revelation of God to mankind in the person of Jesus Christ. This is also the day when the *Magi* (the three wise men) visited baby Jesus in Bethlehem, according to the account in Matthew's gospel (see Matthew 2:1–11 for all the details).

Other Christian Holidays

Christians, unlike Jews, recognize very few holidays. In fact, Christianity has so many sects that not even all Christians accept Christmas as a religious holiday. The Roman Catholic faith observes minor holidays that are named for saints whose lives served as an example for others, but Protestants often don't recognize these holidays.

As a result, Valentine's Day, named for the Catholic Saint Valentine, has become a secular romantic holiday. Saint Patrick's Day, named for an Irish Catholic saint, has become another secular holiday with green beer and parades.

Hallelujah! He is risen: Easter

Spring is a time for rebirth, which is why almost every religion has a holiday then. (Passover is the Jewish spring holiday; see Chapter 4.)

Easter is a spring holy day that commemorates the death of Jesus and his resurrection. According to the Bible, Jesus was crucified and died on Friday, but he rose from the dead and was seen by his disciples on Sunday. His victory over death provides a model for the faithful to follow. They believe that because Jesus overcame death, they, too, will obtain immortality.

The only religious holiday accepted by all Christians is Easter.

Spring forward

Winter celebrations were commonplace in ancient cultures. Most people found the winter very discouraging with the ice, snow and cold, and shorter days. They weren't sure spring would ever arrive.

They often made sacrifices to encourage their gods to hurry the warming process. In Germany, the evergreen tree eventually replaced the human sacrifice. The Yule log of Christmas is a remnant of that ancient ritual. The evergreen, which retained its color and was assumed immortal, became a phallic symbol tied to fertility rituals. Other winter plants that are associated with Christmas have their roots (sorry, bad pun)

in ancient customs. To ancient Germans, holly depicted the queen of heaven (Mary, Jesus's mother), while white berries on the mistletoe represented drops of semen.

The winter holidays go back even further than Europe. The ancient Egyptians set aside 12 days to celebrate at the end of the year. They, too, used greenery — in this case, palm fronds — as symbols of eternal life. The Egyptians created the holiday because their calendar was originally only 360 days long. When they realized they were five days short, they extended the calendar. That was a great reason for a party.

Easter history

No one celebrated Easter in the early years of Christianity. Instead, when Christians decided to observe Easter, they borrowed elements from other spring holidays. The principal model was Passover, the Jewish holiday, which celebrates the Exodus from Egypt. That's because, according to the Bible, Jesus died during the holiday.

By the fourth century, Church fathers wanted to separate themselves completely from Judaism and decreed that the holiday would fall on a Sunday.

How Easter is celebrated

The days leading up to Easter Sunday are solemn ones, typically used for religious services and contemplation.

Palm Sunday is celebrated the Sunday before Easter and commemorates Jesus's entry into Jerusalem. In Christian tradition, his arrival represents the first time the public welcomed him as their redeemer. In the Gospel of John, palm fronds are laid along Jesus's path. They represent victory and triumph. People lining the streets also waved fronds, adding to the symbolism and giving the holiday its name.

Practices vary according to the sect of Christianity. In the Roman Catholic faith, for example, baptisms are held on Easter. Many groups hold candlelight vigils, read sections from the Bible that concentrate on creation and rebirth, and renew their faith. Many churches will troop down to a body of water to hold group baptisms.

Why is Easter on a different date every year?

Easter bounces around the calendar in tandem with the Jewish holiday of Passover. That's because the day when the Passover festival begins is based on the lunar calendar. Aside from some complicating factors that aren't interesting or important, the date of Easter Sunday falls, follow us now, on the first Sunday after the first full moon after the vernal equinox. The vernal equinox is usually March 21, so the earliest possible date for Easter is March 22; the latest possible date is April 25.

Because Jesus died after celebrating Passover, according to biblical accounts, the two holidays are inevitably tied together.

Easter is the only Christian holiday that isn't fixed to a specific day.

Churches are typically festooned with flowers. Easter lilies are a traditional floral arrangement.

The day is not all solemn. Congregations contemplate the great joy that Mary must have felt when greeting her resurrected son. As a result, music plays a big part in the activities.

Easter symbols

Eggs are a symbol of rebirth, and the early Christians worked this pagan symbol into their observances of Easter. But ironically, these eggs (and today, other goodies) are delivered by the Easter Bunny. Rabbits don't lay eggs, but the connection was made through Oester, a German fertility goddess whose name was converted to Easter. Every deity had a *familiar,* an animal that kept him or her company. Witches had black cats. Oester had rabbits.

A solemn and somber season: Lent

Lent ("spring"), the only other major Christian holy observance, consists of 40 days preceding Easter. It commemorates two aspects of Jesus's life: the 40 days in lived in the desert, fasting and fighting off the devil's temptations; and, in some sects, the 40 hours he was in the tomb before his resurrection.

To Christians, this is a time of sacrifice and prayer. Many give up something they enjoy to emulate Jesus's fast. The money saved is then donated to charity. Lent, too, grew from pagan and Jewish sources.

Early Christians didn't observe Lent. However, festivals for risen Greek gods like Osiris, Adonis, and Tammuz all featured 40-day fasts. Jews commemorated a 40-day period leading up to God giving them the Ten Commandments on Mount Sinai. Eventually, Christians felt a need to develop a holiday that countered those of opposition faiths.

There's no definite date when the holiday was initiated, but it became accepted by the fifth century. The Catholic Encyclopedia suggested there was a 50-day festival, of which 40 were set aside to be less of a party and more devoted to prayer.

Many Christians recognize Lent by attempting to give up unhealthy foods, like chocolate, or stop bad habits, like smoking. Others use Lent as a time to take up charitable causes or attempt personal improvement, such as increasing exercise or praying every day.

Lent is more than a 40-day commemoration. It has several holy days associated with it:

- **Fat Tuesday:** This holiday actually precedes Lent, which begins the following day on Ash Wednesday. Also called Mardi Gras, this day is considered the last day for fun and festivities before the serious work of religious contemplation begins, to prepare for Easter. The city of New Orleans marks the day before Ash Wednesday with a big party that's renowned for excessive and perhaps unsavory behavior.

- **Ash Wednesday:** This is the day Lent begins. Christians go to church to pray and have a cross drawn in ashes on their foreheads. The ashes draw on an ancient tradition and represent repentance before God. The holiday is part of Roman Catholic, Lutheran, Methodist, and Episcopalian liturgies, among others.

- **Holy Thursday:** This is one of the important days in the Easter celebration and is tied to four events in Jesus's life: his washing of his disciples' feet; the institution of the Eucharist (ingesting of bread and wine in Jesus's name) at the Last Supper; the suffering of Jesus at the Garden of Gethsemane; and the betrayal of Jesus by Judas Iscariot, who identified him to the Roman soldiers. It is also known as *Maundy Thursday*. *Maundy* is derived from the Latin word for "commandment."

- **Good Friday:** Another highly significant day, this holiday commemorates the crucifixion and death of Jesus. In some faiths, it is a fast day. For many Christians, it is a day of solemn services and prayer.

A weekly holy day: The Sabbath

Christians very early in their history added Sunday to the traditional Saturday Sabbath (see Chapter 5). At one time, the Roman Catholic Church required parishioners to attend Mass that day.

Early Christians followed the Jewish tradition of setting aside one day each week for prayer. However, soon after Jesus, historical accounts indicate that his followers expanded the Sabbath to include Sunday. The Bible indicates that Jesus died on a Friday and appeared to his followers on a Sunday. In 325, Emperor Constantine declared Sunday as the official Christian day of rest.

Until the 20th century, so-called Blue Laws prohibited American businesses from being open on Sunday. Eventually, that law was challenged in court and ended.

For many Christians, Sunday remains a day for prayer and contemplation of the mysteries of the faith. The Roman Catholic Church used to require attendance at Mass that day, but dropped the rule during the 1960s reformation of the faith.

Today, just as with Jews, many Christians treat Sunday as a day for daily activities away from work.

Happening upon Christianity's Holy Sites

Because Christianity has sprouted so many branches, finding a sacred site depends on which group is providing the directions. For example, Lourdes in France is considered holy to Roman Catholics because that's where Mary, Jesus's mother, reportedly appeared to 14-year-old Bernadette Soubirous in 1858. However, Protestants don't share that belief.

Seeing how sites become holy

In truth, almost any site can be holy as long as something associated with the religion happened there. Some places are considered holy through traditions that developed around them. Other sites have official church endorsements.

As religions develop, they accumulate sacred sites — places where their founders or other leaders walked, worshipped, or had a revelation. Often, these places are shifted from an older religion to a new one. For example, many pagan sites were taken over by the Roman Catholic Church for the simple purpose of building a church there.

On one archaeological site in Israel, for example, a former Greek temple was converted into a Jewish synagogue and then into a Christian church, all within a few hundred years. Today, the locale is deserted except for tourists.

Wandering around Rome and the Vatican

The Roman Catholic Church, like religions before it, carefully selected sites on which it would build churches and where its followers would worship. The grandest site of all is the Vatican, home to the pope, and St. Peter's Basilica. These buildings are located in Vatican City, a tiny, independent country located within Rome, Italy, and they sit on a pagan gravesite.

In Helen's footsteps

For many years after Jesus, Christians didn't designate any sacred sites. They were too busy surviving Roman persecution, the Jewish wars, and battles against heretics.

Finally, in the fourth century, Helen, Emperor Constantine's mother, identified places where Jesus lived and walk, and designated them as shrines. The places where Jesus lived and died were forgotten by the time they were identified by Helen, who waited for inspiration to strike as she wandered around Jerusalem. Unfortunately, she was there about 300 years after Jesus, so many of the important sites were gone. The destruction of Jerusalem in AD 70 pretty much jumbled up the place.

Historians know Helen wasn't correct about Golgotha, the place where Jesus died on the cross. She chose a site that was outside Roman control at the time Jesus lived. Because Jesus was crucified by the Romans, they would not have used that site.

When Christianity became the sole religion of the empire in the late fourth century, Christian leaders often took over Jewish or pagan holy sites and gave them new meaning. Today, visitors cheerfully go to the various, often duplicate, sites in good faith that one of them is correct.

Rome became an important Christian site for several reasons:

- ✔ It was the home of the Roman Empire, the seat of power and significance. When the Roman Empire fell in the fifth century, the Catholic Church seamlessly slid into the power vacuum. The Church had already borrowed titles from the Roman Empire for its own officers.

- ✔ Paul, the great apostle who spread the knowledge of Jesus, supposedly was martyred there around AD 64.

- ✔ Peter, the leading follower of Jesus, also supposedly was killed there.

Other important sites in Christianity are detailed in Chapter 12.

Rituals: Outward Expressions of Faith

Christian *rituals* (ceremonial acts that follow religious customs) often were drawn directly from biblical accounts. The rituals serve as reminders of Jesus's sacrifices. Some Christian sects refer to these rituals as *sacraments*.

Early Communion

The idea that wine and bread can represent a deity reaches back before Christianity.

One such meal was part of the Mithraic religion, which Christianity battled for many years. The ritual was similar to Communion and was accompanied with the words: "He who shall not eat of my body nor drink of my blood, so that he may be one with me and I with him, shall not be saved."

Wine and bread were pagan symbols for the divine long before Mithra, too. In 50 BC, the Roman orator Cicero wrote that equating a god with corn and the vine was only symbolic. He then asked, "Is anybody so mad as to believe that which he eats is actually a god?"

One bread, one body: Communion

When worshippers observe the central Christian ritual called *Communion* (or sometimes the *Eucharist*), they eat a small wafer and sip from a cup of wine (or grape juice). The bread and wine symbolize the body and blood of Christ. This ritual is based on the biblical account of the *Last Supper* (also called the *Lord's Supper*) when Jesus asked his followers to eat bread and drink wine in memory of him.

This ritual is an integral part of many Christian worship services and is derived from the Latin word for "common." Partaking of the ritual allows a Christian to remember Christ and to contemplate his or her own life. Many faithful Christians participate in the ritual on a weekly basis.

At one time, the Christian world was hotly divided over the question of whether the wine and bread is actually *transmuted* (changed form) into the real flesh and blood of Jesus after being ingested. While the debate has faded, some Christian faiths still believe in *transubstantiation*.

Now most Christians focus on the metaphorical idea that Jesus is the "blood and body" of life — that is his sacrifice represents the essence of existence. No eating of human flesh is involved, an idea that nauseated the Romans and helped fuel their anger against the early Christians.

Welcoming new Christians through baptism

Baptism is a sacred rite in Christianity. Babies are brought into churches to be welcomed into the faith with holy water. In some sects, adults are led to rivers or to the ocean for ritualistic baths.

Doing a little spiritual cleaning

Water, a rare commodity in the dry Middle East, played an important part in Jewish rituals at the time of Jesus.

Sluices found at Qumran, an isolated desert site inhabited by very religious Jews until AD 70, for example, are thought to have fed ritual baths, called *mikvahs*. Today, converts to Judaism and women undergoing purification are required to bathe in a mikvah.

Leviticus in the Old Testament lists a variety of laws regarding ritualistic cleansing, which can be seen as primitive baptism: ridding walls of mildew (Leviticus 14:33–53); purifying a woman after childbirth (Leviticus 12:1–8); and accepting a healed leper back into the community (Leviticus 13:1–36, 14:1–32).

Jars holding baptismal water were commonplace in Jesus's day. Those jars show up in the biblical story of the Cana wedding where Jesus turned the water into wine.

"Nearby stood six stone water jars, the kind used by the Jews for ceremonial washing, each holding from twenty to thirty gallons. Jesus said to the servants, 'Fill the jars with water'; so they filled them to the brim. Then he told them, 'Now draw some out and take it to the master of the banquet.' They did so, and the master of the banquet tasted the water that had been turned into wine."
—John 2:6–9

Although the Bible never says that Jesus baptized anyone, the sacred texts describe a man named John the Baptist who baptized Jesus in the Jordan River. According to several accounts, John felt that people awaiting the end of the world needed the last baptism as final proof of their belief. Modern baptism serves that same idea: to cleanse away old sins and to symbolize birth. To some, baptism represents their acceptance in the salvation promised by Jesus.

The concept draws on Jewish teachings, which encouraged cleanliness. In fact, Jews were mocked by Romans for insisting on ritual cleanings on a daily basis. John the Baptist, who was Jewish, drew on the ritual cleansing idea, but insisted that one final baptism was necessary for a person to repent of his sins and to seal the individual in preparation for the coming end of the world. That view was incorporated into Christianity.

The Roman Catholic Church made baptism a sacrament, in accordance with the biblical accounts of Jesus's baptism, and requires infants to be baptized to receive God's saving grace. The debate over whether baptism is for babies or for anyone, however, led to bloody battles in the Middle Ages.

Today, baptism remains a key component of Christian faith. Some sects insist on infant baptism; others allow children to be older. A person who feels "born again" — that is, returning with full faith to Christianity — is often baptized again as well to symbolize that status.

Celebrating additional sacraments

Many Christian sects have more than the two basic sacraments of Communion and baptism. The additional ones range from ceremonies involving marriage, confirmation of faith, death, reconciliation to the faith, and the taking of *holy orders* (becoming a priest or a nun). These sacraments are accepted by orthodox Christians and members of the Roman Catholic Church.

Groups like the Salvation Army and Society of Friends don't see the need for additional sacraments. They believe they are living a sacramental life.

The Different Symbols of Christianity

Christians have developed many symbols to reflect their beliefs. The most common symbols are the cross, halos, and fish. These symbols can show up on the walls of homes, as well as in everyday life, in religious services, and on clothing or even cars.

The old rugged cross

The cross, which Romans used as an instrument of torture, became the symbol of eternal life for Christians (see Figure 6-1). According to biblical accounts, Jesus died by being nailed to a cross. Because he symbolized victory of life over death, the instrument of his torture took on special significance in the faith that developed around him.

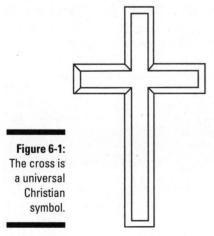

Figure 6-1:
The cross is a universal Christian symbol.

Christians had a model to draw on. Prior to Jesus, the cross had been used by Jewish zealots who fought against the Roman occupation of their land. So many of them were crucified as punishment that the cross took on special significance. Early Christians saw the cross in the same way.

In early years, all images of Jesus on a cross didn't depict his suffering. Realism crept into artwork in the Middle Ages, just as it did in other types of paintings. Eventually, some sects refused to showed a bloody Jesus and only use a cross as a symbol. Other sects insist that Jesus must be part of the sacred image.

The cross appears in the flags of many countries, including Great Britain and Sweden. Many athletes make the sign of the cross before, during, and after athletic competition. One baseball player used to draw a cross on the ground with his bat before batting.

At one time, the cross was used as a kind of protective mark against illness and was even placed on cattle to shield them.

The cross symbol and accounts of crucifixion also show up throughout world history.

- ✔ Easter occurs shortly after the time of the vernal equinox, an event considered important by astrologers during the Roman Empire, who viewed the astrological event as the time of the crossing of two astrological celestial circles. They symbolized the equinox by a cross.

- ✔ Many pagan gods were crucified. Divine or semidivine figures who are crucified appear in the mythology of civilizations stretching from the British Isles (the farthest extent of the Roman Empire) across the Middle East to India. Osiris, the Egyptian god of the underworld, is described with his arms stretched out on a tree like Jesus on the cross. This tree was sometimes shown as a pole with outstretched arms — the same shape as the Christian cross.

- ✔ In the worship of the Greek god Serapis, the cross was a religious symbol. Indeed, the Christian "Latin cross" symbol may be based directly on the cross symbol of Osiris, an important Egyptian god.

The biblical description of Jesus's death on the cross fits what we know about crucifixions throughout history, including his *scourging* (whipping) and the use of guards around the cross to prevent a rescue.

The Gospel writers may have added other details based on texts that preceded them:

- ✔ "He is despised and rejected of men; a man of sorrows and acquainted with grief; and we hid our faces from him; he was despised and we esteemed him not." —Isaiah 53:3

- ✔ "For dogs have compassed me; the assembly of the wicked have enclosed me; they pierce my hands and feet." —Psalm 22:16

- ✔ "Give strong drink to him who is ready to perish." —Proverbs 31:6

- ✔ "They gave me also gall for my meat; and in my thirst they gave me vinegar to drink." —Psalm 69:21

- ✔ "He was numbered with the transgressors." —Isaiah 53:12

- ✔ "The sun and the moon shall be darkened, and the stars shall withdraw their shining. The Lord shall also roar out of Zion, and utter his voice from Jerusalem, and heaven and earth shall shake." —Joel 3:15–16

- ✔ "They shall look upon me whom they have pierced, and they shall mourn for him as one mourns for his only son." —Zechariah 12:10

What's the bright idea behind halos?

Many Christian religious icons and paintings feature *halos,* an aura of light hovering over a holy person's head, as shown in Figure 6-2. That image was actually banned in ancient times by the early Church because it was used in pagan artwork. After several centuries, Christian artists could use halos, but they had to be square to distinguish them from pagan versions. Finally, around the ninth century, the Church felt that the pagans had been overcome and permitted artists to incorporate the now-familiar round halos.

Figure 6-2:
Jesus is often depicted with a halo.

Check out that hat!

One article of dress specifically tied to Christianity is called a mitre hat. Long and thin, it ends in a pointed, open top. The hat takes its design from the fish symbol used for Mithra (again, the Zoroastrian god of truth and light), along with the pope's famous fisherman's ring. Only Roman Catholic officials can wear this hat.

Fish, lamb, doves, and more

You may have seen a fish on the back of a car on a necklace. It, too, is a symbol of Christianity. The letters of the Greek word for fish, *ichthus*, spells out the first letters of "Jesus Christ, Son of God, Savior." Early Christians used a fish to symbolize their faith. Today, the image of a fish reflects the Christian faith without the need for words.

Other symbols often associated with Christianity actually have other roots:

- ✔ **Lamb:** Jesus is called the "lamb of God," reflecting his role in a sacrifice for man's sins. That idea is borrowed from Judaism and shows up in Passover as the animal sacrificed so the Angel of Death would bypass Jews during the ten plagues.

- ✔ **Dove:** A dove appears when Jesus is baptized by John the Baptist. As a result, a dove is often associated with Jesus. Once again, this is a Jewish symbol. Today, the dove represents Israel as well as peace.

- ✔ **Rainbow:** This is both a Christian and Jewish symbol, representing God's promise. It comes from the Bible. In Genesis, after a terrible flood destroys all of mankind except Noah and his family, God sends a rainbow as a promise never to destroy all humans again.

Many Christians, Many Sects

After Martin Luther broke with the Catholic Church (see Chapter 5), he inspired many other religious leaders to offer their own ideas. As a result, Christianity today has more sects than it's possible to count. The sincere efforts made by the Church fathers at Nicaea (see Chapter 5) to develop a single, universal view of Jesus and eliminate any others has failed.

Worldwide, Christianity claims about 2.1 billion members among its many sects. They include the African Independent Churches, the Aglipayan Church, Amish, Anglican/Episcopalian, Armenian Apostolic, Assembly of God, Baptists, Calvary Chapel, Catholic, Christadelphians, Christian Scientist, Church of Jesus Christ of Latter-day Saints, Coptic Christians, Eastern Orthodox, Ethiopian Orthodox, Evangelicals, Iglesia ni Cristo, Jehovah's Witnesses, the Local Church, Lutherans, Methodists, Monophysites, Nestorians, the New Apostolic Church, Pentecostals, Plymouth Brethren, Presbyterian, Seventh-day Adventist, Shakers, Disciples of Christ, Churches of Christ, the International Church of Christ, Quakers, United Church of Christ/Congregationalists, the Unity Church, Universal Church of the Kingdom of God, Vineyard churches, and others.

And of course, each of these sects can be separated into additional categories, ranging from fundamentalist to liberal.

Overall, American Protestants outnumber Catholics — 52 percent to 24 percent — but Protestants are broken into so many smaller units that no one denomination is larger than the Catholic bloc. The largest single group of Christians in the United States is Catholic, with about 67.2 million members in 2001. Baptists are second with 47.7 million members.

Here are the top ten Christian denominations in the United States based on 2006 membership.

1. Roman Catholic Church: 67.2 million

2. Southern Baptist Convention: 16.4 million

3. United Methodist Church: 8.2 million

4. Church of Jesus Christ of Latter-day Saints: 5.5 million

5. Church of God in Christ: 5.4 million

6. National Baptist Convention USA: 5 million

7. Evangelical Lutheran Church in America: 4.9 million

8. National Baptist Convention of America: 3.5 million

9. Presbyterian Church (U.S.A.): 3.2 million

10. Assemblies of God: 2.7 million

All believe in Jesus. Members of each are sure they are saved, but they're not so positive about anyone else.

Chapter 7

The Birth of Islam: The Prophet Submits to Allah

In This Chapter

▶ Understanding how the Arab world gave birth to Islam

▶ Welcoming Muhammad to the ranks of great religious leaders

▶ Developing two Islamic points of view

Mark went fishing recently in upstate New York with his new rod. On a remote road in the woods by a lake, a van pulled over in front of him. Mark stopped behind the van, thinking there might be a good fishing hole nearby, and what he saw surprised him. The driver was a man dressed in a robe. He took out a small rug, laid it on the ground, knelt on it facing east (in the direction of Mecca), and began reciting his prayers. His face expressed his deep devotion, and in those moments, the world became his temple. There was hardly a ripple on the lake.

Years ago, a *Muslim* (a follower of the Prophet Muhammad) in a Western country would have seemed unusual. Today, the Muslim religion, called *Islam,* is commonplace. *Mosques,* the Muslim religious buildings, exist in many major cities throughout North America and Europe. In fact, Islam may be the fastest-growing religion in the world.

Yet Islam started in a small, out-of-the-way community lost in a desert. This chapter explains the origins of the youngest of the major monotheistic faiths and introduces Muhammad, the great prophet of Islam.

Islam, Born in the Desert

Islam is much younger than Judaism and Christianity. This monotheistic faith emerged in the Middle East with a distinct face and a solid historical base.

Islam arose in the deserts of the Arabian Peninsula — a part of the world Abraham would have felt comfortable in, but a place very alien to Jesus. Here, ancient civilizations thrived and desert gods ruled the arid land.

Then Islam changed everything. When Islam was born, it confronted Christianity, which had replaced the Roman Empire and towered over the religious landscape as the controlling force. Around AD 391, Emperor Theodosius closed the pagan temples and demanded that all Roman citizens worship one God and his son, Jesus. For the next 200 years, Christianity tightened its grip on people's lives, even as Goths and Vandals destroyed the Western Roman Empire.

However, in the swirling sands of the Arabian Peninsula, Christianity made only modest inroads. By the sixth century, the last of Abraham's offspring was about to be born. The entry of Islam continued a pattern of monotheism begun with the Babylonians more than 2,500 years earlier.

All roads lead to Mecca

The Arabian Peninsula, where Islam originated, is mostly desert with sandy dunes, grayish camels, and white stone buildings. Here and there, the green of an oasis sparkles in the sunlight.

Most of its residents (then and now) lived along the coast or in a few major cities that served as crossroads for goods heading west to Egypt or east toward Mesopotamia (or present-day Iraq). Most of the inland residents were nomads, wandering through the dunes from oasis to oasis in a perpetual search for water and food for their herds.

The city that drew them was *Mecca,* which served as the heart of the region. Mecca had long been a religious center of Arabic culture and would become the birthplace of Islam.

Today people sometimes call an alluring or popular site a *mecca* (for example, Graceland is a mecca for Elvis fans).

Travelers bringing goods along the desert route that led to Mecca also toted their religions. Books had been invented hundreds of years earlier, so salesmen didn't have to lug around heavy scrolls. Books were still rare and copied by hand, but at least they were available.

As a result, Christianity and Judaism became widely known among the pagan Arabs. Jews dominated some cities, such as Yathrib, while Christians populated many other cities. Both religions had penetrated Arabic culture by the fifth century AD.

These nomadic *Bedouins* (which means "desert" in Arabic), who were pagans and believed in many gods, did far more than shepherd their livestock from one oasis to another. Some became businessmen and kept the trade going. Their most important achievement, however, was the conquest of Mecca by the tribe of Quraysh around AD 500.

Meccans become traders with the world

The Quraysh turned Mecca into a city-state that was ruled by a council of ten chiefs who enjoyed a clear division of power. A group of ministers aided the chiefs with foreign relations, taking care of the temple, and of course, overseeing the military. The Quraysh developed solid institutions that made Mecca successful.

This organized system helped the Meccans create treaties with distant empires such as Iran, Byzantium, and Abyssinia, and to work out pacts with the Bedouin tribes who carefully watched the caravan trade routes. The agreements created a lively import-export business through Mecca and gave residents the ability to travel safely. At the same time, foreigners felt comfortable coming to Mecca.

The intermixing cultures throughout the Middle East inspired poetry and the growth of folk tales. They also opened the Arabs' eyes, leading to new ideas about the treatment of women, who were usually viewed with contempt by tribal leaders. As a result, women could own property in Mecca. They had to consent to a marriage and could divorce their husbands. They could remarry, too. Many of these ideas would eventually seep into Islam.

The Prophet Arrives

Muhammad, who announced Islam to the world, was born in Mecca, where religions and commerce mixed freely.

Tradition indicates Muhammad's name originally may have been *Amin,* which means "faithful" or "trustworthy," and was changed later. The moniker *Muhammad* was common then (and still is today) and means "praise" or "popularity."

Muhammad was born into a reasonably well-off merchant family in the late 500s, but his circumstances changed quickly.

Historians can detail Muhammad's life because many people in his lifetime wrote biographical sketches. As with the Bible, the stories are often intermingled with mythology and *hyperbole* (exaggeration). Fortunately, Muhammad was also mentioned by non-Arab historians. The resulting merger of evidence creates a clear, consistent account of an extraordinary life.

Muhammad's early life

Muhammad's father, Abdullah, died shortly before his son's birth. So Muhammad's grandfather took him in. By custom, a Bedouin foster mother handled Muhammad's upbringing, something akin to Moses being raised by a foster princess in an Egyptian palace. Muhammad's "palace," however, was the desert.

Eventually, Muhammad was returned to his family when he was barely beyond toddler age. His mother, Aminah, took him to his maternal uncles in Yathrib to visit his father's tomb. When Aminah died, Muhammad went back to live with his grandfather, who also died abruptly soon after. Orphaned and alone in a harsh culture, the 8-year-old Muhammad was adopted by his uncle, Abu-Talib, who barely scratched out a living as caretaker of the sacred *Ka'baa,* one of the holiest monuments in Islam.

Starting out as an average guy

As a child, Muhammad didn't attend school. He worked as a shepherd, tending the neighbors' flocks. He also traveled with caravans to Syria. Along the way, he was introduced to a hodgepodge of faiths, including Bedouin polytheism, Judaism, and a little bit of Christianity.

At some point, Muhammad opened a small business in Mecca. He couldn't read or write, but he apparently loved to talk with the priests and rabbis he met at caravan trading posts on his travels. He must have remembered those conversations. The *Koran,* the Islamic holy text that contains his inspirational thoughts, includes many mentions of Old and New Testament patriarchs and events.

At age 25, Muhammad met and married Khadija, a wealthy widow who eventually presented him with six children. At that point in his life, Muhammad seemed unlikely to achieve greatness. Like Abraham before him, his early years were commonplace and of little apparent significance.

Unlike Jesus and Moses, of whom there are no extant pictures, Muhammad has been fully described. He was "sturdy and thickset, of medium height, with heavy shoulders and a thick black beard. He was beetle-browed and blessed with long black silken eyelashes, which he painted with kohl. They fell over eyes which were very large and piercing, and often bloodshot. His skin was rosy . . . and he had a Roman nose, thin, aristocratic with flaring nostrils. He had dazzling white teeth, but was gap-toothed toward the end of his life," according to historian Robert Payne.

The influence of the Ka'baa on Mecca and Muhammad

Mecca was home to the *Ka'baa,* which means "cube." The building served as the temple for the Bedouins' pagan religion, and it's the one reminder of the pre-Islamic days. Various historians have noted that no other object of veneration has been worshipped longer than the Ka'baa has. At one time, the Ka'baa may have been a temple devoted to the sun, the moon, and the five planets. It featured 360 idols, which seems to have an astrological symbolism.

The Ka'baa is 35 feet x 40 feet x 50 feet and covered by a black cloth that has verses from the Koran written across it in gold lettering. The Ka'baa also contains a sacred rock called the Black Stone. This stone is small (11 inches x 15 inches) and rests in a silver frame some 5 feet off the ground in a corner of the inner Ka'baa. Because of its religious significance, the stone has never been examined by scientists, but is thought to be a meteorite. Meccans considered it sacred long before Muhammad was born.

A second rock, called the Stone of Good Fortune, is also built into the Ka'baa, but is not considered as sacred.

In the Koran, it is written that Adam built the first Ka'baa. Abraham and his son Isaac later rebuilt the monument, it is also written. The Ka'baa is a replica of the house of God. The pilgrims who come each year to Mecca move in circles around the Ka'baa with the belief that they are like the angels who circle God's throne in heaven (Sura 3, 90).

Muhammad knew this ancient artifact well. The founder of Islam saw the stone many times, both as a youngster and as an adult. Reportedly, he helped rebuild the Ka'baa in 605 when the black cloth on the outer walls caught fire. The building weakened and collapsed in subsequent rains, so the Meccans set out to reconstruct it. Muhammad's shoulders were reportedly injured while carrying stones.

The Ka'baa still exists in Mecca and is visited by many thousands of visitors each year during their *Hajj* (pilgrimage). In the old days, this journey often took years to complete.

Beginning of a faith

As a young man, Muhammad began to have regular revelations, some apocalyptic in tone:

> "And when the book of fate is open wide,
> And when the heavens are stripped bare
> And when Hell is set ablaze,
> And when Paradise comes near,
> Each soul shall know what it has done!" —Sura 81:10–14

Many of the verses, which Muhammad said were dictated to him by the angel Gabriel, declare that mankind is doomed unless people follow the ways of God.

Muhammad accepted his role as the mouthpiece of God, but like Jewish prophets in earlier times, he wasn't sure how to respond to an inner tugging that called on him to proclaim his message.

Solitude leads to action

Troubled by the revelations but initially reluctant to face down the dominant pagan faith in Mecca, Muhammad spent days quietly thinking about the angelic messages while in a cave, supposedly imitating his grandfather. The tale parallels biblical accounts in which David, Elijah, and Jesus went to mysterious caverns and spent long periods of isolation in prayer.

At age 40, again on a retreat in a cave, Muhammad was visited by an angel who announced that God had chosen Muhammad as his messenger to all mankind. Muhammad said Gabriel told him:

> "With the name of God, the Most Merciful, the All-Merciful.
> Read: with the name of thy Lord Who created,
> Created man from what clings,
> Read: and thy Lord is the Most Bounteous,
> Who taught by the pen,
> Taught man what he knew not." —Sura 96:1–5

After delivering this divine message, Gabriel taught Muhammad how to worship God, pray, and conduct *ablutions* (a religious cleansing of the body).

Muhammad shared this revelation with his wife but hesitated to speak out for another three years. Moses, too, demurred when God called him, insisting he needed a spokesman.

The faith develops: Introducing the five pillars

Stories about Muhammad and his heavenly visitor began to circulate. In response, Muhammad began to talk first to his family, and then to his friends. Muhammad's message was simple: They were to believe in one God, in the resurrection of believers, and in a final judgment before God. Muhammad also removed all other gods from the Arab world and insisted *Allah* (the Arabic name for God) was alone. Muhammad encouraged charity and proper behavior. In this, he was duplicating Jesus and the Jewish prophets.

The basic rules of behavior were codified into five pillars of faith (see Chapter 8). The fundamental pillar requires followers to pray five times a day. All Muslims repeat a daily affirmation of faith, called the *Shahadah:*

"There is no God but Allah, and Muhammad is his messenger."

Anyone who cannot repeat this sentence wholeheartedly is not considered a Muslim. Anyone who says it three times in front of witnesses is officially a member of the faith.

Other pillars include

- **Prayer *(Salate):*** These are required daily prayers. The fisherman who Mark saw was fulfilling this requirement.

- **Purifying tax *(Zakat):*** Muslims are required to donate a portion of their income to the needy.

- **Fasting *(Sawm):*** Muslims must fast during the holy month of Ramadan. They eat only after the sun sets.

- **Pilgrimage *(Hajj):*** At least once in a lifetime, a Muslim is obligated to visit Mecca and pray at the holy shrine.

Muhammad called the resulting faith *Islam* (meaning "submission"), which was based on heavenly dictates.

Like many ancient Jewish prophets, Muhammad was often scorned by those who listened to him and was the subject of bitter jokes.

Writing the Koran

Muhammad did something for which later scholars are grateful. He ordered his revelations to be written down and memorized by converts to his new faith.

Muhammad's revelations were dictated and collected in the *Koran* (also spelled *Qur'an* and meaning "recitation"), which Muslims believe to be the perfect words of Allah. The Koran also accepts Jewish and Christian sacred texts as divinely inspired and even encourages readers to compare the Koran's words with those beloved books.

- "If you have any doubt regarding what is revealed to you from your Lord, then ask those who read the previous scripture;" —Sura 10:94

- "This is a revelation from the Lord of the universe. The Honest Spirit (Gabriel) came down with it, to reveal it into your heart that you may be one of the warners, in a perfect Arabic tongue." —Sura 26:192–195

- "Say, 'Anyone who opposes Gabriel should know that he has brought down this (the Koran) into your heart, in accordance with God's will, confirming previous scriptures, and providing guidance and good news for the believers.'" —Sura 2:97

The Koran and Bible offer different views, different bloodlines

Although the Bible and Koran recount similar stories, they often contain contradictory details. For example, the Koran explicitly denies Jesus's crucifixion (Sura 4:157–158), while all four Gospel accounts clearly portray Christ as crucified. Muslims believe that a prophet is always saved by God, not murdered by Romans or others.

One major contradiction in particular separates Muslims and Jews. The founder of Judaism, Abraham, had two sons, Isaac and Ishmael. In Jewish teachings, Isaac is the patriarch of the Jews (see Chapter 3).

"And the Lord visited Sarah as He had said, and the Lord did for Sarah as He had spoken. For Sarah conceived and bore Abraham a son in his old age, at the set time of which God had spoken to him. And Abraham called the name of his son who was born to him — whom Sarah bore to him — Isaac." —Genesis 21:1–3

Jews believe that God made an agreement (also called a *covenant*) with Abraham and Isaac: If they worshipped him, he would protect them, bring them to a holy land (see Genesis 12:4 for one example), and make them prosper.

However, the Koran insists that Ishmael was the child of promise (Sura 19:54; also compare Sura 37:83–109 with Genesis 22:1–19). Muhammad said Arabs descended from Ishmael, giving Muslims claim to God's promised land. So Muslims believe that God's covenant was meant for Ishmael's descendants, not Isaac's. Since 1948, when Israel was created as a Jewish state by the United Nations, Israel and her Arab neighbors have displayed unceasing hostility toward each other, with major armed conflicts in 1948–49, 1956, 1967, 1973, 1982, and 2006.

Christianity is caught up in this disagreement. Christians believe that Jesus came into the world through the nation of Israel, and according to Christians, he fulfilled the covenant that God had made with Abraham.

The Scriptures referred to in the Koran are the Torah, the Psalms of David, and the Gospels of Jesus Christ (Sura 4:163; 5:44–48).

The Koran, like the Jewish and Christian sacred books, is divided into chapters (called *suras*) and verses. However, the Koran is organized by length, not chronologically. The longest suras appear first. No other writers contributed to the text, unlike the Jewish Bible where books are ascribed to David and Solomon, or in the Christian New Testament, where books are ascribed to the disciples of Jesus and to Paul, among others. (For more on the holy texts of all three religions, see Chapter 9.)

Muhammad Takes Command

As news of Muhammad's revelations spread, people began to join him. With a surge in membership came the usual, violent reaction of authorities. Officials tend to get upset whenever someone speaks out against the accepted faith. (That happened in both Judaism and Christianity. Jesus ended up getting crucified for his efforts.)

The official punishment for a *heretic* in Mecca was to strip the culprit naked and leave him to die in the desert. City leaders were eager to see how long Muhammad could endure that kind of treatment. He was reportedly subjected to verbal attacks and being doused with dirt. Others Muslims were stretched on burning sands, branded with red-hot irons, and imprisoned with chains on their feet.

Muhammad was spared some agony because he didn't introduce a new god. Instead, he said that Allah, who was worshipped among the pagan gods, was the only deity.

Nevertheless, the threats reached a dangerous level. He had few followers, and authorities were threatening a violent response. Finally, Muhammad ordered his followers to flee. Many did. Ironically, Muhammad's strongest enemies included his uncles. One, Abu-Lahab, took over leadership of the Meccans.

Despite the maltreatment, Muhammad refused to give up. In time, he began to envision himself as an apostle of God like Paul, who had carried the Jewish message of salvation to the Gentiles. Muhammad would take that same divine information to the Arabs.

After continued harassment and other troubles similar to the ones that the Bible says Jewish prophets and Christian apostles experienced, Muhammad and his few followers finally fled Mecca in 622 and set up a base in the northern community of Yathrib (later called Medina).

That escape, called the *Hegira,* changed history. Muslims began to follow a cultural path that took them away from Judaism and Christianity. They even have an alternative calendar.

Muslims mark July 16, 622, as the beginning of the new era when, after years of struggle, Muhammad was welcomed to Yathrib as a king.

Battles with the Jews begin early

Although Muhammad encouraged his followers to look at the Jewish holy texts, he did not gain the support of Jews living in Arabia.

Disagreement with Jews started soon after Muhammad and his small band arrived in Yathrib. He thought Jewish residents would welcome him in line with other biblical prophets. Instead, one of their leaders, Ka'b ibn al-Ashraf, aligned himself with the Meccans and promised to help kill Muhammad.

The basic problem was that the Jews liked their religion, no matter how many times they were conquered or harassed by other religions, and they rejected Muhammad's vision. He also banned alcohol, gambling, and games of chance. Jews could have done without the latter two, but wine was a sacred part of their rituals.

Muhammad wanted to advance the cause of his new and vibrant religion through conquest. Success followed quickly, including a triumphant return to Mecca, battles against the Persians who ruled the Holy Land, and a showdown with the Byzantine governor of Egypt. Muhammad even sent a letter to the Byzantine emperor, who ruled the last remnant of the great Roman Empire, asking for surrender (the emperor didn't give in).

Spreading the new faith

Muhammad was busy sending out missionaries to spread the word of the new faith. As with the early Christian missionaries, the public wasn't ready to endorse his teaching. The Byzantine emperor's daughter accepted Islam but was promptly lynched by the Christian mob. When the leader of Palestine accepted Islam, he was promptly decapitated and crucified by order of the emperor.

A Muslim ambassador was assassinated in Syria-Palestine. The Roman emperor didn't care about this violation of diplomatic courtesy. Instead, he sent an army to battle the angry Muslims.

Considered the last and greatest of all God's prophets, Muhammad himself wasn't sitting back, watching everyone else do all the work, however. He led a 10,000-man army into Mecca and conquered the region's key city. People flocked to his side, obeying the age-old view that whoever won the battle must have a stronger god. Muhammad didn't even have to leave any soldiers to guard the city against insurgents when he returned to Yathrib. Mecca was firmly in the Muslim camp.

The Farewell Sermon

Muhammad fought continual wars against non-Muslim forces for more than ten years. By 632, Muhammad met 140,000 Muslim pilgrims from around the Mediterranean region at the Ka'baa. This led to his most famous sermon, the Farewell Sermon, akin to Jesus's Sermon on the Mount.

Muhammad told his followers to obey several important rules:

- ✔ Believe in one God.
- ✔ Do not use images or symbols.
- ✔ Treat all believers as equals.
- ✔ Treat life as sacred.
- ✔ Treat women better.
- ✔ Be sure to help the poor and needy.

Muhammad insisted that the holy Koran and the examples he set of how to live according to Allah's will were to be the basis for laws and behavior in every aspect of human life.

Breakdown at the Start-Up: Sunnis and Shi'ites Can't Get Along

On June 8, 632, Prophet Muhammad died. His impact, however, didn't fade. Nor has his presence waned in the last 1,400 years.

> "Of all the great visionaries who at various times have come to torment an evil world with visions of Paradise," noted modern historian Robert Payne, "he was perhaps the most human, the most like ourselves."

Muhammad's death unleashed the fury of Arab armies driven by a religious ideal. Many times, Muslims simply approached a country as religious missionaries, only to find the people welcoming them as rescuers. Many of the lands were so badly managed that people were eager for these fiery horsemen from the desert to take control.

As a result, Muslims swept quickly across the Middle East, avoiding only Byzantium, the last remnant of the Roman Empire, and then leaping the Mediterranean Sea into Spain. They were stopped from conquering Europe by the Frankish army at Tours in 732. The Arabs call the battle site "the pavement of martyrs." This battle was a major defining event for the West.

As Arab armies marauded, the religion began to splinter because Muhammad had named no successor. The divisions within Islam echoed what happened to Christianity after the death of Jesus. (Jesus had no successor either, but eventually, the newly risen Christian leaders settled on the view of Jesus that dominates Roman Catholic thinking to this day.) Islam was broken in two and never healed. Among Muslims, two factions developed

- ✔ **The Shi'ites,** who wanted someone from Muhammad's family to continue in leadership
- ✔ **The Sunnis,** who preferred that the most capable individual available at a given time take charge

Choosing a leader causes strife early on

The Shi'ites and Sunnis went their separate ways from the moment Muhammad died. Many members of the faith nominated Ali, Muhammad's son-in-law, cousin, and early convert, to step into Muhammad's leadership role, a position known as the *caliph* (successor). Instead, Ali waited patiently as Abu Bakr (632–634), Umar (634–644), and Uthman (644–656) served as caliphs.

When Ali finally became caliph after Uthman was assassinated, he found himself locked in a struggle with Aisha, Muhammad's wife and the daughter of Abu Bakr. Aisha accused Ali of laggardly pursuing Uthman's assassins. After a fierce battle between the two sides, Ali won and forced Aisha into retirement.

However, Ali then had to fight Mu'awiya Umayyad, Uthman's cousin and governor of Damascus. Mu'awiya also declined to back Ali unless the assassins were caught. Once again, soldiers on opposing forces clashed.

At the Battle of Suffin, Mu'awiya's soldiers stuck verses of the Koran onto the ends of their spears. It was a clever move. Ali's pious troops refused to fight them.

Backed into a corner, Ali worked out a compromise with Mu'awiya. His gesture, although politically advantageous, undermined his popular support, and Ali was killed by one of his own men in 661.

Mu'awiya promptly seized the title of caliph. Ali's elder son, Hassan, wanted to do the same thing. His existence threatened Mu'awiya's budding dynasty, but not for long. In a pattern familiar from Roman history, Hassan died within a year, allegedly poisoned. Ali's younger son, Husayn, didn't protest openly, but bided his time. He was sure that the caliphate would return to him when Mu'awiya died. Instead, Mu'awiya son, Yazid, claimed the throne when his father passed away in 680.

Husayn then recruited an army, but it proved no match for his rival. He and his troops were annihilated in the Battle of Karbala. Husayn's infant son, Ali, survived. *Shi'ites* (meaning "party of Ali") rallied around him as a descendant of Muhammad, while *Sunnis* (meaning "custom" or "tradition") went with the strongest man, Yazid. The two political-religious parties have never reconciled.

To complicate matters, Muhammad's line ended in 873 when the last Shi'ite leader, Al-Askari, who had no brothers, disappeared within days of inheriting the leadership mantle at the age of 4. The Shi'ites refused to accept that he was gone, and still insist the toddler is merely in hiding and will return someday.

Shi'ites currently view virtually all Islamic rule — whether by Sunnis or outsiders — as *illegitimate* (not the real thing), or *provisional* (temporary) at best. The well-known guerilla organization, *Hezbollah,* now heading the Palestine Liberation Organization, follows Shi'ite beliefs.

How Sunnis and Shi'ites practice Islam

First the good news for Islam: Sunnis and Shi'ites do agree on the core fundamentals of Islam and recognize each others as Muslims. Unfortunately, the sects have developed different ways of following Muhammad's directions (Chapter 8 has more on Islamic practices). Many Sunnis believe that Shi'ites are more interested in the death of their early leaders than in the tenets of the faith.

This is best illustrated at *Ashura,* a ten-day Muslim holiday in which the Shi'ites commemorate the Battle of Karbala. Each evening a wailing *imam* (someone who leads prayers in mosque) whips the congregation into a frenzy of tears and chest beating.

Sunnis, however, don't consider Ashura a major holiday, nor do they associate it with the battle. Instead, it celebrates several traditional events, like the day Noah left the ark.

The differences between the two sects run deep. Shi'ites, for example, don't believe Muslims will see the face of Allah after death, while Sunnis do.

The two sects have different calls to prayer and follow different rituals. To the horror of Sunnis, Shi'ites combine prayers, sometimes only saying them three times a day, instead of the prescribed five. Sunnis may say different prayers, too, drawing on verses written by Ali and Muhammad's daughter, Fatima, which Shi'ites consider the worst options, unless the writings support their claims that the descendants of Ali should rule Islam. Shi'ite Muslims also permit *muttah* — a fixed-term, temporary marriage — which is banned by the Sunnis, although it was permitted when Muhammad was alive.

The groups have worked together occasionally, but the current war in Iraq has highlighted their differences. Sectarian attacks are commonplace, with each group desecrating the other's favorite mosques. The same conflict is being played out in Pakistan.

The disparity in size doesn't help. Census figures show that Shi'ite Muslims dominate Iran. They control the population in Yemen and Azerbaijan and represent about half the population of Iraq. Sizeable Shi'ite communities exist in Bahrain, on the east coast of Saudi Arabia, and in Lebanon. Worldwide, Shi'ites only constitute 10 to 15 percent of the Muslim population. The largest group of Shi'ites is in Iran, but they can be found in Iraq, Afghanistan, and Pakistan in significant numbers.

Arab geniuses keep knowledge alive

In the first centuries after Muhammad, the Arabs were lords over a vast empire. When their religious fervor cooled, the Arabs settled down to rule their lands. Occasionally, interludes of peace were broken by bouts of civil war, changes in dynasties, and tiffs with the Greeks, who were still holding onto Byzantium and the tarnished Roman Empire name.

During this era, the Muslim world contributed a stream of great scholars and scientists to the world, including:

- Mathematician Al-Khwarizmi

- Physicist Alhazen, whose works were translated into Latin about 1,000 years ago

- Physician Avicenna, who was known throughout Europe and whose textbook was required in European universities

- Alburundi, a geographer who, among other feats, worked out latitude and longitude

- Averroes, a philosopher who translated Aristotle for his people

Many of the translations of Greek works only existed in Arabic and were rediscovered by Europeans during the Crusades. The ancient writings helped fuel the Renaissance.

Arab intellectuals created the first space observatories, set up the first universities, and propelled mathematics into more complexity.

Some critics of the faith look at this early strength of Arabic culture and at these original minds in science and philosophy and wonder what happened in more modern times.

Muslims have a strong sense of divine intervention and fate. They believe that all things happen because of God's will, and the notion of surrendering to God's will (*Islam* means "surrender," after all) is central to Islam. Outside critics look at the early accomplishments of Arab intellectuals and argue that this fundamental belief in Islam slowed down Islamic culture, especially in the sciences.

A Muslim might counter and say that his focus on pure faith is more important than anything else as he prepares himself for the next life.

The Ottoman Turks Dominate Islam

Arab power, however, did not last long. In 1273, a group of Turkish tribesmen under Ertughrul came to the aid of the sultan in a battle against Mongols, the invaders from the Far East. In 1288, Ertughrul died and was succeeded by his son, Osman — in the West known as Ottoman. The Crusades had brought Christian armies into Jerusalem in the 1100s. For two centuries, the Christians watched as Arabs battled each other. They knew they were no match for a united Arab front.

They were right. Within the next 200 years, the Ottoman Turks had seized power in the region. Their approach was simple: They started with cattle raids and then bought land. Neighboring farmers paid *tribute* (a sum of money they were forced to cough up) to avoid being killed, and then converted to Islam to avoid further payment. In that way, Islam continued to spread throughout the Middle East. This time, however, the Turks rather than the Arabs carried the Prophet's message.

The Turks built their capital in Adrianople, on the European side of the straits, across from Byzantium. After recovering from fresh attacks by the Mongols under Tamerlane (Timur the Lame) in the early Middle Ages, the Turks resumed their conquests.

In 1453, Byzantium fell, and as a result, all of Asia Minor now belonged to the Ottomans. By 1517, they controlled Egypt, Palestine, Syria, and Iraq. Attacks on Europe followed, leading to an unsuccessful siege of Vienna in 1683. That failure in the Austrian snows — essentially a stalemate — ended Turkish hopes for power outside Asia Minor.

Despite success on the battlefield, the Ottoman Empire was weakened for centuries by ill-suited sultans. Eventually, other countries labeled the empire "the sick man of Europe."

The end came after World War I. Arab dominance of the region was dead. The Turks were pushed back behind their current border. Modernized in the 1920s by Kemal Ataturk, the residents use a Western alphabet and have moved away from their Islamic roots. The Turks are led by a secularized government and are part of the European Common Market.

The religion of Islam, however, continues to expand, reaching all areas of the world with the message once heard in a lonely cave in a desert.

Chapter 8

Islam: Submission of the Faithful

These days, concerns about terrorism tend to overshadow understanding of Islamic religious tenets and ideas, at least in Christendom and the West. Lost in the uproar is a religion with rich traditions and detailed beliefs that has enlightened millions of people for centuries.

Muhammad, the founder of the faith and its great Prophet, encouraged education and the accumulation of knowledge. He created many of the rituals, including daily prayers, as well as festivals. Others were added over time.

In many ways, Islam today continues to be a direct reflection of the ideas he presented to the Arab world about 1,400 years ago.

This chapter provides an overview of this robust and expanding faith.

The Core of Islam: One God with Muhammad as His Last Prophet

Central to Islamic belief is the absolute power of God. Islam is strictly monotheistic in believing there is only one God, who is omnipotent and merciful. Associating any human being or image with God is an unforgivable sin. That, of course, parallels the second commandment against graven images.

This rule explains in part the Muslim rejection of Christianity, because Islam doesn't acknowledge the divinity of Jesus. It also helps clarify why Islamic armies were so brutal when confronting Arabic tribes that worshipped idols.

Muslims believe that Muhammad was the last of a series of prophets that God sent to earth. Although Muslims respect the teachings of the earlier prophets like Moses, Jesus, and Elijah, they believe that Allah sent his final message to Muhammad to correct the corruption that occurred after previous revelations. Like Christians, Muslims believe that their faith is the whole of God's revelation to mankind, and also its final expression. There is nothing more to be changed or added, in other words.

They revere the Prophet as the embodiment of the perfect believer and accept his actions and words as a model of ideal conduct (Muhammad's words and deeds, and also the things he *affirmed* like good acts by others, are called *hadith* in Arabic). Unlike Jesus, whom Christians believe was truly God's son, Muslims accept that Muhammad was a mortal with extraordinary qualities.

Today, many Muslims insist that pictures of Muhammad are improper and against their faith. However, at one time, they created many images of important Muslim leaders, although none became holy icons, as in some Christian sects.

A passage in the second *sura* (chapter) of the Koran sums up what it means to be a Muslim:

> "Verily, righteousness is he who believes in God, in the day of Judgment, in the angels, in the Koran, and in the prophets; who bestows his wealth, for God's sake, upon kindred and orphans, and on the poor and homeless, and upon all who ask; also for delivering captives; he who is steadfast in prayer, gives alms, who stands firmly by his covenants once he has entered into them, and is patient in adversity, and in hardship, and in times of trial. These are the righteous, and these are the God-fearing."
> —Sura 2:177

Allah: The Almighty of Islam

The name for God in Islam is *Allah*. God's name is not something to be trifled with in any of the monotheistic religions. The prohibition against using God's name in vain remains in the Ten Commandments. God's name in Islam, of course, is used in prayers and in pious comments, but as in Judaism and Christianity, the sacred name is not to be uttered improperly.

Jews were adamant that God's name, Yahweh, was not to be spoken at all, except by the High Priest and only on the holiest day of the year. Sages ruled that the only heresy was saying the holy name aloud. The control of the use of that name was so complete that historians today have no idea how the four letters of God's name were actually pronounced.

God, in turn, spoke to mankind in different ways. In Judaism, God often spoke to patriarchs. Abraham even argues with him over the possible destruction of two cities. However, in Islam, God sends an intermediary, the angel Gabriel, to speak to Muhammad. The idea that a deity could select someone to speak to the people for him wasn't uncommon. Many religions began with this premise.

The history of Allah

Allah, as the name Muhammad identified with his God, has a long family tree. The name existed well before Muhammad ventured forth from Mecca. After all, Muhammad's father's name was Abdullah, which means "servant of Allah." The Koran contains evidence that the name Allah was used in pre-Islamic Arabia. Some pagans called the god who created heaven and earth Allah. They also believed that Allah was the top deity in the gods' hierarchy.

The name Allah shows up in various Middle Eastern inscriptions, including several in the Southern Arabia region. The most interesting is the one found in Libyan inscriptions from the fifth century BC. Libya, which evidently got the god from Syria, was the first center of the worship of this deity in Arabia.

The name is also found as part of certain proper biblical names, like the *el* in Daniel or Rachel. "El" was once the bull god of the Canaanites, but came into Judaism as a synonym for Yahweh. In the same way, the feminine form of Allah, which is *Allat,* is found commonly among the names on inscriptions from North Arabia.

Arabs also would have heard the term "Allah" used when traveling Christians and Jews came through Arabia and discussed religion. To the visitors, the word Allah was simply a designation for God. For Arabs, however, the same word had a meaning rooted in their own culture.

In the pre-Muhammad days, Allah had company, what the Koran now disdainfully labels *associates:*

- Ailat ("goddess") may have stood for one aspect of Venus, the morning star.
- Uzza ("the all-powerful") also shared traits with Venus.
- Manat, the goddess of fate, held the shears that cut the thread of life and was worshipped in a shrine along the coast of the Arabian Sea.

In support of Allah's status as the one and only god, there were no idols of Allah. In addition to the black stone of the Ka'baa in Mecca, as many as 360 idols were housed there, the kind of idols Abraham would have been familiar with; but, interestingly, there was not even one idol of Allah, perhaps reflecting his superior status.

The Satanic Verses

The three goddesses Ailat, Uzza, and Manat were the subject of *The Satanic Verses,* brought to recognition in the West after Salman Rushdie's book of the same title. Rushdie was targeted for punishment by radical Muslims for writing the book.

Ailat, Manat, and Uzza were all goddesses worshipped by the pagan Meccans — Muhammad's neighbors whom he hoped to convert. It was very hard for them to grasp the idea of one god, at first, and these goddesses were revered by them.

The belief is that Satan tempted Muhammad to utter the following lines in Sura 53, after verses 19 and 20 ("Have you thought of Ailat and al-Uzza and Manat the third, the other?"):

"These are the exalted *Gharaniq,* whose intercession is hoped for."

Gharaniq means "something written or uttered only once in a book or culture," making it very rare.

The goddesses were offered (and then retracted) by Muhammad as real deities (in addition to Allah) whose "intercession" would affect people's lives. They were a threat to Allah's almighty power and thus a threat to strict monotheism. Again, remember that Muhammad retracted the verses.

Allah's divine role

At first, Allah was only the god of contracts who watched over travelers. As he became more important in the years leading up to Islam, he assumed other tasks. He became the moon god, a role familiar to Abraham, who grew up surrounded by the rituals for a powerful moon goddess. He also evolved into the god of sky and rain, a key necessity of life in the desert.

In the view of Muhammad, Allah becomes God of the world, of all believers, the one and only who admits no other associates in the worship of him. This conforms with Jewish and Christian monotheistic views. Muhammad identified Allah as the one God.

The Prophet's mission was not only to proclaim God's existence, but to deny the existence of all lesser deities. The Koran regularly refers to Muhammad's adversaries in Mecca, swearing by Allah, invoking him, and recognizing his sovereignty as creator. That's because Allah, to them, was one of many gods, not the sole deity as claimed by Muhammad.

Conflict between Muhammad and the Meccan leaders arose because the people of Mecca didn't understand or allow that Allah alone should be worshipped. They insisted that if Allah had willed it, they would have refrained from believing in other deities (Sura 6:148). The Meccans believed that Allah was okay with their worship of other gods.

Muhammad's success changed that thinking forever. From Muhammad on, Allah was the one true god of Islam.

Before God was God

It's interesting to note that both Allah and Yahweh were worshipped *before* becoming associated with Islam and Judaism.

Archaeologists found three variations of Yahweh in Canaanite written inscriptions — Yahh, Ya/El, and Yah. The deity was shown in association "with radiance, as from the sun, and a radiant serpent." (That iconic snake might have survived, but for King Josiah's reforms in the seventh century BC. See Chapter 3.)

Allah also appears in historical records prior to Muhammad. The *name* itself may derive from two Arabic words that mean "the God." The *word* Allah, however, is Aramaic and derives from a descriptive term used in pagan faiths to identify their superior deity. It translates as "top god."

As a result, Allah is comparative to the Jewish *Elohim,* which means "gods," or the Greek *theos*, which also means "gods." The name revealed by God, according to the Bible, for Elohim is Yahweh. The revealed name for theos is Jesus.

Muslims never were given a revealed name for their God, but over time, the word Allah took on that connotation.

The Pillars of the Faith

Each religion has sacred texts to base its faith on. Judaism stands on the Torah. Christianity has the New Testament of the Bible to support its beliefs. In addition to the Koran, Islam has *arkan ud-Din,* or in English, "pillars of the faith." These are five religious duties expected of every pious Muslim.

The five pillars are cited throughout the Koran on an individual basis, but Muhammad listed them together when he was asked to define Islam. After his death, Islamic leaders designated these pillars as "anchoring points" within the Muslim community. Believers who obey the five pillars are thought to receive rewards both in this life and in the afterlife. The pillars are a ready-made formula for becoming a believer, and they make transitioning to the faith very accessible.

First pillar: Creed (Shahada)

A Muslim must make a public declaration of the faith (called a *Shahada*) at least once in a lifetime, although most Muslims recite it daily. Here's the declaration in Arabic:

"Ashhadu al-la ilaha illa-llah wa ashhadu anna Muhammadar rasulu-llah."

Shi'ites erect a few additional pillars

All Muslim sects endorse the five pillars of faith in Islam. The Shi'ites have increased the total by adding four more:

✔ The jihad: This is a "holy war" declared by the religious leader (*imam*).

✔ Payment of the imam's tax: This is a tax to support the religious leader in addition to tithing.

✔ Encouragement of good deeds.

✔ Prevention of evil.

In English:

"I bear witness that there is no God but Allah, and I bear witness that Muhammad is his messenger."

Converts can join the Muslim community simply by reciting the Shahada in complete sincerity. The vow is also echoed in the regular call to prayer, included in the daily ritual prayer, and recited in the moments before death.

By saying the Shahada, a person is accepting the tenets of Islam, including beliefs in angels, the Koran, the Bible, the prophets, and a Day of Judgment.

Second pillar: Prayer (Salat)

Muslims must pray five times daily — at dawn, noon, midafternoon, sunset, and nightfall. The prayers (*salat* in Arabic) always contain verses from the Koran and must be said in Arabic. Muslims believe that prayer provides a direct link between the worshipper and God.

The Muslim holy day is Friday, when congregations gather just past noon in a mosque. An *imam,* or religious leader, gives a sermon and leads the congregation in prayer. The Friday service matches the Jews, who also have a singular prayer — the *Shema* — which characterizes their faith. The Catholic Creed would have the same role (see Chapter 5), but not all Christian sects have such a statement.

As a result, in most Muslim countries, the weekend begins on Friday, not on Saturday as in Western countries.

The three holiest places of worship in the Islamic world are

✔ The Mosque of the Ka'baa in Mecca

✔ The Mosque of the Prophet Muhammad in Medina

✔ The Masjid Aqsa, adjacent to the Dome of the Rock in Jerusalem

Why pray so often?

Muslims are obligated to pray many times each day — the number varies depending on the sect. The inspiration for that requirement may have come from Saint Benedict, who set up the rules for monks and died shortly after Muhammad was born.

Benedict ordered prayers seven times a day. He wanted the monks to focus on their religious duties. However, as an unexpected side effect, the bells ringing for prayers served as a clock. No one had wristwatches in those days. Many communities relied on the calls to prayer to know the time of day.

Today, the only vestige of Benedict's required prayers in Christianity is Vespers, the prayers at dusk.

Muslims don't need to be in a mosque in order to pray, however. As is true for devout Christians and Jews, they may perform this requirement anywhere — a house, office, school, or even outside. All they have to do is face the Ka'baa in Mecca. When Jews pray, they turn toward Jerusalem. The Muslims did that, too, initially, but when the Jews of Medina rejected Muhammad's call after he fled Mecca for there, he shifted the direction of prayers away from David's City.

Unlike Christian churches and Jewish synagogues, mosques are nondenominational. Traditional Friday prayer services are largely similar in every sect, and Muslims of any background are welcome to attend services at any mosque. Still, some Sunnis only will attend a Sunni mosque. Some Shi'ites feel the same way. (To read more about Muslim houses of worship, see Chapter 10.)

Third pillar: Purifying tax (Zakat)

Muslims believe that all things belong to God, and that humans only hold wealth in trust for him. For that reason, they think wealth should be distributed throughout the community of believers, or *umma,* through a purifying tax (called a *zakat*). The usual payment is 2.5 percent of a person's assets. That means everything: grains; fruit; camels; cattle; sheep and goats; gold and silver; other assets and movable goods.

The money is distributed to the poor, debtors, volunteers participating in a *jihad* (holy war), pilgrims, and the collectors of the tax. At one time, slaves seeking to buy their freedom got a handout. There's even Web sites where Muslims can use a calculator to figure out how much *zakat* they should donate. Here's one such site, created by Council of Islamic Organizations of Greater Chicago: www.zakatchicago.com. Additional charity work is also encouraged.

The Koran explicitly requires zakat (Sura 9:60) and often places it alongside prayer when discussing a Muslim's duties. ("Perform the prayer and give the alms." —Sura 2:43, 110, 277) For those who believe in taking their wealth with them, the Koran minces no words: The fires of hell will heat up the coins, and the greedy will be branded with them (Sura 9:34–35).

The zakat is designed to ensure that the wealthy help the poor, a practice that boosted Christianity in the eyes of pagans during its early years. Muhammad may have been motivated to add this rule because of the overt poverty he endured as a child. He was known to have been very kind toward orphans.

The Islamic state used to enforce zakat, but, today, it's an individual's choice unless a country, like Saudi Arabia, demands strict adherence to religious law (called *shari'a*).

The Shi'ites emphasize this pillar by requiring an additional one-fifth tax (called *khums*) that must be paid for the benefit of orphans, the poor, travelers, and the imams.

Zakat is similar to voluntary *tithing* (the act of giving one-tenth of your income to the church) in both Judaism and Christianity. In the Church of Jesus Christ of Latter-day Saints, in contrast, tithing is a religious requirement.

Fourth pillar: Fasting (Sawm)

During the month of *Ramadan,* the ninth month in the Islamic calendar, Muslims fast between dawn and dusk (this act is called *sawm*). (Because Islam follows a lunar calendar, Ramadan moves around each year.) Muslims must abstain from food, liquid, and intimate contact during those hours of the day. Muslims fast to commemorate the descent of the Koran from the highest heaven to the lowest, from which it was then revealed to Muhammad over the next 22 years. Fasting is seen as a method of self-purification by cutting oneself off from worldly comforts.

The sick, elderly, travelers, and pregnant or nursing women are permitted to break the fast during Ramadan, provided they make up for it during an equal number of days later in the year. Children begin the ritual at puberty. The end of Ramadan is celebrated by the *Eid al-Fitr,* one of the major festivals on the Muslim calendar.

Jewish and Christian calendars are also dotted with fasts, but none longer than a day.

Westerners probably know the Islamic holiday of Ramadan more than any other. That's because Islamic athletes, like former Houston Rockets center Hakeem Olajuwon, often try to compete while fulfilling their fasting duties. In

Olajuwon's case, many commentators filled the airwaves with their thoughts about his efforts to maintain religious obligations amid athletic requirements.

Fifth pillar: Pilgrimage (Hajj)

All Muslims are required to make one pilgrimage to Mecca in their lifetimes, called a *hajj,* provided they are physically and financially able to do so. Muhammad probably made this mandatory to gain support of Meccan merchants who were losing money because Islam didn't initially recognize the Ka'baa. That cut off visits by pagan pilgrims and undercut support for Islam. The required pilgrimages ended that concern.

Today, the requirement helps bring Muslims together and adds cohesion to the faith.

The hajj begins in the 12th month of the Islamic lunar calendar which means, like Ramadan, it doesn't correspond to a specific month in the solar calendar.

Modern transportation methods, particularly the airplane, have made it possible for many more Muslims to fulfill the hajj today than 1,400 years ago.

Like Ramadan, the end of the Hajj is also celebrated with a festival, the *Eid al-Adha,* which is marked by all Muslims, whether or not they made the pilgrimage. This festival and the *Eid al-Fitr* at the end of Ramadan comprise the highlights of the Islamic year.

Pilgrimages are encouraged in both Judaism and Christianity, but none are mandatory.

Meeting Some Muslim Sects

Both Judaism and Christianity have divided into multiple sects and have been that way for centuries. Islam is no different. The biggest sects, the Sunni and Shi'ite, were introduced in Chapter 7.

The four Sunni schools of law (called *madhahib*) — the *Hanafi,* the *Maliki,* the *Shafi'i,* and the *Hanbali* — are sometimes thought of as different sects, but are not. The schools refer to four great Islamic scholars who may have taught slightly different ideas but were actually students of one another.

The Shi'ites have one major school of thought known as the *Jafaryia* or the "Twelvers," and a few minor schools of thought, known as the "Seveners" or the "Fivers." These names all refer to the number of imams Shi'ites recognize after Muhammad's death. The term *Shi'ite* is usually meant to be synonymous with the Jafaryia.

Shi'ite and Sunni communities are splintered into thousands of smaller sub-sects and cults with an incredible diversity of beliefs. The multiple sects have created friction within Islam, just as the various groups in Judaism and Christianity have bred conflict within those faiths. In reality, as one historian noted, "Every single person practicing Islam in the world today is a heretic in the eyes of at least one other such person."

What follows are descriptions of some of the larger Islamic sects, listed in alphabetical order.

Ahmadiyya

A messianic arm of Islam, the *Ahmadiyya* sect was founded by Mirza Ghulam Ahmad (c. 1839–1908) in India. He claimed to be everything from the biblical Messiah to Muhammad, Jesus, and the Hindu god Krishna. After his death and the death of a successor, the sect divided in two. One recognizes Ahmad as a prophet; the other sees him as only a reformer. Today, about 170 million Ahmadiyya Muslims reside mainly in Pakistan.

Ahmadiyya Islam is also associated with several Sufi orders, most notably the Al-Badawi order of Egypt, named for an Islamic saint who died in 1276.

Ismailis

An offshoot of the Shi'ite sect, *Ismailis* accept the Aga Khan, an honorary title dating back more than 1,000 years, as their spiritual leader and refuse to join other Muslims in prayer. The most recent Aga Khan is a Harvard-educated businessman living in Switzerland. The Ismailis left the fold not long after Muhammad's death by accepting one son of the sixth imam, Ishmail, as their titular head while other Shi'ites accepted a different son.

Ismailis gave birth to their own subsects, including one of the most famous groups in Islam, the *Nizaris*. The Crusaders had another name for them, the Assassins. Formed in the 1200s, they were Shi'ites who would commit murder to protect the interests of Ali's descendants. They fought with the Knights Templar, the power behind the Jerusalem throne, under a leader called the "Old Man of the Mountains."

Kahrijites

In Arabic, the name *Kahrijite* means "to go out." The sect earned that title by leaving the main sects almost as soon as the religion was founded. They simply disagreed with some of the teachings. For example, they originally supported the idea that any Muslim who violated Islamic law should be put to death. Other sects were not as harsh. As a result, Kahrijites believe the members of the main sects have stepped off the true Islamic path.

Kurds

Although not a sect, *Kurds* nevertheless are outside the mainstream because of their insistence of a separate country. Although mostly Sunni with a smaller portion Shi'ite, they inhabit land about the size of Spain that stretches from Turkey through Iraq and Iran.

Many of the residents there follow traditional Islamic and pre-Islamic practices. They also speak a different language related to Persian, not Arabic.

Ethnically related to Iranians, the Kurds once had their own country and have endured conquerors of all stripes, including Sumerians, Assyrians, Persians, Mongols, Crusaders, and Turks. Eventually, in the tenth century, the Kurds accepted Islam.

They are prominent now because many supported the Americans in battles with Iraq and even tried to revolt against their Iraqi overlords. Their goal is independence in a new Kurdistan.

Sufis

The *Sufis* represent a mystical tradition in Islam, seeking an alternative way of approaching the faith through a direct experience of God. Prominent throughout Islamic history, more than half of the male Muslim population was attached to a Sufi order *(tariqa)* in the 19th century. To the Sunnis, Sufism is considered to be integral part of Islam.

Whirling dervishes, a group known to spin in religious ecstasy until collapsing, are members of this sect.

Jews who became attracted to the *Kabala,* a mystical book introduced around the 1100s, share the same interests as the Sufis in reaching out to the divine through spiritual means. So did the ancient Gnostics.

Wahhabis, or Muwahiddun

Wahhabis are strictly traditionalist, an approach popular on the Arabian Peninsula. Founder Muhammad ibn Abd al-Wahhab argued in the 1700s that every concept added to Islam after the first three centuries after the

Prophet's death was erroneous. He was objecting to a variety of new ideas that had seeped into Islam, including the worship of saints and sacrificial offerings.

The term *Wahhabi* was first used by opponents of the founder, and is considered derogatory and not used by supporters of the sect, who prefer to be called "Unitarians" *(Muwahiddun).* Also, the terms *Wahhabism* and *Salafism* can be used interchangeably, but Wahhabism is seen by some as ultraconservative.

Gender Equality in Islam

Women have gotten short shrift in all three monotheistic religions. In Judaism, women are responsible for taking care of the house and family. The important task of handling religion is left to the men. In Orthodox Jewish services, men and women are seated in separate areas so the men won't be distracted from their sacred duties.

In Christianity, women often are shunted aside. Early theology insisted that women don't possess souls and are inherently evil, because of Eve's original sin of getting Adam to munch on a forbidden apple in the Garden of Eden. Although Protestant sects may be led by women, the Roman Catholic Church to this day still limits female roles and refuses to allow women to be priests.

The Koran paints a different picture, at least in writing. In Islam, men and women are created equally. Neither gender is superior. Both can go to heaven. Adam and Eve both were responsible for losing Eden, but because both repented, both were forgiven. Women are here, the Koran says, to give birth, but also to perform good deeds, just like the men.

As such, women aren't possessions of men. They can choose their husbands, keep their own names, build capital, divorce if necessary, and keep property.

The Koran also requires men and women to dress modestly. For women, that has translated into the *hijab,* a piece of cloth that many women use to cover their heads and body, except for the eyes and hands. Other women limit it just to hair.

Muhammad's farsighted guidelines, however, ran smack into the real world and, today, are rarely followed. Muslim women are often kept away from schools and live restricted lives unlike anything the Prophet seems to have recommended. More orthodox views, such as those expressed by the Taliban in Afghanistan, have completely isolated women from society. In some cases, Muslim leaders supplied interpretations of sacred texts which overturned earlier teachings. In other instances, culture trumped religion.

It has been said that any culture that denies women equality denies the society half of its dynamic force and creativity.

In some Middle Eastern countries, women can't walk outside alone. Those who do may be considered prostitutes. Muslim males believe they are protecting women rather than inhibiting them.

Observing Muslim Holidays

Muslims observe several holidays throughout the year with prayer, gatherings in the mosque, and occasional feasts. Muslims do not have holidays like Christmas with lights and decorated trees. Each holiday is typically a solemn religious occasion, although, as you see below, there are exceptions. Different sects may have varied rituals or may not even celebrate some of the same holidays. Ramadan is considered the most important.

Muslims, like Jews, follow a lunar calendar. That's much shorter than a solar calendar, so holidays move around every year based on lunar cycles.

Ramadan

Ramadan is the best known Islamic holiday perhaps because of its unusual length and the novelty of a hefty fast. Devout Muslims fast for 30 days from sunup to sunset to thank God for giving them the Koran. Muslims use the last ten days of Ramadan for devotions and good deeds in an effort to draw closer to God.

The holiday comes with special foods, prayers, and readings from the Koran, the same as the Jewish Passover.

The 27th day of Ramadan is set aside as *Lailat-al-Qadr,* the day the archangel Gabriel introduced the first words of the Koran to Muhammad. Muhammad reportedly stayed awake all night. Some Muslims duplicate that feat, praying for forgiveness of any sin. In a way, the holiday also resembles the Jewish Yom Kippur, when devout Jews gather in synagogues, fast, and ask God to pardon their sins.

Hijra: Turning the page to a new year

The *Hijra* holiday commemorates Muhammad's exit from Mecca to the city of Yathrib (Medina) in AD 622. This event, called the *Hijra,* marks the start of the Muslim calendar. Islamic years are numbered starting from the Hijra.

Ashurah: A day of many remembrances

The holiday of Ashurah recalls the martyrdom of Imam Husain, the grandson of the Prophet in 663. The Shi'ites consider this day extremely important, and they still bemoan Husain's death.

In addition, the day is also linked to an old holiday once followed by Jews in Medina. They would fast to remember their salvation from the Pharaoh in Egypt. Muslims multiplied the reasons behind the occasion by saying, on this day, Noah's Ark also came to rest on Mount Ararat, Abraham was born, and the Ka'baa was built.

Id Milad al-Nabi: Marking Muhammad's birth and death

The Muslim Christmas without the commercial hoopla, Id Milad-al-Nabi commemorates the birth of the Prophet and is celebrated on the 12th day of the month *Rabee-ul-Awwal,* the third month of the Muslim calendar. The day is not totally joyous because Muslims also mark Muhammad's death at the same time.

As with Christmas, this holiday wasn't celebrated in earlier times and has not attained universal status in all Muslim countries. In addition, as with Jesus, Muhammad's birth date is unknown.

Milad, which means "birthday" and is spelled in various ways, is an official holiday in most Muslim countries. Like Christmas, the holiday lasts 12 days. Muslims whoop it up with carnivals and processions. Of course, time is also devoted to prayers and religious activities. There are even songs, reminders of Christmas carols in other lands.

More conservative sects, such as the Wahhabis, reject the idea of celebrating Muhammad's birthday. In the same way, some conservative Christian groups still refuse to acknowledge Christmas.

Id al-Adha: Honoring Abraham's dedication to God

The Festival of Sacrifice, *Id al-Adha,* recalls the biblical account of Abraham being asked to sacrifice his son Isaac. A sheep or cow gets it in the neck on this day, and much of the meat is donated to the poor. In some Muslim countries, this is a public holiday.

Lailat al-Baraa: Seeking and granting forgiveness

Borrowing from the Jewish Yom Kippur, on this "the night of repentance," forgiveness is granted to those who repent.

15th of Sha'ban: Shaking things up

The 15th day of the eighth month, *Sha'ban,* is when the tree of paradise is shaken. According to tradition, each leaf of the tree bears the name of a living person. If the leaf bearing a person's name falls off during the shaking, Muslims believe, the person will die that year.

The holiday is marked with prayer and, in some countries, ceremonies that honor the dead.

The day probably gained some distinction because it marks the anniversary of Muhammad's return to Mecca as a conqueror in AD 630.

27th of Rajab: A heavenly holiday

On this day in AD 632, Muhammad reportedly traveled to Jerusalem to ascend to heaven to greet Allah. Some sects believe he rose physically and then returned to earth. Others insist the visit was in spirit only. The day, akin to Christianity's Easter, is marked with prayers and processions in many Muslim countries.

Getting to Know Saints in Islam

Muslims revere saints, although the process of becoming a Muslim saint differs from the Christian *canonization.* A Catholic person thought to be a *saint,* or a devout person whose life can serve as an example to others, must meet certain criteria to merit that status, including the performance of miracles.

However, in Islam, anyone revered as a saint instantly becomes one — alive or dead. Called a *Wali* (or "friend of God"), a saint can be very popular or completely ignored. Some countries that recently became Islamic cheerfully include pagan figures among Muslim saints.

The Pakistani authors estimate there may be more than 1,000 saints from their country alone.

As with Christian saints, their Muslim counterparts have shrines that are sites for worship and prayer.

Here are a few Muslim saints:

- **Ahmad Ibn Hanbal** (780–855): He was tortured by declaring the Koran was not created. His view won eventually, and he was honored as a saint in his lifetime.
- **Ahmad al-Badawi** (1228–1297): He founded a sect of the Sufis and was believed to have performed miracles.
- **Rabi'a al-'Adawiyya** (c.717–801): A mystic whom some followers called the second Mary, she taught her students to love God completely.

Common Rituals and Daily Practices

Muslims practice some familiar rituals. They circumcise their male children. Unlike the infant circumstances in Judaism, Muslim boys can be as old as 15 at the time of the ceremony. Some Muslims insist on circumcising girls, a practice that has been attacked in recent years as being mutilation.

Although there is no bar mitzvah or similar coming-of-age ritual, Muslims become adults by demonstrating an ability to read the Koran. That parallels the procedure in Judaism prior to the creation of the bar and bat mitzvah.

Getting hitched in Islam

Muslims are expected to marry. Having more than one wife *(polygamy)* is illegal in countries that ban it, but may be acceptable in Muslim lands. The Koran talks about the issue specifically in what is known as the Noble Verse: "And if you fear that you cannot act equitably towards orphans, then marry such women as seem good to you, two, three and four, but if you fear that you may not do justice to them, then (marry) only one" (Sura 4:3).

Muslim women are also expected to provide a *dowry,* which is a gift from the bride's family to the husband.

Love may not play a part in a marriage, which is often based on family relationships and economic considerations.

A Muslim wedding is seen as a contract between the parties. As a result, there is no ceremony akin to a Jewish or Christian wedding. Instead, the man makes a formal offer that the woman accepts.

The actual ceremony involves a gathering of the bride and groom and their respective attorneys and two male witnesses. No religious prayers are said. Instead, the bride and groom may choose to recite passages from the *Fatihah*, the first seven verses from the Koran. These verses call for God's guidance and emphasize his power and mercy. The same verses are often included in traditional daily prayers.

After the brief ceremony is completed, the groom goes to a room where women in the bride's family are gathered. He offers gifts to the sister (if any) and receives a blessing from the older women there. Men then gather in one place for a large meal; women in another. After dinner, the bride and groom are seated together for the first time. A single cloth *(dupatta)* is used to cover their heads as they say prayers.

Other ways of keeping the faith

Other Muslim rituals include

- ✔ A sacrifice of sheep and goats is made when an infant is named in the first week after birth.

- ✔ Burial occurs on the day of death. Judaism is the only other religion requiring prompt burial, but Jews have up to three days to inter the body.

- ✔ Mourning lasts three days for friends. Widows are to mourn for four months and ten days.

- ✔ Dress is restricted. Some sects insist on veils for women, but the Koran only calls for loose coverings over the head and shoulders. Men are to wear tunics or loose-fitting gowns.

   The rules are generally overlooked in Western lands, although arguments over security risks arose in France and the United States when Muslim women hid their faces behind veils on official photographs. Veils were eventually banned in France.

Muslim men may grow beards but are not required to. Men and women are required to remove pubic and underarm hair. No one is allowed to alter eyebrows. The idea is that the face was created that way and must be left alone. On the other hand, a woman who has facial hair may remove it to avoid looking like a man.

Music in Islam: Not a big deal

You won't find an organ in a mosque. To many orthodox Muslims, music is not acceptable in religious settings. The prohibition is based not on the Koran, which doesn't mention music, but on Muhammad's sayings that supposedly condemned listening and singing to music.

The four legal schools of the Sunni Muslims, representing the largest sect of believers, have ruled against listening to music.

Muhammad objected to music in religious ceremonies because music was a big part of pagan rituals. However, soon after his death, music crept into Islam via war. Persians and Greeks were known for their music and shared it with their conquerors, including Muslims, who apparently found the sounds rather appealing.

As a result, Muslims do enjoy hymns, some of which were also inherited. The Arabs, like the Jews, eliminated any connections with other deities, even changing accepted hymns to reflect Islamic ideology. The Hebrew Bible (the Old Testament) contains psalms copied from the Egyptians; the hymns originally praised the sun god, Aton, but they now praise Yahweh. In Islam, the same alteration took place. After all, pagans Arabs included Allah in their pantheon before Muhammad showed up.

Islam's dietary requirements

Foods are limited for Muslims, akin to Jewish kosher laws. The Koran stresses the need for a healthy body so the believer can worship Allah properly.

> "O' Believers! Eat of the good and pure (lawful) that We have provided you with and be grateful to Allah, if you truly worship Him." —Sura 2:172

To accomplish that, a variety of foods are banned. Muslims can't eat the meat from a pig, animals that are found dead, or animals used in sacrifices by other religions.

In addition, Muslim scholars outlined several more prohibitions:

- Animals killed by strangling.
- Animals killed by a violent blow. Muslims practice humane slaughtering techniques pioneered by the Jews.
- Animals killed by a headlong fall or gored to death.
- Animals partially eaten by wild animals.
- Animals sacrificed in the name of idols.

The Story Behind Symbols and Colors

Islam largely shuns icons, liturgy, music, and drama, as well as processions, festivals, and myths. As a result, the religion avoids symbols and symbolism, so Islam has no visual symbol like the Jewish star or the Christian cross. A few symbols have, however, become unofficially associated with Islam:

- ✔ The crescent moon, which appears on the flags of various countries, such as Turkey and Pakistan, is really not a religious icon, but was the insignia of the Ottoman Empire.

- ✔ The single star is often joined with the moon (see Figure 8-1). Westerners saw the two paired so often in Middle Eastern countries that they simply assumed the crescent moon and star were symbols of Islam.

- ✔ Among the Muslims, only the Shi'ites have a symbol, a sword. They associate it with Caliph Ali, who was killed in battle.

On the other hand, colors have long been part of Islamic symbolism. They were associated with various dynasties as battle standards. Three colors — white for the Ummayads; black for the Abbasids; green for the Fatimids — have become traditional in Islamic countries, along with red.

Green receives a particularly high status because it was reportedly Muhammad's favorite color. He was supposed to have worn a green cloak and turban, and fought under a green banner. The Koran gives some credence to that claim, saying that the "inhabitants of paradise will wear green garments of fine silk" (Sura 18:31).

Figure 8-1:
This symbol is often associated with Islam, but it's not an official symbol.

Part III
Shared Aspects of the Faiths

The 5th Wave   By Rich Tennant

In this part . . .

Despite their differences, the three faiths actually have a lot in common. You probably won't confuse a mosque with a church, but members of the three religions have similar approaches to worship and to expressing their faith.

They each have sacred texts. The Bible and Koran came together along different routes, but each provides the moral and ethical underpinning of its respective faith. Christians, Jews, and Muslims erected buildings of all sizes to honor God and to provide places of worship.

Each religion also generated historic figures, as well as congregational leaders. They also have created their own holy sites, and all regard Jerusalem with awe, as well.

Chapter 9

Reading the Holy Words

In This Chapter

▶ Seeing how the Bible and Koran came into existence

▶ Understanding the problems of translating sacred books

▶ Checking out other sacred books in Judaism and Islam

*I*n high school, Bill took a required class called comparative religion. In it, he and other seniors were introduced to many of the world's religions.

As a final project, Bill read the Jewish and Christian Bible and the Muslim Koran to see if any of the laws in them still applied to modern life. To his surprise, he filled dozens of notecards with rules that still having meaning in modern life.

His teacher declined to read the project. She was used to getting just a couple of lines from disinterested students, not a mound of paper.

His research revealed one reason why these sacred texts remain important to modern believers: Their stories and lessons continue to motivate and direct billions of people worldwide.

The Bible and Koran came together in different ways, but each holy text provides the moral and ethical underpinnings for its respective faith. Each one also has its own history and challenges to understanding.

To believers, the books represent the words of the divine filtered through human writers. As such, the manuscripts are studied to find guidelines for behavior and belief.

In some sects, the holy books have taken on such status that no challenge to the words is accepted. The books themselves have almost become objects of worship. It's important to note that they didn't start that way. The books required time to acquire their mantle of true faith.

This chapter looks at each sacred text in turn, starting with what Jews call the Bible or Tanakh and Christians label the Old Testament.

The Hebrew Bible

The Hebrew Bible has a long history. It contains books that were written thousands of years ago, and its study has continued for thousands of years.

The Hebrew Bible texts, called the Old Testament by Christians, were written to demonstrate how God is involved in daily life. They also helped priests (rabbis arrived after the sacred texts were written) keep historical records. The holy men feared that successive conquerors would kill so many learned Jewish leaders that vital memories would disappear unless committed to paper.

Sections of the Hebrew Bible

Jews divide the Hebrew Bible into three units:

- The Law, also known as the *Torah,* which contains the first five books of the Bible
- The Prophets
- The Writings

Later editors separated the books into separate chapters and verses. The earliest versions of the books don't even have spaces between words.

The Law (Torah)

This section of the Bible, often called the *Torah,* contains the first five books. These books reached final form at least 2,400 years ago. The Torah (meaning "law") reflects basic Jewish history and teachings.

- **Genesis:** This book tells the story of the creation of man through Abraham and his grandson's fateful decision to move to Egypt.
- **Exodus:** The second book of the Hebrew Bible recounts the story of Moses and his courage to face Pharaoh and lead the Jews from Egyptian slavery.
- **Leviticus:** This book continues the story of the Exodus while outlining the rules of the religious community.
- **Numbers:** The story of the Exodus goes on (and the story's still not finished in Numbers). The book was named "Numbers" because the text enumerates the Jews who left Egypt.
- **Deuteronomy:** This book recaps the events of the Exodus and concludes with Moses's death. It's often been called the "last will and testament" of the great leader.

The Prophets (Nevi'im in Hebrew)

This section of the Bible follows the first five books and includes what many people might think of as histories.

- ✔ **Joshua:** Here, you can read the story of the man who led the conquest of Canaan. This book was probably once part of the first five, but later separated.

- ✔ **Judges:** This book gives an account of the various tribal leaders who followed Joshua.

- ✔ **Samuel:** This is the story of the last judge, a prophet who named the first king of Israel. The story is split in two parts (1 Samuel and 2 Samuel) and includes the life of King David.

- ✔ **Kings (1 Kings and 2 Kings):** These books are an accounting of the rulers of Judah and, after the country divided in two, Israel.

The 15 books that round out this section of the Bible are named for individual prophets. Three of these volumes are linked to *major prophets,* a term used for prophets whose surviving writing is extensive — Isaiah, Jeremiah, and Ezekiel.

The other prophets, like Hosea, Amos, and Nahum, are considered *minor.* That's because little of their writings survived, not because their words are considered less important.

The Writings (Kethuvim in Hebrew)

This last section of the Jewish Bible includes writings from a prophet like Daniel, to Psalms, Proverbs, the Song of Songs (some sects call this book Song of Solomon), Esther, and 1 and 2 Chronicles, among others.

Early Jewish scholars, called *sages,* recognized that these books weren't necessarily factual, but rather philosophical and ethical volumes designed to guide readers.

When were the books written?

The biblical books appear to have been written at various times. Many Jews think the first five books (the Torah) were written by Moses, who must have lived anywhere from 1200 to 1400 BC. Moses probably shouldn't get the credit for writing these books because internal evidence, such as word choice, reflects a much later time period. The text of the Torah was finalized about 2,400 years ago.

Not-so-sacred texts

Of course, many more books were written than what are included in the Hebrew Bible. Some may have been considered sacred at one time.

Many of them have survived and have been included in what is called the *Apocrypha*. Those books aren't considered holy, but are important to understanding the thoughts of the people during the time they were written. Books in the Apocrypha include Tobit and 1 and 2 Maccabees.

Some additional books have been found at various times. In 1945, for example, archaeologists dug up old Gnostic texts in a stone jar in the Hag Hammadi Valley in Egypt. The *Gnostic Gospels,* as they are called, include Jewish and Christian themes.

Many of these books are still read for their inspirational messages. They also help scholars understand ideas that were current at the times when the books were written. In some cases, they contrast with sacred texts, helping scholars see how various beliefs developed.

Jewish tradition credits a man named Ezra for putting together the Torah. Ezra the Scribe came from Babylon in the fifth century BC. His account of what he found in Jerusalem and his actions appear in the Bible under his name. In his book, he describes reading the law to the people who had also returned from Babylonian exile.

However, the book of Joshua reports that the law was read to the tribes before Ezra lived. Unfortunately, whatever Joshua read wasn't described in the account.

Other books in the Tanakh are credited to David, the second king of Israel, or to his successor, Solomon. There's no question that some of the text is old enough to have been written during their lifetimes, but most of it is not.

No one knows who wrote individual biblical books. In those days, there was no such thing as "pride of authorship" or copyrights.

When did the books become holy?

The books in the Hebrew Bible gained sacred status at different times. By the third century BC, the books in the Torah were already considered holy. Other books obtained that lofty position later. The prophets' writings were the next to be revered, followed by the assortment of books in the Writings section.

One reason the New Testament authors quote books from the Writings so often is that those texts had only recently become considered holy.

Understanding the Bible through JEPD

Historians are sure of one thing: The first five books of the Bible contain multiple stories describing the same event. Jean Astruc, the doctor to King Louis IV of France, first noticed the overlap in the 1700s.

His careful inspection of the Torah revealed multiple accounts of the most beloved stories: creation, Noah and his ark, the renaming of Jacob to Israel, the appearance of David, and so on. One version was written by authors among the northern tribes; the other, by writers in the southern tribes.

Because a later editor didn't know which tales were correct, historians believe he kept all versions. Many explanations have arisen to address the discrepancies. For example, Jewish sages argue that the second creation story (Genesis 2: 7, 22) merely amplifies the first (Genesis 1:27). However, the texts clearly are different and don't agree. For example, man and woman in Chapter 1 are created at the same time. In Chapter 2, man (Adam) is created first from dirt, and then woman (Eve) is created from man's rib.

Astruc's insight is called the *JEPD theory* and is the most widely accepted explanation for the writing of the Torah. In Astruc's scheme:

- ✔ **J stands for Jehovah:** Material using the name Jehovah for God came from the tribe of Judah, the last of the 12 original tribes to survive.

- ✔ **E for Elohim, a Hebrew word for God:** These writings were produced by the northern tribes, which were led by the tribe of Ephraim.

- ✔ **P for priestly requirements:** That section was created by priests.

- ✔ **D for Deuteronomy, the last of the five holy books:** Deuteronomy recaps what was in the first four books. It seems to have been written independently of (and possibly later than) the other four.

It's just coincidental that the J in Jehovah matches the J in Judah. However, generations of scholars are grateful for the parallel. Imagine how confused everyone would be if the J god went with the E section and vice versa.

Today, few scholars doubt Astruc's inspiration.

It's all Greek to me

In the third century BC, the Hebrew Bible was translated into Greek in Alexandria, Egypt, so Jews who read and spoke Greek could use the text. Called the *Septuagint* — from the Greek word for 70 — the translation helped spread Judaism's stories throughout the known world. The Septuagint contains the books of the Tanakh plus apocryphal books.

The books in the Septuagint became a model for other writers. After Jesus's death, books began to appear that dealt with his life and the beginnings of Christianity.

The Christian Bible

Pick up a Bible today, and you'll find that it has two parts: the Old Testament (the Hebrew Bible) and the New Testament. The New Testament was written after Jesus died and focuses on his message. While Jews only use the Hebrew Bible, Christians use both the Old and New Testaments.

Christian texts appear to have been written to resolve questions arising after Jesus's death. Early followers of Jesus thought the world would end promptly. When it didn't cease with his death, they thought he would return sooner, rather than later, to complete the task. However, as years passed, they began to have questions. The texts may have been written to answer those concerns.

The structure of the New Testament

Here's how the 27 books of the New Testament break down:

Four Gospels

The Gospels are biographies of Jesus, each written by a different author:

- Matthew
- Mark
- Luke
- John

Acts of the Apostles

This book describes events after Jesus died, and concentrates largely on the activities of Paul, the first great evangelist of Christianity. He toured the Mediterranean region in a tireless effort to set up colonies and to introduce Jesus to distant lands.

Epistles

The Epistles are 21 letters. Many are attributed to Paul, although scholars think he wrote six or seven at most. Each is identified by the church Paul wrote to, such as Rome, Corinth, and Galatia. They were edited extensively.

The rest of the letters are by unknown writers, although names of famous early leaders of the church, such as James and Titus, have been attached to them.

Early writers didn't care about who got credit. They just wanted their message distributed, so they often listed a famous person as the author. That's true in the Old Testament, too. The book of Daniel, for example, is named for a famous Jewish prophet who lived hundreds of years before the book could have been written.

The Revelation of Saint John

This book provides a prediction of the end of the world. In it, the author describes a terrible war between heavenly armies ending in the return of Jesus, the reward of heaven for the faithful, and the condemnation of nonbelievers. The climatic conclusion of life is discussed in detail in Chapter 15.

Who wrote the books?

As with the Old Testament, no one knows who wrote most of the material in the New Testament. The Gospels each carry a name from their title pages — Matthew, Mark, Luke, and John — but they first appeared without any authors on them. The names, which were chosen from among the followers of Jesus, were added around AD 150.

The Gospel of Luke and the Acts of the Apostles are thought to have been written by Clement, a doctor in Rome, and may have been combined into a single book at one time.

As noted earlier, Paul did write some of the letters attributed to him. Based on computer analyses of word choice and style, scholars think at least six (and maybe seven) of the epistles in the New Testament are authentic. The rest were produced by people who used Paul's name to get their thoughts accepted by a wider audience. All the epistles were extensively edited, so no one is sure exactly what Paul wrote and someone else added.

The book of Revelation is attributed to John, a disciple of Jesus, but most scholars believe it was written too late for that to be the case.

Where were they written?

No one knows where Old Testament books were written, although many seem to have originated in Israel. The New Testament contains more clues.

Intense study has concluded that the Gospel of Matthew was probably written in Egypt; the Gospels of Luke and Mark in Rome; and the Gospel of John probably in what is now Turkey. Not all scholars agree, however.

No one is sure where the epistles were written. Only those by Paul contain biographical material, but even that is skimpy. Some scholars believe Acts was written in Rome.

When were the books written?

The New Testament was compiled within a relatively short time — between AD 70 and 120. By analyzing words that the authors used, events occurring at the same time, and other factors, historians have narrowed down the chronology.

The Gospel of Mark is clearly the oldest book in the New Testament, an idea first suggested in the 1800s, but now universally accepted. That's because 80 percent of the stories in the Gospel of Matthew also appear in Mark, not the other way around. These similarities suggest that the writer of Matthew took the older texts and updated them with additional material or new ideas that had come into the early faith. In addition, Mark is written in rougher language, while Matthew is smoother and written by someone who was better educated.

Mark is dated to about AD 70 because the writer infers that the Temple was destroyed, which took place in 70. Matthew and Luke probably were written in AD 85, which gave the Gospel of Mark time to circulate and reach the authors of those Gospels.

The Gospel of John is the youngest Gospel and dated from AD 90 to 105. That Gospel writer didn't read the Gospels of Matthew and Luke. His book has more historical data, but Jesus is presented as a divine figure far removed from the earthly figure who walks through Mark.

Paul started writing his letters as early as AD 39 and probably continued until his death around AD 64. Some of the epistles believed to be written by other early Christians were probably written after the Gospel of John.

Drawing material from many sources

The Old Testament mentions sources, such as the Book of Jasher, that the writers used as reference material. However, those original texts have disappeared in time. The situation is more complex with the New Testament.

The writers of the Gospels of Matthew and Luke relied on the Gospel of Mark as their source. They also had another document, known as *Q* (from German for "unknown"), that provided additional information. However, neither writer read the other's book, which is why they disagree in many areas.

In addition, all four Gospel authors draw on various other sources, including

- ✔ Word of mouth. People in the first century would memorize and pass on stories to their children.
- ✔ Gnostic documents like the Gospel of Thomas, which was rejected as canonical and survived only by being buried in the desert.
- ✔ Jewish stories available in what became the Old Testament.
- ✔ Writings in pagan texts about their gods.

By the fourth century, despite the lack of a good publisher, many books were floating around. No one knew what to believe. Church fathers were upset, as was Emperor Constantine. He figured that one empire deserved one holy book and demanded that all the philosophical debates stop.

Jerome gets an assignment: Revise the Bible

In AD 382, Pope Damasus commissioned a young priest named Jerome to revise the Latin versions of the Gospels.

Jerome was the pope's private secretary, but he was also a linguist who could speak, write, and understand Latin, Greek, and Hebrew. Jerome even knew Aramaic and was trained in Latin classics.

Jerome began with the Jewish books first, and then went to work on the Christian texts. (Jews had sacred books, but had not decided that more holy texts couldn't be produced. After the destruction of the Temple in AD 70, Jewish sages met in the small Israeli town of Jamnia to collect the holy books. However, debates recorded in the Talmud show arguments raging as late as the fifth century over which books were truly holy. That implies that the holy men at Jamnia didn't make a final decision on the Jewish Bible. Jerome changed that with his translations.)

Eventually, Jerome's successors produced what became the official Bible. The text became known as the *Vulgate,* because it was written in "vulgar" Latin, rather than the sophisticated Greek language. Suddenly, in the fifth century, as the western Roman Empire was being overrun by pagan hordes, the world had a Bible. The translation wasn't accepted right away by Church leaders, but eventually it became the primary Bible for millions of Christians through the centuries.

The Koran

The Jewish and Christian Bibles came together almost by accident. The process for creating Islam's holy text, the *Koran* (also spelled in English as "Qu'ran" and "Quran," among other alternatives), was very different. However, it's similar to the Bible in some ways. The Koran contains revelations from God, similar to those in the Bible, but presented through the Prophet Muhammad. Some history of the Arab people is also included.

Revealing the Koran's history

Muhammad didn't write anything down on stone, papyrus, paper, or anything else, but his revelations were eventually collected and placed in manuscript form. The process must have been complicated.

No record of a Koran exists for at least 20 years after the death of the Prophet in 632. That's when Ali, Muhammad's son-in-law, and other early companions of Muhammad began amassing the Prophet's revelations, but not before several different versions were cobbled together.

Some historians have conjectured that later believers wrote additions to the Koran and backdated them to Muhammad.

According to Muslim tradition, about 20 years after Ali died, Caliph Uthman gathered together all the copies of the Koran, reportedly changed some passages, destroyed the other versions, and made six copies of the new edition. He relied on two sources to create the Koran that Muslims use today:

- ✔ The written text that had been ordered by Abu Bakr, Muhammad's initial convert and the first leader of the Muslims after the Prophet's death
- ✔ The various oral texts provided by Muslims who had memorized them during Muhammad's lifetime

The text has been unchanged since then.

Muhammad called on his followers to preserve his words. He may have been inspired by the example of the Bible, which Christian missionaries and Jewish travelers brought with them into Arabia.

Devout Muslims, of course, believe that Muhammad dictated every word in their sacred book. They use the book in legal, religious, and daily life, in much the same way the Bible is used in the Western world.

Outlining the Koran's organization

The Koran contains many chapters (called *sura*), but they aren't in sequential order. Instead, unlike the Bible, the longest ones have been placed first and the shortest ones are in the back. Like the Bible, however, suras are divided into verses to help in memorization and location.

According to tradition, followers of Muhammad wrote down his teachings on palm leaves, stones, and other objects. After he died, many of his close companions were either killed in wars or died from old age. To protect and preserve the revelations, scholars brought all the writings to Abu Bakr. He then had them compiled into a single unit with 114 chapters.

The book contains many Biblical characters, but provides alternative versions of familiar stories. For example, Abraham is commanded to sacrifice Ishmael, not Isaac (Sura 2). The Koran records Haman as a minister of the Egyptian pharaoh who oppressed the Jews, not the prime minister of Persia, as listed in the biblical book of Esther (Sura 28:6).

The text is written in poetic style and in rhyme. Muhammad spoke in Arabic, but limited words in the vocabulary forced him to borrow many foreign terms to express ideas. The combined languages add a universal element to the revelations.

Understanding the Texts

The Bible and Koran are hard to read. The Old Testament was written in Hebrew and Aramaic, which is closely related to Hebrew. The New Testament was written in Greek and Aramaic. The Koran was written in Arabic.

Unfortunately, what the Bible and Koran actually say are not as clear as many people think. No one today is reading the same book, nor are they reading what was actually written centuries ago. That's because modern languages didn't exist when the holy texts were written. Each sacred text had to be translated.

How accurate are the translations? Not very. They can't be. This section looks at what that limitation means to the understanding of the holy books.

Translating can be such sweet sorrow

You can read these sentences easily because there are periods, commas, capital letters, and other marks to help you. Those marks weren't around when the Bible and Koran were written. Ancient Hebrew writing was simply a steady stream of letters from right to left. There were no capital letters, commas, periods, exclamation marks, or any other kind of grammatical notation. That's also true in Greek and Arabic, another language closely related to Hebrew.

Hebrew did develop a few final letters to indicate to readers when a word ends, which is one reason Hebrew sentences sound so similar. However, there are only a handful of final letters. As a result, reading the exact words can be difficult.

Actually, that's a minor complication. There's a far bigger one: Hebrew has no vowels. That means that words spelled the same but pronounced differently have different meanings. Translating the correct meaning can only be done with vowels. Hebrew, however, didn't add vowels until the ninth century, long after the Bible's text had been codified. The result can be confusing.

Translators have to find ways to reproduce the words in a way that is acceptable to their readers. That has meant taking liberties to capture the sense or meaning of the passage, while not necessarily repeating it word for word. That approach, although necessary, can lead to confusion.

In the Gospel of Matthew, for example, Jesus rides into Jerusalem astride two animals. That's because the writer of Matthew, relying on the Greek translation of the old Hebrew texts, read that the Messiah would appear on the back of an ass. That line is followed by "foal of a horse." The writer thought that meant two animals. But in Hebrew poetry, the second line duplicates the first line, but uses different words. Matthew tripped over a translation.

Scholars are well aware of this problem. In the 11th century, a great French scholar named Rabbi Solomon Isaac (better known as Rashi) wrote a beloved commentary on the Torah. His thoughts are still read today in synagogues around the world. Repeatedly, Rashi was forced to write "Hebrew unintelligible" as he tried to make sense of the Bible. And that was 1,000 years ago.

That's not what that says

The holy texts also use *idioms*. Those are phrases that meant something thousands of years ago, but now seem strange. There are many of them in every language. For example, an American might note a heavy storm and say, "It's raining cats and dogs." No one thinks that little furry creatures are falling from the sky. But, someone translating that phrase from English into another language years from now might not know the true meaning and conclude the heavens amazingly dropped kittens and puppies all over the place.

Without knowing the original meaning, however, any translator is hard pressed to explain various terms and to translate them adequately into another language. Translators simply don't know what the idioms mean and, after so many years, can only guess at their proper sense.

At the same time, the holy Scriptures are filled with *colloquial* terms. These are words that have a meaning at a particular time, but that meaning has changed. We see that all the time in English. Our vocabulary changes constantly. Look at William Shakespeare, considered the greatest of all English writers. He lived from 1564 to 1616. We can't read his works today without a dictionary because new words have replaced some of the words he used in his day, and meanings have shifted dramatically. That's true of any language. Many of the words of French author Victor Hugo or Russian novelist Leo Tolstoy, both of whom lived in the 1800s, no longer have the same meaning.

Think how many word meanings have changed in the Bible, which contains writing as much as 3,200 years old, or the Koran, which is about 1,400 years old. Unfortunately, translators don't necessarily know what the words meant originally and can only estimate what they mean now.

I can read it, but what does it mean?

Then, too, there are strange sentences in the texts which defy understanding. Take the story of the prophet Samuel and the first king of Israel, Saul (Samuel 13:1). Samuel is able to locate Saul and anoint him king because the new monarch was the tallest man in the crowd when Samuel makes his selection. Then we are told that Saul ruled for one year and 21 years.

Why didn't the Bible say 22 years, which would make more sense? That's because the Bible clearly says, "Saul was one year old when he began to rule." That would seem to eliminate the possibility that he was the tallest man in the crowd. Obviously, there is some confusion in copying the words. At this late date, however, no one knows what the original text said.

The end result is that the Bible has to be taken on faith. Scholars have done the best job they can to translate the ancient words and to give modern readers a good idea of what the texts say.

Things get really complicated in the Koran

Translating the Koran is hampered both by the language barrier and politics.

Although the Koran is in Arabic, today only about 20 percent of the population uses that language. As a result, like the Latin of the first Bible prepared by Jerome in the fourth century, the Arabic language is slowly being reserved for religious documents. That means more difficulty in understanding the nuances, metaphors, and idioms expressed in the text.

As a result, many Muslim scholars today believe the Koran can't be correctly translated. That leads to immense misunderstandings as journalists and writers try to communicate the ideas of the Koran in a language non-Muslims can understand. It's no wonder the Western world is puzzled by behaviors that seem alien compared with what supposedly is in the Koran.

The reality is that the Koran, like the Bible, is hard to translate. The language is archaic. The structure reflects seventh century Arabia, not modern ideas. Add in the cultural biases, and the book becomes a minefield for any intrepid interpreter. "Muslim scholars believe that any translation cannot be more than an approximate interpretation, intended only as a tool for the study and understanding of the original Arabic text," according to Khaleel Mohammed, writing in the *Middle East Quarterly.*

To heighten the tension, during the Crusades and the brief establishment about 800 years ago of a medieval Christian state in what is now Israel, Muslim scholars reinterpreted the Koran to remove any idea that Muhammad may have been influenced by the Bible or Jewish commentaries, even though he often quotes them. Today, those interpretations remain the standard teachings of the Koran, adding to the division between Muslim and non-Muslim worlds.

To aggravate the problems even more, the Koran has achieved a status akin to the Bible. Like many modern readers of the Bible, Muslim believers now claim that the Koran reflects the unchangeable views of God. That has led to further estrangements both within Muslim society and without.

The end result is the same as in the Western world: a poorly understood document from another era remains the guide for a people living in a different time and place, and under totally different conditions.

Where are the originals?

Some of the questions raised in the Bible and Koran could be answered if historians could find the original books. However, no one expects to find the first edition of any sacred book. That's because they were often written on *papyrus,* a writing material made from a reed that grows in Egypt. It's not very strong or durable.

Some books were written on dried, smooth animal skin, called *vellum,* or on really excellent animal skin, called *parchment.* However, because the materials were passed hand to hand, they quickly deteriorated.

Because all copies had to be made by hand and were very expensive, the old text was discarded as soon as the new one was ready.

At some point, Jewish sages ordered that any text with the name God in it must be preserved, so the old books were buried. That's why archaeologists have found some forgotten books.

Still, the oldest Torah ever found dates from about 200 BC, at least 250 years after it was first compiled. The oldest complete New Testament dates from around AD 340, at least 250 years after it was written. The oldest complete Koran comes from the late seventh century.

All the texts probably contain numerous editing changes and simple human errors made while copying. One historian called the changes "pious editing."

Unrolling the Dead Sea Scrolls

Our understanding of the Jewish and Christian holy texts received an enormous boost in 1947 with the discovery of what are called the *Dead Sea Scrolls.*

Young Bedouin shepherds claim they were walking near the Dead Sea in Israel and tossed rocks into caves built into the steep walls. A rock supposedly hit something. The boys heard a crash. Using a rope ladder, they went to investigate.

They found huge ceramic jars containing old manuscripts. The papyrus on which some of the writings had been made dissolved instantly when exposed to air, but the manuscripts written on prepared animal skin (or *vellum*) survived. The Arabs knew the value of old manuscripts. Pieces were torn off and sold in open marketplaces. Eventually, the various shreds came to the attention of scholars interested in ancient documents.

The scraps were traced back to the caves, and a thorough investigation began. In time, more than 900 scrolls have been recovered from various caves. A few are shown in Figure 9-1.

What's in the Dead Sea Scrolls?

Every book of the Old Testament is represented in these scrolls, except Esther, which was a later addition to the canon. In addition, the scrolls contained many other books that we don't think of as sacred today, but obviously the writings had that connotation then. In some cases, the scrolls are the only copies ever found of texts quoted by later authors.

Scholars have learned several important lessons from the Dead Sea Scrolls:

- ✔ They date from about 200 BC to AD 70. That places them a lot closer to the original writing. The oldest complete Hebrew Bible prior to the Dead Sea Scrolls was written about AD 1000.

- ✔ The texts were obviously thought of as sacred. As a result, the original wording was retained for many years until these copies were made. Still, there are multiple versions of almost every book. So historians still don't know what the original manuscripts contained.

- ✔ Some books were not considered as important. There are many copies of three books now in the Torah — Genesis, Exodus, and Deuteronomy — but only a couple copies of the two other books in the Torah (Leviticus and Numbers).

Why were the scrolls there?

Historians have debated the source of the Dead Sea Scrolls since they were discovered in 1947.

Options include:

✔ They had been placed in storage centuries ago because of the Jewish prohibition against destroying the name of God.

✔ They represented the library of residents in the nearby city of Qumran.

✔ They may have been brought to the caves for safekeeping around AD 70 when Roman troops threatened the Temple in Jerusalem and its sacred archives.

Historians can't agree on who lived in Qumran, site of the scrolls. Some suggest it was an isolated community where people who thought themselves holy, called *Essenes*, had separated from the rest of Jewish society. They left society in the first century BC to await the end of the world.

Others think the tiny town was a resort for wealthy Romans and Jews, or a factory for producing documents or ceramics.

✔ Some of the material in the New Testament was influenced by the texts in the Dead Sea Scrolls. For example, the Essenes (an isolated community of Jews) are awaiting the return of a Teacher of Righteousness, a man persecuted and either killed or executed at least 90 years before Jesus lived. No one argues that the Teacher of Righteousness was Jesus, only that the idea of a returning leader preceded Christianity.

How do they help us translate the Bible?

The Dead Sea Scrolls help bridge some of that empty space in time. Artifacts from thousands of years ago are rare. Many items simply were worn away through use, discarded, and destroyed. Others may have been buried in areas where water or weather eventually ruined them. Some were reused.

Because the Dead Sea Scrolls contain so many ancient books — books written in the same limited vocabulary that appears in the Bible — historians can isolate idioms, colloquial terms, and strange writing. Then by comparing the documents, translators can get a better sense of what the author may have meant. That has led to new translations, relying on the old texts.

The work continues. Most of the Dead Sea Scrolls were translated and published in the 1950s. The rest, a mixture of fragmentary letters and words torn from scrolls and seriously damaged texts, have required additional decades to decipher. Today, very little of the Dead Sea Scrolls is not in the public domain.

Although not all the writings contained in the scrolls are historically signifi-cant, they help us appreciate and understand the Bible better than before.

Perusing Other Sacred Books

Although the Bible and Koran serve as the mainspring of faith in their respec-tive religions, other books have been written over time to help explain or amplify the holy texts.

The insightful Talmud

To help explain the Bible, the Jews developed a second book, called the *Talmud* (meaning "teachings"), which provides insight into sacred writing. It's actually a compilation of two earlier books. There were originally two Talmuds, one in Jerusalem and one in Babylonia. The Jerusalem one was closed in the fifth century. The Babylonian version continued to grow for another 200 years after that. Eventually, the texts were combined into one book.

When the Torah was first read to the people, not everyone understood what the words meant. Occasionally, the wording was clear — "Remember the Sabbath and keep it holy." That sounds obvious enough. Or "Do not seethe the kid in the mother's milk." That seems to prohibit boiling some goat meat in milk. But what do these sentences really mean? How could someone "honor" the Sabbath, which, according to the Jewish calendar, extends from sundown Friday to sundown Saturday? What was wrong with boiling meat?

Everyone had some ideas. People began to discuss these laws and try to understand them. Because the requirements were part of God's law, failure to obey could be catastrophic.

Soon, scholars known as *sages* began to study the texts and issue rulings to help guide the people. For example, "honor the Sabbath," they decided, meant the people should pray all day, rest, and do no work. Rest meant not doing anything that might force someone else to work. As a result, even today, very Orthodox Jews cook during the day on Friday so they don't have to work in the kitchen on Saturday. They won't even turn on lights, because that means someone at the electric company has to work.

The biblical prohibition about cooking goat meat has been linked to a Canaanite ritual that involved boiling meat in milk and offering it to a god.

For years, people memorized the various decisions that carefully controlled their lives. In time, sages realized that every time a person died, enormous amounts of information vanished, too. So, they wrote down their commentaries, discussions, and rulings in what became known as the *Mishna* (meaning "repetition").

The text included stories about the patriarchs, like Abraham destroying the idols, as well as commentaries on holy books and debates. One version was created in Babylon, where some Jews remained after being allowed to return to Israel under the Persians. A second version was drafted in Israel.

Both versions constitute the "oral" law, which sages insisted was handed down to Moses on Mount Sinai along with the Ten Commandments.

After the Mishna was produced, sages tried to stop all the bantering, but scholars are hard folks to keep quiet. In time, another book appeared, called the *Gemara* (meaning "tradition" in Aramaic; "completion" in Hebrew) and written in Aramaic. It provides commentary on the Mishna. In the third century AD, the two were combined into what is called the Talmud.

Some Jews didn't like the use of the oral law, preferring to limit their beliefs to what was written in the holy texts. The oral law would eventually become an area of contention between two large Jewish political-religious groups at the time of Jesus. The *Pharisees* supported the oral law; the *Sadducees* rejected it.

In time, the Talmud was almost equal to the Bible in importance to Jews. In the Middle Ages, the Talmud was actually put on trial for supposed anti-Christian sentiments and burned by Christians who thought it was the Jewish holy text.

The mysterious Kabbalah

One other book deserves mention, the *Kabbalah,* which contains several books with it. The largest text in the Kabbalah, the Zohar, was probably written around the 1200s by Moses de Leon — although believers argue it is far older.

The Kabbalah contains Jewish mystical thought. It became very prominent in Jewish life through the 1600s, especially because of its efforts to pinpoint the arrival of a Jewish messiah. However, the failure of false messiahs reduced enthusiasm for it. Still, many people continue to read the text and appreciate the Kabbalah's basic idea that a spark of divine exists in all people.

Christians stick with the original reference book

No other books have attained the sanctity level of the Bible. However, Protestant and Catholic Bibles are not the same. Some books of the Apocrypha are included only in the Catholic version.

Catholics originally relied on the Greek translation of Jewish sacred books, the Septuagint. As a result, their Bible includes such books now in the Jewish apocrypha as 1 and 2 Maccabees, Baruch, Tobit, Judith, The Wisdom of Solomon, Ecclesiasticus, Susanna, and Daniel. They also have a longer version of Esther and Daniel. Catholic Old Testaments also include 1 and 2 Esdras, Prayer of Manasseh, Psalm 151, and 3 Maccabees.

Protestant sects followed the Jewish canon and did not add these excluded books. Protestants opposed some of the teachings in the books. For example, 2 Maccabees discusses purgatory, an idea that Protestants rejected. Instead of picking and choosing from the list of books, Protestant leaders rejected all but those in the Jewish Old Testament.

Some sects, like Lutheran and Anglican, may include the apocryphal books as an appendix to the Bible, but most Protestants never see them in church.

Several other books have some religious significance, at least within Christian denominations. *Catechism of the Catholic Church,* published in 1992, is a 900-page exposition on Catholic beliefs and has been translated in many languages around the world.

In addition, the Book of Mormon, which is the sacred text of the Church of Jesus Christ of Latter-day Saints, tells the story of refugees fleeing ancient Israel and coming to what eventually became the United States. According to tradition, the founder of the faith, Joseph Smith, translated the books in the 1820s from golden tablets the angel Moroni pinpointed for him.

The Hadith collects Muhammad's sayings and teachings

During Muhammad's life, many of his sayings were written down. In addition, stories about him circulated. After he died, Islamic leaders added to this mass of material, including their own interpretations, creating what is known as *Hadith.* In many ways, this is similar to the New Testament stories about Jesus and to the Talmudic interpretations by Jewish scholars.

The Hadith eventually was divided into books. Many Muslims accept all the Hadith material as divinely inspired. Some sects eliminate comments and ideas they believe were added later and not authentic.

An array of books was originally produced that purported to contain the sayings of Muhammad. Over time, six have become accepted by the vast majority of Muslims. The same process occurred in the eras when the biblical books were produced.

The six Hadith books rank only behind the Koran in importance and value in Islam. The books are

- **Sahih al-Bukhari** (810–870): Bukhari spent a quarter of his life on his great work, the most revered in all Hadith literature. He pared more than 600,000 sayings attributed to Muhammad down to 7,275. In addition, he linked the sayings to specific areas of Islamic law.

- **Sahih Muslim** (817–874): Muslim also took thousands of existing sayings and compiled a collection of about 3,000 authenticated ones. Like Bukhari, Muslim was trying to weed out false teachings. He carefully established the validity of accepted sayings, creating a verification pattern still followed today.

- **Sunna** (meaning "path"): This text consists of four books that focus on Muhammad's actions and decrees, creating the basis of Islamic law. They were passed along orally for decades before being written down.

  - The most prominent is the **Sunan of Abu Dawud** (817–889). Some of his material duplicated writing in the first two books, but he also included new sayings. He also recognized some may not be authentic and identified those which may be suspect.

  - Two other books are by **at-Tirmithi** and **an-Nasai.** Each compiles the sayings in accordance to the laws, but an-Nasi also added traditions.

- The last of the Sunna books, written by **Ibn Maj,** is considered the weakest of the books because the author didn't identify sayings that may not be authentic. All the other authors did.

All these books were completed by the end of the ninth century. Eventually, they were brought together by Shaikh Wali ud-Din (1377?–1440?) and entitled *Mishkat ul-Masabih* (meaning "niche of lights").

The two principal sects of Islam, Sunni and Shi'ite, follow the teachings of the sacred books, but have different views. The Sunnis look to the ancient texts for guidance; the Shi'ites believe a modern scholar can provide an authentic reinterpretation. As a result, each sect may follow a different law regarding an activity or behavior.

Interpreting sacred Islamic texts

Average Muslims, like Jews and Christians with their sacred texts, need help to interpret the holy words. Like Rashi for the Jews, Islam produced a great scholar, Muhammad Ibni Jarir Abu Jafar Al-Tabari (AD 838–923), who carefully interpreted the Koran. He also wrote a detailed history of the religion, the first and still considered one of the best.

The mystical sect of Islam, the Sufi, produced a great leader whose writings and poetry continue to resonate today. Mawlana Jalal-ud-din Mohammed (1207–1273), better known as Rumi, wanted to return to what he saw as pure Islam, leaving behind accepted interpretations of his day. In that, he resembled many Jewish and Christian leaders who tried to "purify" their own faiths.

Rumi saw man as perfect. In his last book, he wrote, " Do not look (at the fakir who is looking for a treasure) as a treasure-hunter: he is the treasure itself. How could the lover be anything but the beloved?"

Chapter 10

Houses of Prayer

· ·

· ·

*F*riends of Bill attended services at a Methodist church in New Haven, Connecticut. The church was probably 150 years old and was located along the city's central green, which was at one time the heart of the community. Bill used to join his friends there for Sunday services to admire the impressive structure with its stained-glass windows and glistening wooden interior.

Such buildings abound in all religions. People like to congregate in a special site specifically designated as a house of prayer. Jews troop into synagogues and temples to pray; Christians typically go to churches, although some sects prefer private homes. And Muslims walk to mosques.

There is a long history behind the design and adornment of such buildings, as you find out in this chapter.

Early Sacred Sites: Stone Mounds and Altars

Holy buildings are relatively new. Although the few big cities in ancient times may have featured a temple or two, nomadic herdsmen and farmers living in tiny villages didn't have the means to build large structures. Besides, they believed in gods of nature, who were worshipped in the fields and on mountaintops.

To honor them, the people set up stone altars, called *cairns,* to mark a holy site and to make sacrifices to their gods. The Middle East is littered with such locales.

In early years, Jews worshipped stones, and some of those altars still exist today. The Bible, too, contains evidence in that belief. Joshua sets up stones to "listen" to him read the law and "bear" witness (Joshua 24:27). Psalms talk about the "stone that bore you" in reference to the old idea that God, as a stone, gave birth to his people (Psalm 18). Even today, the song "Rock of Ages" reminds us of that nearly forgotten concept.

The idea of a stone mound peaked in Babylon, where Abraham probably saw giant pyramids, called *ziggurats,* with huge stones laid on top of each other so a priest could climb to the top.

A Greek visitor left this account of what one temple in Babylon looked like.

"Below, in the same precinct, there is a second temple, in which is a sitting figure of Marduk, all of gold. Before the figure stands a large golden table, and the throne whereon it sits, and the base on which the throne is placed, are likewise of gold. The Chaldeans told me that all the gold together was eight hundred talents' weight. Outside the temple are two altars, one of solid gold, on which it is only lawful to offer sucklings; the other a common altar, but of great size, on which the full-grown animals are sacrificed. It is also on the great altar that the Chaldeans burn the frankincense, which is offered to the amount of a thousand talents' weight, every year, at the festival of the God." —*History of the Persian War* by Herodotus

Jacob climbs a ladder

A biblical story about Jacob, Abraham's grandson, reflects the strong tradition of rock altars.

According to an account in Genesis, Jacob ran away from his angry brother and found himself in a small Canaanite community.

"Jacob left Beersheba and set out for Haran. When he reached a certain place, he stopped for the night because the sun had set. Taking one of the stones there, he put it under his head and lay down to sleep. He had a dream in which he saw a stairway resting on the earth, with its top reaching to heaven, and the angels of God were ascending and descending on it. There above it stood the Lord, and he said: 'I am the Lord, the God of your father Abraham and the God of Isaac. I will give you and your descendants the land on which you are lying.' When Jacob awoke from his sleep, he thought, 'Surely the Lord is in this place, and I was not aware of it.' He was afraid and said, 'How awesome is this place! This is none other than the house of God; this is the gate of heaven.' Early the next morning Jacob took the stone he had placed under his head and set it up as a pillar and poured oil on top of it. He called that place Bethel ('house of God'), though the city used to be called Luz." —Genesis 28:10–14, 16–19

The Many Lives of the Temple in Jerusalem

The First Temple may have been the most revered building of its day. Erected in the tenth century BC, it served as the home of God for about 400 years.

Whether living under foreign control, serving as slaves in Egypt, or traveling to distant countries, Jews dreamed of a great building to house their God, similar to religious structures used in Egyptian and Babylonian cultures. Until the reign of David around 1000 BC, however, the Jews didn't have a leader who was strong enough to rid the land of enemies and redirect resources into the construction of what became known as the First Temple.

The Bible says that David started to build the Temple, but was prevented from continuing by God because his hands were too stained with blood from so many wars. His son, Solomon, was assigned the task. In the fourth year of his reign, Solomon hired Phoenician craftsmen to build God's house in Jerusalem.

The Temple took seven years to complete and followed the design of Egyptian houses of worship.

The Bible gives a detailed account of the construction in two books, 1 Kings and 2 Chronicles:

> "Then King Solomon raised up a labor force out of all Israel — and the labor force was thirty thousand men. Solomon selected seventy thousand men to bear burdens, eighty thousand to quarry stone in the mountains, and three thousand six hundred to oversee them. And the temple, when it was being built, was built with stone finished at the quarry, so that no hammer or chisel or any iron tool was heard in the temple while it was being built.

> "The house which King Solomon built for the Lord was sixty cubits long, twenty cubits wide, and thirty cubits high. The vestibule in front of the nave of the house was twenty cubits long, equal to the width of the house, and ten cubits deep in front of the house. And he made for the house windows with recessed frames. He also built a structure against the wall of the house, running round the walls of the house, both the nave and the inner sanctuary — and he made side chambers all around. The lowest story was five cubits broad, the middle one was six cubits broad and the third was seven cubits broad — for around the outside of the house he made offsets on the wall in order that the supporting beams should not be inserted into the walls of the house.

"The entrance for the lowest story was on the south side of the house; and one went up by stairs to the middle story, and from the middle story to the third. He made the ceiling of the house of beams and planks of cedar. He built the structure against the whole house, each story five cubits high, and it was joined to the house with timbers of cedar."
—I Kings 5:13, 15–18; 6:2–6, 8–10

The Temple's significance to the Jews

The Temple that eventually was constructed was more than a large building. It served as a solid symbol of God's presence among the Jews and was the central cultic site. All animal sacrifices were conducted there; the high priest lived there; and many Jews regularly made pilgrimages to the building for certain annual holidays. The priests maintained the treasury there, filled with money tithed by the devout.

In many ways, the Bible seems to focus on the Temple as though it were the culmination of Jewish religious beliefs.

No physical evidence of the First Temple survived (the next section talks about the Temple's destruction), nor are there any accounts of anyone visiting it. However, the prophet Jeremiah clearly acknowledged one existed in the seventh century BC and, of course, the Bible described it. Some historians argue that the Temple was built after David's reign and then predated to connect it to the most significant Jewish king. Regardless, the Temple served as a symbol of Judaism for centuries.

The Temple's destruction

The Jerusalem Temple survived probably 400 years. Then the Babylonian army showed up in 597 BC and conquered Jerusalem. The troops returned 11 years later when the Jews tried to revolt against their masters. The Temple was burned down, and the Jews were taken away to Babylon. Only a few residents remained in Jerusalem to remember the glories of the land and God's house.

Then around 538 BC, the Jews' new overlords, the Persians, allowed all captive people to return home. Many Jews marched the thousands of miles back to ancient Israel, where they found a found a pile of rubble where the Temple had been.

The handful of residents who had stayed in the holy city hadn't been able to muster the manpower to rebuild the Temple. Moreover, their neighbors were opposed to a new structure, insisting that the Temple was actually a military fortress.

A Samarian temple

Two temples were built in ancient Israel. The one in Jerusalem is the most famous, but after the northern tribes rebelled against Solomon's son and created their own country, they erected a temple on Mount Gerizim. That temple eventually was destroyed by the Assyrians.

Later, a prophet around the time of Jesus led a movement to rebuild the Samarian temple. He told the people that he would show them the sacred vessels which Moses had buried on the site. The Roman governor, Pontius Pilate, who became notorious for his connection to Jesus, crushed that effort and killed the prophet, according to the Jewish historian Josephus.

A new Temple rises

The returning Jews expected that God would restore their independence so they could worship him without Persians hovering around. They turned to the words of the prophets Jeremiah and Ezekiel for guidance. Both had predicted the rebirth of Israel, a rebuilding of the Temple, and the return of the holy priests. Yet, despite such hopes, the Jews had remained under foreign control. Zechariah asked why God had not responded, and God answered that the Temple had not been rebuilt yet (Zechariah 1:12–16). The prophet Ezekiel also suggested that God was waiting for the Jews to build a new Temple (Ezekiel 40).

Eventually, Jewish leaders got permission from the Persians to rebuild their glorious Temple in the fifth century BC. Lacking money for ornate furnishings, they erected a smaller version of the First Temple, but one that assured Jews that God had come home.

The new residents of Jerusalem built the Temple on the site of the old structure. Over time, it again became the center of the religion and was greatly expanded later by King Herod in the first century BC.

A battle for the Temple and its rededication

Lacking independence, Jews often found their religion and their Temple threatened. The situation bottomed out around 167 BC, forcing them into a guerilla war with their Syrian masters.

The Second Temple served as the heart of the faith while the Persians were conquered by the Greeks. Then the Greek Empire divided into three parts. Syria, the eastern third, eventually took control of Israel.

Late in the second century BC, a new ruler in Syria tried to ban basic Jewish beliefs involving kosher food and prayer to God. Antiochus IV was determined to instill Greek culture. He ordered his Israeli governor, Jason, to conduct improper sacrifices in the Temple. As far as Jews were concerned, that action polluted the sacred altar.

Antiochus had gone too far. Led by a family known as the Hasmoneans, Jews revolted against the Syrians around 167 BC. After two years of hard fighting, Jewish forces entered the Temple and purified it. By then, Antiochus lay dying of consumption, and soon after, Jason died in Egypt.

Unable to celebrate the fall harvest holiday of Sukkoth because of earlier battles, the victorious Jews held the priestly mandated, seven-day feast in December to rededicate and purify the Temple.

The new holiday immediately took on special significance and is remembered each year under the name of *Hanukkah,* which means "rededication." The holiday would have been a minor one on the Jewish calendar, but it falls near Christmas. As a result, Jews felt the need to add additional emphasis to their ancient holiday.

No Jewish officials who had supported the Greeks were around to enjoy the celebration. Victorious Jews, nicknamed *Maccabees,* had dropped them over the Temple's 100-foot walls.

Romans defile the Temple

The independent Jewish state fell in 63 BC to the Romans, who had a tradition of respecting the religion of conquered people. However, Roman General Pompey was curious about the Temple. He had heard about it and wanted to see what was housed there.

When he reached the Temple, he didn't stop at the front gate, but chose to enter uninvited the *Holy of Holies,* the inner sanctum of the Temple that was reserved for the high priest. Along the way, he and his men saw the golden table with the bread topped with frankincense, the menorah (the seven-stemmed candelabra), the vessels used to pour oil, and bowls filled with various spices. The Temple walls were coated with the blood of sacrificed animals.

In the small room in the back, where God supposedly lived, the Romans found nothing.

Pompey was amazed, because his temples were filled with idols. Roman historians refused to believe his reports and suggested there was a statue of a donkey there. Later, Romans would revive that charge and accuse Christians of worshipping donkeys.

Herod's version of the Temple

The Temple enjoyed a rebirth under Herod the Great, who succeeded his father around 38 BC. He built temples for Roman gods and dedicated cities to the emperor, but wanted to please his Jewish subjects. So he began a mammoth reconstruction of the Second Temple to make it more magnificent. Work continued long after Herod's death and resulted in a huge structure renowned around the Mediterranean.

The Temple's entryway opened onto a huge courtyard, known as the Courtyard of the Gentiles. Anyone could go there except lepers, those with diseases of the sex organs, and menstruating women. The Temple's inner courtyards bore signs (written in Greek) that warned all non-Jews to stay away on pain of death.

Herod's Temple served many purposes and was thus a busy place with soldiers, pilgrims, priests, scribes, scholars, and vendors assembled for business. Pilgrims could buy pure doves or pigeons to use in sacrifices in the Temple. The birds were less expensive than a lamb or cow, which were also available.

Classes were held there, too, by sages. These wise men devoted their lives to studying the holy scrolls stored at the Temple and passing along knowledge to eager students. That information was important: Jews believed that God punished them for misbehavior, so they had to learn the sacred texts to be sure not to do anything wrong.

Jews living far from Jerusalem would send representatives to the Temple to acquire information, get answers to questions, and report back to their communities.

Money-changers waited in a long row to convert unacceptable pagan coins marred with human images into proper Temple *shekels* (ancient Hebrew currency). Their crowded stalls stood side by side with tax collectors and priests gathering tithes. Jesus would scatter the money-changers one day, but they were actually performing an important function for the visiting pilgrims.

The whole area swarmed with crowds of people from all walks of life — rich and poor, beggars and sages. The noise was overwhelming, with the bleating of frightened animals piercing the confusion, and the odor of burned meat hung in the air.

The Romans' view of the Temple

The Temple remained under construction for decades. It faced destruction several times as fighting between Jews and Romans continued.

Wise men lead the faith

Because Judaism doesn't have any kind of organizational structure, teachers would have their own schools and develop the ideas later collected in the Talmud. The most famous teacher (or *sage*) was Hillel, who lived just before Jesus.

The *high priest,* a title dating back to the time of Moses, served as the director of the Temple, not as the presiding officer of the religion. By the time of Jesus, the high priest was appointed by the Roman governor of the region and had become a political position.

The high priest and sages met in what was called the *Sanhedrin,* mimicking the group of 70 elders who advised Moses. The Sanhedrin decided questions of Jewish law and issued rulings.

The Romans recognized Jewish belief in one God and didn't require Jews to pray to the Roman emperor. In the Temple, however, the Jews offered regular sacrifices on the emperor's behalf. The sacrifices were their way of expressing gratitude for the Romans' tolerance.

That wasn't enough for every Roman ruler. In AD 41, Emperor Gaius, better known to history as Caligula, tried to have a statue of himself placed in the Second Temple. The *Abomination of Desolation,* as Jews called it, almost led to a national strike.

The aged Jewish philosopher Philo headed a Jewish delegation that hurried to Rome in hopes of changing Caligula's mind. Philo's diplomatic mission failed. In Judea, however, the Syrian governor Petronius Publius hesitated to obey Caligula's orders, well aware that a revolt that would ensue if he followed the imperial demand. He wrote Caligula, asking for a delay. In rage, the emperor commanded him to commit suicide.

That order and the requirement that the Temple be desecrated were never obeyed; Caligula was assassinated before any actions could be taken.

The Romans burn the Temple

Herod's rebuilding project ended around AD 64, but didn't endure. Two years later, Jewish rebels, called *Zealots,* seized Jerusalem and ousted the Roman troops stationed there. They recruited armies to fight the Romans and prepared for a long siege.

The Romans quickly swept through the countryside and surrounded Jerusalem. Inside, people began to fight each other and starve. In AD 70, troops under General Titus finally broke through the massive walls of Jerusalem. They began to slaughter everyone.

Somehow, amid the turmoil, the Temple caught on fire. Titus later said it was an accident. Nevertheless, the Temple burned down.

The destruction of the Second Temple was absolutely cataclysmic in the Jewish world and, according to the Bible, predicted by Jesus.

God apparently had fled his house once again and broken the contract with the Jews. Sages insisted such an event must be man's fault and was thought to be the first step toward the cleansing of the world.

As surviving Jewish sages sought answers in ancient prophetic wisdom, Christian missionaries hurried through the Roman Empire trying to "save" as many people as possible before the end of the world arrived.

Because Jews no longer had a Temple, they needed someplace else to pray. That's when *synagogues* became prominent.

After the Temple was destroyed, Jerusalem was razed by angry Romans. The only part of the Second Temple that survived was one wall, which has become venerated as the *Wailing Wall.* (The "wailing" part of the name refers to the grief the Jews felt when the Temple was destroyed; it has nothing to do with actually expressing those feelings.) Jews who visit the wall pray in front of it and often leave written prayers in its cracks. Figure 10-1 shows the Wailing Wall today.

Figure 10-1:
Jews pray in front of the Wailing Wall.

© MedioImages/Corbis

Synagogues become the Jewish houses of prayer

For generations, Jews living far away from Jerusalem used private homes to hold services on Saturdays. The rooms were bare without any religious adornment, such as an altar or a container for sacred scrolls. Families didn't own any scrolls, and the Temple contained the holy objects.

With the Temple gone, the homes became the only places to worship. The houses were designed so they faced Jerusalem. A container for sacred scrolls was added and called an *ark*. In addition, a light was required to burn constantly to indicate God's presence, an idea borrowed from the Zoroastrians. Eventually, one home was used solely for worship. The *synagogue* (from the Greek for "meeting") was born.

Such places had existed away from Jerusalem, but they were more commonly used as gathering rooms for discussion. The apostle Paul described visiting synagogues on his travels around the Mediterranean. There were many of them: An estimated 10 percent of the Roman Empire was either Jewish or supporters of the religion at that time.

Synagogues (*shul* in Yiddish) in the early years may have had tile mosaics of animals and people on the floor, but they vanished as Jews began to accept that the second commandment banned images. In time, ornate Hebrew script began to serve as the artwork.

A synagogue's architecture rarely had any symbolic meaning. In fact, as Jews were harassed in the Middle Ages, synagogues became very simple. The faithful never knew when local authorities would force them to leave the community, so they erred on the side of caution and built nondescript synagogues to help them remain anonymous.

In Eastern Europe, synagogues were often tall. The Babylonian Talmud required that the synagogue be the tallest building in town. That rule wasn't usually followed, especially if there was a church in town. Christians didn't let anyone build a religious structure taller than a church. However, some ingenious Jews fulfilled the letter of the law by building deep basements and floors below ground so that the entire building was bigger.

Synagogues are also required to have windows because, in the book of Daniel, the hero prays with "open windows in his upper chamber" (Daniel 6:10). However, because the prayers could be heard by non-Jews and misunderstood, windows often were not included in synagogues. If they existed, they simply were designed for better air flow.

Ancient synagogues featured several basic elements that live on today:

> ✔ *Bimah,* a raised platform that officials stand on to read from the Torah. Today's bimah has been replaced by elevating the entire altar area.
>
> ✔ *Aron hakodesh,* the ark that holds the sacred scrolls. Many are more like ornate closets built into a back wall.
>
> ✔ *Ner tamid,* an eternal light that signifies the constant presence of God. Today, electric lights usually replace candles.

Music was commonplace, as it had been the days of the Temple. Today, a *cantor* serves as the music director in many synagogues. Many prayers are sung, often accompanied by a choir. Some synagogues have added organs or pianos.

Christians Choose Churches

Early Christians, who were a sect of Judaism, naturally prayed in the Temple and in the small synagogues around Judea. As a result, when Christianity became an independent religion, leaders had a Jewish model on which to base their houses of worship. They drew on other designs as well.

For their places of worship, Christians often took over existing sites abandoned by another religion. On one Israeli historic site, a Greek temple was first turned into a Jewish synagogue and then a Catholic church.

The churches of early Christians

For several hundred years, Christians worshipped in simple structures that were easy to abandon if the Romans started persecutions. (The Jews used this strategy too; see the "Synagogues become the Jewish houses of prayer" section.) Most services took place in private homes with an open courtyard used for meetings.

Historians aren't sure what an early church looked like when the Second Temple existed. As with Judaism, the first churches probably started as private houses. One part of the house would have been set aside for worship, while the rest was the living quarters.

The leader of the service would sit in a chair called a *cathedra.* Everyone else stood. Eventually, large churches, where the bishop kept his chair, would be called *cathedrals.* (Figure 10-2 shows the famed Notre Dame Cathedral). There would have been a table, too. Early Christians shared everything, including meals, in remembrance of Jesus.

Parishioners set up a screen to separate the altar from the image of Jesus, while hanging sacred pictures (called *icons*) on the screen, which was called *iconostasis.* The icons depicted saints, holy objects or locales, and Jesus.

Figure 10-2:
Notre Dame
Cathedral
in Paris,
France.

Church design evolves

When Emperor Constantine legalized Christianity early in the fourth century, construction began in earnest on more permanent religious structures.

The most common and popular design at the time was a *basilica* with two rows of columns supporting the roof. Eventually, more columns were added so the buildings could be expanded sideways, but they kept the same design: an altar set in front of a seating area. The basilica often was oriented so the priests could face the rising sun, which symbolized resurrection.

Churches gradually began to take on the design of a cross, with the altar at the head and an aisle down the center. The Greek version featured arms of equal length.

Churches contained several basic structures:

✔ *Apse,* the semicircular recess, usually at the east end of a church, which held the cathedra and was designed to focus everyone's attention on the altar.

✔ Lecterns, which were placed in front of the congregation for Scripture reading and sermons.

✔ A large table that originally was used for communal meals in the altar area. In time, the table would become the altar. Sometimes martyrs would be buried there. Historians report that bread and wine prepared on the table were often dropped through a hole into the sarcophagus below.

✔ To reduce observations by those who didn't know the faith, screens were set up to shield the priest and altar from the congregation. In the Middle Ages, the altar was attached to the back wall, like the Jewish ark. Today, it may be flush against the wall or free standing.

Until the 1500s, congregants stood during worship services. Often, the only seating was a thin wooden bench running along the side of a massive cathedral. And that was just for the ill or feeble to use.

Churches often have two distinct units:

✔ *Nave,* which holds the congregation

✔ *Sanctuary,* the area around the altar reserved for the priest

The Protestant Reformation, beginning in 1517, affected church architecture, too. The *pulpit* (a raised lectern), home to thundering bishops and priests, was moved above and behind the Communion table. The altar vanished. Organs were often front and center, a concession to musicians, not theology.

Altars later were brought back to some sects, but many Protestants today worship in churches with no altars.

Artistry and music abound

Christian basilicas weren't much to look at from the outside, but they were filled with artwork inside. They often featured tile mosaics and *frescoes* (watercolors painted on wet plaster), gold leaf, and elaborate paintings.

Images from Jesus's life and biblical accounts often brightened the walls, providing visual stories to illiterate parishioners.

Churches, like synagogues, reveled in music. References to church music during a Christian religious services date as far back as AD 129. A Roman bishop soon after suggested that a song called "Angel's Hymn" should be included in Christmas services in Rome. A Christmas song (which has been lost to history) dates from the fourth century and is attributed to several people.

Choirs were common, too. Singers needed *pews* (benches with backs), which were set up across from each other. Congregants still stood until more modern times. And they had no need for hymnals, because most were illiterate.

Byzantine style moves in

After Constantine shifted his capital from Rome to Constantinople, churches were infused with a new style of architecture, called *Byzantine,* after the region of the country.

This style of architecture featured a dome in the center of the building. Smaller domes often were placed near the central dome. This lofty ceiling rested on great pillars, creating a feeling of grandeur and extending the heavenly reach of the building.

Later styles emerge, but some things don't change

Eventually, architects found all sorts of new ways to design churches, including massive Gothic structures, Romanesque ones that imitated ancient Roman art, and many more. Some of the most famous churches in Europe took decades to complete.

Today, churches display a variety of architectural styles depending on the sect and the architect's imagination.

But church interiors have been fairly consistent in recent years, depending on the denomination.

- ✔ Virtually all have some image of Jesus, either vividly depicting the crucifixion or in an abstract form.
- ✔ Candles abound.
- ✔ Pictures from Christian history hang on walls, and stained-glass windows depict biblical scenes.
- ✔ Pews face an altar, which typically contains a central table.

Mosques Reflect the Prophet

The Islamic *mosque* (where Muslims go to worship), unlike the religious structures in Judaism and Christianity, is directly linked to the faith's founder.

Muhammad's house in Medina, the city he fled to in 622, provided the design for the first Muslim religious buildings. Unlike Jews and Christians, Muslims don't believe that their religious buildings come from divine inspiration or house God.

The baptismal font

Initially, adult Christians were baptized in rivers and streams. The free-flowing water followed Jewish requirements for ritualistic cleansing. Early churches sometimes had circular or octagonal tubs so an initiate could kneel in the water.

Later, adult immersion was replaced by infant christening. The font was then moved to the entryway to the church, signifying the door into the fellowship of the religion.

Today, Catholic churches feature fonts by their entrances. Parishioners enter the building, dip the fingertips of their right hand into the water, make the symbol of the cross by touching their forehead, chest, left shoulder, and right shoulder, and then find a seat.

Mosques quickly became the hub of a community. Social programs as well as judicial trials took place there. They have retained much of that importance today.

As Muslim armies conquered new land, commanders would build a mosque in the center of a captured community as a symbol of the new religion and authority. Military camps were placed around it to emphasize the power.

Often, as Christians and Jews did before them, Muslims would take over a town's sacred site and turn it into a mosque. Buildings for other religions had to be smaller than the mosque.

At first, criers *(muezzin)* would walk through the town to announce the times of mandatory prayer. By the beginning of the eighth century, distinctive towers *(minarets)* were erected by each mosque so foot-weary muezzin could stand in one place and be heard long distances. Minarets remain the most obvious architectural element of a mosque.

How mosques are designed

There are two types of mosques:

- The large, significant mosques are called *jama'as*. They host the Friday prayer and feature thick carpets and rich adornment. In English, they are known as "great" mosques.

- The smaller version is called *masjid*. They can feature lots of designs, but are not as big or ornate as the jama'as. They serve as houses of worship in communities without great mosques.

Like synagogues and churches, mosques were based on local designs. They all have several required features:

- They point toward Mecca.

- They contain a niche *(mihrab)* in the appropriate wall aimed at Mecca to orient believers in the correct direction. Scholars think the structure was borrowed from prayer niches existing in Christian churches. Many Muslims today consider the mihrab as the holiest site in a mosque.

- The area in front of the mihrab must be covered by a roof. No doors may be built in that wall.

- A pulpit *(minbar)* is placed in front of the mihrab.

Inspecting the interior of a mosque

Mosques have no seats, but the floors are usually covered with rugs. Worshippers bring rugs as gifts to the mosque. Muslims also carry prayer rugs with them so they can pray when required during the day. Many rugs feature pictures of mosques, so the Muslim "carries" his own mosque with him.

Mosque walls show no images because of the religious commandment banning graven images, but Arabic letters are often used to decorate walls.

Other elements in a mosque include:

- *Dakka,* a platform the muezzin uses to call the faithful to prayer after using the minaret

- *Kursi,* a desk to hold the Koran and a seat for the reader

- *Reliquaries,* where bodies, parts of bodies, or belongings of deceased religious personalities are kept

- Candles and lamps used for illumination

- Incense used with festivals

- Water for ritual cleansing and drinking

There is no music, nor anyone leading the service. In many mosques, men and women worship separately.

Who's Welcome for Worship?

Anyone can enter a church or synagogue. Even synagogues that require skull-caps and prayer shawls set them out for visitors who don't have them.

Mosques are different. Non-Muslims aren't always allowed inside. That rule was put into effect long after Muhammad. Today, many mosques do allow non-Muslims to enter, provided the visitor respects Muslim law and is there for a sincere purpose. Some of the great mosques, such as the Dome of the Rock in Jerusalem, are still off-limits to non-Muslims.

When a Muslim enters a mosque, he removes his footwear to avoid soiling the prayer rugs. He is obligated to put his right foot into the mosque first while blessing the Prophet and the Prophet's family.

Inside the mosque, a Muslim must talk quietly so as not to disturb others in prayer. He also must dress nicely on Friday nights and, if possible, wear perfume.

Women aren't always allowed in a mosque. Of course, Muslims believe prayer requirements can be fulfilled anywhere, so the inability to go to a mosque isn't a hardship.

Christian churches have no such rule; men, women, children, and seniors are welcomed to services. Orthodox Jews allow women to enter the synagogue, but during services, women are segregated from the men. In Reform and Conservative synagogues, women and men can sit together during the service.

Muslim men are obligated to attend Friday night services and listen to the accompanying sermon. No such rule exists in Judaism, but Catholics are required to attend Sunday Mass, but not necessarily take Holy Communion each week.

Chapter 11

Religious Leaders: Keeping the Faith

. . . .

In This Chapter

▶ Meeting religious leaders who built the faith

▶ Understanding each faith's organization

▶ Knowing what titles to call the clergy

. . . .

*T*oday's religious leaders come in varied forms:

- ✔ If you go into a Roman Catholic church, you'll be greeted by a priest, who reports to a bishop, who reports to an archbishop, who reports to a cardinal, who reports to the pope.

- ✔ Go into a Greek Orthodox church, and you'll still meet a priest, but the ultimate authority lies with a patriarch.

- ✔ If you go into a *synagogue* (a place where Jews worship), you'll be greeted by a rabbi, who reports to a board of directors.

- ✔ If you go into a *mosque* (a place where Muslims worship), you'll be greeted by an imam, who reports to no one.

Every religion has spiritual leaders. You are about to meet them, including a few who became great figures in their faith.

Each religion has generated historic figures as well as congregational leaders. Many of the Jewish and Christian leaders found a place in the Bible. Their names live on, although historical evidence is slight. Muslim leaders, on the other hand, weren't included in the Koran, but have left a strong legacy throughout the world.

Great Jewish Leaders of the Past

Moses was the first great voice in Jewish history. Unlike Abraham, Moses is the focus of several books of the Bible. We are told of his birth, of his rescue from the Nile River, and how God called him to free the Israelites from bondage.

He is followed by a long line of important individuals who played major roles in monotheism. Judges and kings, discussed in Chapter 3, begin the procession. They are followed by men who had a profound effect on human thinking. We call them *prophets*. They were the teachers directed to bring the Yahwist message to believers.

Prophets emerge from the shadows

The first significant prophet in the Bible is Nathan, the advisor to King David. Prophets before Nathan were likely to go into trances and have ecstatic experiences, as Saul and Samuel did. A story about those two prophets reveals how both men rolled around on the ground and spoke in strange languages, just as believers in some sects of Islam and Christianity do today.

In contrast, Nathan spoke for God, but with the voice of a serious consultant who guided David's actions. You can almost picture him in a business suit and tie.

Nathan is called the first real prophet. His model may have been the Egyptian religious leaders who counseled pharaohs.

Nathan was fearless. In one case, he chastised the king for having Bathsheba's husband killed in battle and then marrying Bathsheba. Prophets after him followed his example.

There are 21 prophets included in the Bible. They stood up to royalty and demanded that their people listen to God's word and behave accordingly. For example,

- ✔ Jeremiah spoke harshly to kings in his day as the Babylonian army closed in on Jerusalem. He felt that God would protect his country and wanted his ruler to stand up to the enemy.

- ✔ Isaiah called for justice: "And I will make justice the line, and righteousness the plummet; and the hail shall sweep away the refuge of lies, and the waters shall overflow the hiding place," giving voice to mankind's longing for peace. (Isaiah 8:6, 7–10)

- ✔ Amos advised, "Do justly, love mercy and walk humbly with your God," rejecting sacrifices and outward shows of piety. (Amos 6:3–7)

The prophets were often punished and ridiculed; for example, some were thrown into pits by monarchs who didn't like what they had to say. Elijah had to hide in a cave for safety. Some inflicted suffering on themselves, walking around with heavy yokes on their shoulders or no clothes. Hosea deliberately married a prostitute. The prophets did everything they could to convince people to follow the law.

After the prophets: Sages

When the age of prophets passed, Judaism moved into the hands of scholars. They were called *sages* and were wise men who read and interpreted the texts. Jewish sages fell into two basic schools: liberal and conservative. They argued and debated until one view would prevail on a particular issue.

Akiva, one of the most famous sages, studied Scripture for 20 years with other sages at the Temple and finally went home. In a Talmudic story, his wife asked him why he had returned so soon. So he went back to study for 20 more years. He was eventually martyred by the Romans.

During the Roman era, the sages met in a parliament called the *Sanhedrin*. This form of government was based on the way Moses collected elders to lead the tribes. It issued rulings on religious questions.

The greatest sage was probably Hillel, who lived just prior to Jesus and whose common-sense rulings still guide Jewish behavior. He once said that all of the Torah can be condensed into a single phrase: "Do not do unto others as you would not have others do unto you; the rest is commentary."

Some of his decisions continue to be followed today. For example, during Hanukkah, Jews still light an additional candle each day and start on the left side because Hillel decided that's how the holiday should be celebrated.

Here's an interesting aside: Hillel's grandson, Gamaliel, is mentioned in the New Testament as a teacher in the school Paul attended. He also commented on early Christian philosophy.

Rise of the Rabbi

The destruction of the Temple in AD 70 ended the rule of sages and led to the rise of *rabbis*. Many sages were killed by the Romans when Jerusalem was conquered. Those who survived were disorganized. They were gradually replaced by teachers. In Hebrew, the word for teacher is *rabbi*.

Rabbis started out as community leaders who would go into Jerusalem regularly to learn from the sages and to bring back teachings to the Israeli towns and villages. With Jerusalem gone, the Temple razed, and sages dispersed, the rabbis were the only leaders left.

Today, rabbis are trained in seminaries and ordained in a particular Jewish denomination. They sign contracts to lead a synagogue and serve at the behest of a board of directors. When a rabbi retires or leaves, the board interviews and auditions replacements until one is hired.

There is no Jewish hierarchy, such as a chief rabbi. Congregations in each sect, such as Reform or Conservative, are members of a national council, but they operate independently and can reject council decisions.

A rabbi's job description

Rabbis do more than lead religious services. Many direct the synagogue's education program as well. They visit the sick in hospitals, counsel troubled congregation members, and officiate at weddings, funerals, and bar mitzvahs. Some are trained to perform circumcisions.

All rabbis must earn a four-year degree from a seminary, be able to read from the Torah in Hebrew, and, for the sake of their congregations, have some speaking ability.

Women can become rabbis, but only in less-Orthodox sects.

Education: The key to leadership

Rabbis maintain the emphasis on education begun by the prophets and sages. As a result, many great Jewish leaders throughout history have been recognized scholars.

In the 11th century, scholar Moses Maimonides brought Jewish ideas into the philosophical mainstream. Born in Spain, Maimonides revised the biblical commentaries while producing immortal works that influenced Christian philosophers. Jews still say about him: "From Moses (from the Bible) to Moses (Maimonides), there is none like Moses."

His works disappeared and were found hundreds of years later, preserved in an attic because they contained the name of God. Jews are banned from destroying any writings in which God's name appears.

The rabbi's man (or woman) Friday

Although many rabbis handle all the religious chores alone, many have a companion on the pulpit called a *cantor.* This person oversees the musical requirements in a religious service.

Some great cantors, like Richard Tucker, have gone on to have careers in opera and popular music.

Other cantors answer the calling after pursuing other interests. Riselle Bain, for example, acted in Hollywood movies like *The Ten Commandments,* and then had hit songs in Japan before deciding to become one of the few women cantors. She works for a synagogue in Tampa, Florida.

Another great scholar, Moses Mendelssohn, lived in the 1700s. He had overcome prejudice in his native Germany to help free his fellow Jews from ghettos and persecution. Weak, hunchbacked, and poor, Mendelssohn entered Berlin through a gate available only for animals and Jews.

Yet, with his intellectual talents, Mendelssohn rose to become a leader of his people. He was known as a *court Jew,* a rare Jewish person tolerated in the upper levels of society because of his abilities. (His grandson, Felix Mendelssohn, became a prominent composer.)

Modern Jewish leaders

Jewish religious leaders in more recent days helped found the sects of Judaism. One scholar gained worldwide recognition for his philosophical writings.

Martin Buber, who died in 1965, was heavily involved in boosting the religious consciousness of fellow Jews by retelling old stories and promoting the rebirth of Israel. He was such a significant figure that many Jewish soldiers wrote to him for answers to difficult moral, religious, and ethical questions during World War I. That made him an early Ann Landers and Abigail Van Buren (the ladies of "Dear Ann" and "Dear Abby" fame), who, by the way, were sisters and Jewish.

Other famous Jewish leaders include:

✔ **Benjamin Disraeli** (1804–1881), a British prime minister in the mid-1800s who oversaw the expansion of the British Empire. Disraeli converted to the Anglican faith so he could run for office. He then worked with Lord Lionel Rothschild, a Jewish financier who had been repeatedly elected to office and refused to convert. Together, they succeeded in ending Britain's Anglican-only law for public officials.

- ✔ **Theodore Herzl** (1860–1904), founder of the Zionist movement that eventually led to the modern Jewish state of Israel.
- ✔ **Elie Wiesel** (1928–), a Holocaust survivor who went on to win a Nobel Peace Prize.

Christian Leaders

In the early years of Christianity, many people taken by Jesus's message began to offer guidance and direction to the fledgling church.

James, the leader of the Nazarenes, was described in the Jewish historian Josephus's account as being so devout that his knees were calloused from so much praying. Paul (whom we talk more about in Chapter 5) wrote letters that are now part of the New Testament. His words offered advice and philosophical teachings to converts to Christianity.

Other great teachers included Tertullian, Origen, and Justin Martyr, men who wrote profound arguments in support of Christianity and whose works carried the ideas throughout the Western world. Many such people died in the various Roman persecutions until the religion became legal in the fourth century.

The pope becomes the point man

Initially, the Church was divided into sectors. Leaders in Rome, Alexandria (Egypt), Jerusalem, and the eastern portion of the Roman Empire all jockeyed for power. These fellas were called *bishops.*

In time, the bishop of Rome became the dominant figure. The *pope,* as he was called, gained some of his clout from the legend that both Peter and Paul died in Rome, as well as from living in the empire's capital.

Pope is derived from the Roman word for "father," *poppa.*

The pope took over the title *pontifex maximus,* a title used by priests serving Roman pagan gods and often conferred on Roman political leaders such as Julius Caesar. As a result, today the pope is also known as the *pontiff.*

By the fourth century, the pope had become the leader of the western half of the Roman Empire, negotiating with invading Huns and organizing assistance to residents.

Despite various problems over the years, the pope has remained the central figure for the more than 2 billion Roman Catholics. In modern times, Pope John XXIII reformed the church in the 1960s. One of his successors, Pope John Paul II, revived and energized the religion with his powerful speeches and ceaseless travels.

Historians recognize three great popes:

- ✔ **Pope Saint Leo I (reigned 440–461):** In 452, he bravely met Attila the Hun and succeeded in saving Rome from being sacked. He also instituted many reforms, including imposing strict discipline on the bishops.

- ✔ **Pope Saint Gregory I (reigned 590–604):** He restored clerical discipline, protected the Jews from persecution, and negotiated peace treaties with the barbarian invaders. A renowned teacher, Pope Gregory wrote a book on the role of bishops that remains necessary spiritual reading. He revitalized the Mass and is credited with instituting a type of singing that is commonly called the *Gregorian chant*.

- ✔ **Pope Saint Nicholas I (reigned 858–867):** Like prophets of old, he fearlessly denounced kings. He was a champion of the poor, an art patron, and a reformer.

Christianity's organization

The leadership of Christianity developed a logical hierarchy over time. What follows is a breakdown of the chain of command.

The first heads of Christian congregations were called *presbyters*. That's from the Greek word meaning "leaders." They were responsible for supervising the morals of their members.

As the membership grew, that task became too difficult. So the presbyters began to focus on administrating the sacraments, such as baptism, communion, and the like. Eventually, one person in the congregation was awarded that authority. He became a *priest,* using a word already familiar from pagan and Jewish services.

The financial officer in each community was known as *episcopos* or *bishop.* It means "overseer" in Greek. Initially, the bishop handed out alms to poor Christians in his community. He also had to divvy up money to the various priests in his area. In time, he became their supervisor. When the tasks grew too great, the bishop was able to hire assistants. They were called *deacons* from the Greek word for "servant."

The *archbishop* lived in the capital of a religious region, called a *diocese*. The archbishops began to supervise bishops in smaller communities.

If an archbishop lived in a city tied to an apostle, such as Constantinople, he took on special connotation and was known as a *patriarch,* from the Latin word for "father." Other patriarchs were in Antioch, Jerusalem, and Alexandria.

The patriarch of Rome became the pope, as discussed in the preceding section. He then elevated bishops to serve as his advisors. They became known as *cardinals.*

The patriarch of Constantinople has evolved into the head of the Greek Orthodox Church.

The requirements and roles of Christian church leaders

As mentioned in the last section, while the Church was still getting set up, it borrowed Roman and Jewish nomenclature to create a hierarchy to oversee the faith. Priests lead the people. They are still ordained and, in the Roman Catholic Church, required to be celibate.

To become a priest, an individual must obtain a degree from a seminary. Protestant faiths also require their congregational leaders to have an education. They may be called by a variety of familiar names, including:

- Brother
- Deacon
- Elder
- Father
- Minister
- Reverend

In some faiths, a member of the congregation can be named a minister. That's true for the Unitarian Universalist, but the individual has that position only with the particular Society. Full ordination requires a college degree obtained from the Society's seminary.

Roles vary depending on the denomination. A Roman Catholic priest may not marry and serves as an intermediary between God and man. He has some administrative duties as well. Women aren't allowed to be priests, but some women devote themselves to the Church and are called *nuns.*

In the Methodist Church, in contrast, the minister may marry and is seen as a role model for proper Christian behavior. He also is the administrator of the church and oversees its functions. In the Presbyterian Church, elders are the top officials. Some elders are called ministers; they are responsible for church services and teaching. Others, called deacons, handle administrative duties.

Women can be ordained in almost all Christian denominations, except Catholicism. However, more conservative churches may discourage women from assuming religious duties.

Church Leaders from the Early Days Until Now

Clement of Rome was probably the first pope. Previous leaders, such as Peter, were called popes in church histories, but none exercised wide authority until Clement. Letters that survived the centuries show him trying to solve disputes in Greece around AD 90. Other early Christian leaders were

- ✔ **Athanasius** (293?–373), who is called the Father of Orthodoxy for his determined stand in support of what has become Christian faith.

- ✔ **Jerome** (347?–420), who compiled the books in the Jewish Bible and then started on the New Testament before his death.

- ✔ **Chrysostom** (344?–407), who, like old-time prophets, fiercely denounced immoral behavior on the part of monks and royalty. He must have been quite a speaker. His name means "silver tongued."

Perhaps the greatest of the early Church leaders was Augustus, who lived in the fourth century. A convert to Christianity, he was named a bishop of a small African community. However, his many letters and books carried his thoughts everywhere. He wrote often to Jerome, the man who collected and translated the books in the Bible.

Augustus developed the philosophical base for Christianity while leading attacks on heresies that threatened to undermine the faith. His writings are still read today for guidance, although his advice that nonbelievers could and should be persecuted has somewhat tarnished his status.

Lighting up in the Middle Ages

The Church dominated European life for about 1,000 years. Just before Martin Luther came on the scene and the Protestant Reformation took place (see Chapter 5), a Dutch priest shook up religious thinking.

Desiderius Erasmus (1466–1536) was the best-selling author of his day and the first in history. Taking advantage of the newly invented printing press, he undermined the small-minded thinkers of his day with logic and wit, breathing fresh air into religious philosophy. Not only did he expose abuses in the Church, often by using sarcasm, but he was responsible for bringing learning back into the forefront.

Erasmus died as Martin Luther's efforts to reform the Church were leading to new Christian sects, but his writings continued to delight and inform readers for centuries to follow.

Modern Christian leaders

The list of prominent modern Christian leaders would be almost endless. Here are several who have earned special recognition:

- **Dr. Albert Schweitzer (1875–1965:** A Christian writer and humanitarian. For more, see the nearby sidebar.

- **Dr. Martin Luther King Jr. (1929–1968):** A Baptist minister, he led the fight for civil rights in the United States and was martyred for his efforts in 1968.

- **Mother Teresa (1910–1997):** A Catholic missionary, she worked in the slums of Calcutta, India, bringing hope to thousands of impoverished residents.

- **Billy Graham (1918–):** A Southern Baptist minister, he traveled extensively to bring the word of God to millions worldwide through his crusades.

Dr. Schweitzer put his faith into action

Dr. Albert Schweitzer was a leading Christian writer whose works on Christian history and the Gospels stirred up enormous controversy. The German scholar was also a minister, medical doctor, and a world-class organist.

He is best known as a humanitarian who built rural hospitals for poor people in Africa in the first part of the 1900s. His studies of religious history, however, made him unforgettable.

Nothing is more discouraging than examining the Bible from a historical perspective, he noted. A devout Christian, Schweitzer made a serious search for the historical Jesus by examining the New Testament. He concluded that if all the mythology were removed from the texts, nothing would be left.

That finding didn't deter him from devoting his life to humanitarian efforts based on his view of what Jesus expected of him. In essence, having dismissed any plausible historical elements, Schweitzer concentrated on philosophy.

Following Muhammad

Because Muslims consider Muhammad the final prophet from God, no one has ever claimed to head the religion of Islam, like a pope leads the Catholic Church. However, leaders arose to guide sects. These leaders are called by different names depending on the sect.

- ✔ **Imam:** This is the Arabic word for "leader." The leader of a country can be called an imam. So can the leader of a mosque. For members of the Sunni faith, an imam is one of the founders of four schools of religious law.

- ✔ **Ayatollah:** From the Persian meaning "sign of God," this term is given to a Shi'ite scholar who has gained expertise in Islamic fields of law, ethics, philosophy, and mysticism, and usually teaches in schools of Islamic sciences. Ayatollahs who achieve widespread recognition can issue a legal ruling that gains instant acceptance. Great ayatollahs are the foremost leaders.

- ✔ **Mawlana:** These are experts in the Koran in the Sufi sect. **Mullah** is another term used for the same individual in other Muslim sects.

Islam has no seminaries for training imams or ayatollahs. People achieve that status through community recognition based on religious knowledge and/or scholarship. All religious leaders are expected to know the Koran, the last great holy text given to the world by an offspring of Abraham.

Women can receive religious training, but are not allowed to lead prayers. Those active in mosques are called *morshidat,* or religious guides.

Great Muslim leaders in history

The Muslim world has produced many great leaders. They include:

- ✔ **Abu Bakr (573?–634):** Muhammad's father-in-law was an old man when he was handed the leadership of the fledgling faith after the prophet's death. In two years, he rallied Islam, unified the tribes, and began conquering the Arab world.

- ✔ **Salah Ad-din Yusuf Ibn Ayyub (1127?–1193):** Known in the West as Saladin, he remains the most famous Muslim hero and military tactician. In the 12th century, he served as *sultan* (the Muslim ruler) of Egypt, Palestine, Syria, and Yemen when he faced off and defeated Richard the Lionheart for control of Jerusalem. He also founded the Ayyubid dynasty.

✔ **Suleyman I (1494–1566):** Known as Suleyman the Magnificent, he was sultan in the 16th century and regarded as the most significant ruler in the world by Christians and Muslims. A consummate general, he also wrote poetry that still is considered among the best in Islamic history. Suleyman sponsored an army of artists, religious thinkers, and philosophers who overshadowed the most educated courts of Europe.

✔ **Sidi Ahmad al-Tijani (1737–1815):** This Algerian founded an Islamic movement for the poor in the late 1700s. His efforts brought about reform and grassroots Islamic revival.

Modern Islamic leaders

In recent times, these leaders have made an impact:

✔ **Gamal Abdel Nasser** (1918–1970), an Egyptian soldier whose efforts helped free his country from English rule in the 1950s. His role in wars against Israel didn't make him popular in the West, but he remains a hero to Muslims.

✔ **Ayatollah Rouhollah Mousavi Khomeini** (1902–1989), the leader of the Iranian revolution that ousted the Shah in 1979. Feared by Western countries, the Iranian-born cleric became a national hero after returning from French exile to create a theocratic revolution in his ancient country.

Chapter 12

Sacred Sites

*I*n December 1966, Bill had a chance to visit Israel. Along with thousands — if not millions — of pilgrims there for the Christmas season, he wandered through Bethlehem, where Jesus was reportedly born, and onto Mount Zion, the site of King David's tomb.

At that time, Jerusalem was split into Jewish and Arab sections. Armed sentries marched alongside makeshift stone piles that marked the dividing line between the two portions of the holy city. Jews still claimed Jerusalem as the capital of Israel, but Arabs refused to relinquish their hold on what has always been a sacred city to them.

A few months after Bill was there, Israeli soldiers swarmed over the rubble and took over the old portion of the city during what has been called the Seven-Day War. With that victory, Jerusalem came completely under Israeli control.

Because of Jerusalem's significance, some world leaders have asked that the city be placed outside the rule of any one country. Israeli leaders have rejected that idea, refusing to give up on a site that has meant so much to their faith. Arabs feel the same way about Jerusalem and won't surrender their claim to it. Neither will Christians. No other city in the world carries the hopes and inspirations of three great religions.

Jerusalem, however, isn't the only sacred community in the world. Nor are the various holy places inside Jerusalem unique. The Bible, for example, lists several sacred cities.

Pilgrims or everyday tourists can visit a variety of areas throughout the world that carry a special connotation for one or two of the monotheistic faiths.

The idea of a sacred city or location has been an integral part of all religions, both in ancient times and now. Greeks designated groves of trees they considered sacred, as well as caves, mountains, and temples. So did the Romans and every other culture. This chapter looks at some of the sacred cities and sites in Judaism, Christianity, and Islam.

Jerusalem: Important to All Three Religions

No city has meant more to religion than Jerusalem, as shown in Figure 12-1. This city is important to Jews, Christians, and Muslims alike — but for separate reasons.

- ✔ For Jews, Jerusalem contains the *Wailing Wall,* the last remnant of the Second Temple. Thousands of devout Jews annually pray by the wall and place messages in its cracks. Thousands of Jews are buried near the entry gates on the theory that the Messiah will enter there first (see Chapter 3).

- ✔ For Christians, Jerusalem is the city where Jesus died. In the fourth century, Helen, Emperor Constantine's mother, identified sites where Christ is believed to have walked and was crucified. Those locales remain popular with pilgrims, many of whom have chosen to be buried there.

  Because of the link to Jesus, Christians willingly fought multiple wars to try to recapture and retain the city. Crusading knights marched from Europe and were sure they saw a new Jerusalem hovering in the clouds, waiting to descend and usher in a golden era.

- ✔ For Muslims, Jerusalem contains three sacred sites:

  - **Dome of the Rock:** This monument was built on the site of the destroyed Jewish temple to demonstrate the importance of Islam. It also is supposed to mark the site where the Prophet Muhammad ascended to heaven with the angel Gabriel (see Chapter 7).

  - **Al-Aksa Mosque:** When the Muslims took Jerusalem in the seventh century, they converted an old Byzantine church built on the site of the razed Jewish Temple into the Al-Aksa mosque, a site mentioned in the Koran as where Muhammad also arose to visit heaven.

  - **Al-Burak Mosque:** This is where the Prophet Muhammad supposedly stabled his horse during his nocturnal journeys.

  Modern Jerusalem — divided into new and old sections — also holds 34 mosques. Of those, 27 are located within the walls of the old city.

(c) Kontos Yannis/Corbis Sygma

Figure 12-1:
The
skyline of
Jerusalem.

Jerusalem also features many houses belonging to *Sufi* orders, practitioners of Islamic mysticism, the graves of 24 Muslim leaders, and 15 Muslim graveyards.

"Jerusalem has been a part of Muslim history and identity from the very emergence of Islam until today. Its many meanings for us include victory, defeat, sacrifice, and continuity," according to Muhammad Hourani, a senior researcher and director of the Desk for Dialogue and Teaching for Peace at the Shalom Hartman Institute in Jerusalem.

A city with a fuzzy origin

The meaning of Jerusalem's name has been lost over time, probably because Jerusalem had no special distinction for years after it was founded around 1600 BC. The possible meanings of *Jerusalem* include:

- **City of Salem:** Of course, no one knows who or what Salem was.
- **City of Peace:** *Salem* is related to *shalom,* the Hebrew word for "peace."
- **Complete City:** *Salem* is also related to the Hebrew word for "wholeness" (*shalem*).

Besides, by all rights, Jerusalem shouldn't exist. Ancient people tended to locate cities near rivers or along lakes and larger bodies of water. Jerusalem doesn't have a water supply. A well had to be dug to ensure ample water during a siege.

Moreover, the city wasn't situated along any known trade routes of the time. Communities often sprung up as way stations along these ancient highways. In fact, no logical explanation has ever been found for why the city was located amid a ridge of hills in central Israel.

Jerusalem in history

Jerusalem has endured a long and complicated history, including numerous sieges and the tread of famous people.

Early days

Jerusalem shows up early in the Bible when Abraham stops by to honor the king of Salem (thought to be Jerusalem), Melchizedek.

Then perhaps because of Abraham's unexpected stopover, King David decided that Jerusalem would be an ideal capital for his realm. The residents then were Jebusites, who are mentioned in the Bible as members of the Canaan tribe. *Jebus* was another name for Jerusalem. In Talmudic writing, the Jebusites were protected from attack by Jewish armies because Abraham had signed a treaty with them, and they posted the treaty on the city walls.

In the book of Joshua, the city was supposed to have been seized and placed under Jewish control. According to the Bible, Joshua assigned it to the tribe of Judah. However, in the succeeding book, 1 Samuel, the town is still held by the Jebusites.

Around 1030 BC, David succeeded in taking the city away from the Jebusites. He brought the Ark of the Covenant there, giving the city a strong religious element. From that day on, Jerusalem has been known as David's City (or the City of David).

The symbolism was completed when his successor, his son Solomon, built the Temple there.

Ironically, the Jerusalem of today is nothing like the Jerusalem of King David's time. He ruled over a small city, behind high walls. Estimates of size vary, but most historians agree ancient Jerusalem was probably nothing more than a little town.

Babylonian returnees

Around 724 BC, Jerusalem withstood a ferocious attack by the Assyrians, who had already wiped out Israel to the north. The Bible says God sent mice to gnaw the bowstrings of the Assyrian warriors. However, ancient records show that a lot of *tribute* (a tidy sum of money) convinced the Assyrian leader to take his troops home.

Jerusalem remained the capital of the southern tribes, known collectively as Judah, until the Babylonians showed up in 597 BC. After the Babylonians leveled the Temple and forced the surviving residents into captivity, Jerusalem housed a few destitute farmers.

When the Persians defeated Babylon in 536 BC, Cyrus the Great allowed the Jewish exiles to return home. Naturally, those who chose to go went back to Jerusalem.

Ezra, the man credited with compiling the Torah, also reinforced religious laws and reestablished Jerusalem as the spiritual capital of Judaism.

War inside Jerusalem

Jerusalem's prominent position in Jewish life was highlighted when Jews rose against the Syrians in 167 BC. Their first objective was to retake the Temple in Jerusalem. After they succeeded in 165 BC, they rededicated the Temple.

The resulting celebration became an annual holiday, called Hanukkah (see Chapter 4). The actual war, however, continued for another 23 years.

Jesus's influence on the city

Jerusalem's place in religious history was sealed when Jesus entered the city around AD 30. His death on the cross there guaranteed that Christians would see the city as a holy locale.

In 1997, researchers claimed they had found the tomb of Jesus and his family in Jerusalem. Right or wrong — and few agree with the finding — the archaeologists knew they only had to search David's City.

The city changes hands

Jews lost Jerusalem to the Romans in AD 70, and then were banished from the city after a failed revolt around AD 135.

After that, the City of David became the most important destination for Christian pilgrims. The Church of the Holy Sepulcher and many other Christian shrines were erected there, starting in the fourth century.

Even under Muslim rule, starting in AD 638, Christians continued to pour into the city to pray and to follow in Jesus's footsteps.

Crusaders battle for the Holy Land

Inspired by Pope Urban II, Christian leaders sent troops (called *Crusaders*) to what they called the *Levant* (a region on the East Mediterranean Sea that included Jerusalem) to retake the Holy Land from the Muslims. Heavily armored despite the heat and led by kings of various European lands, the Crusaders conquered Jerusalem in 1099 and established a Crusader state. They massacred everyone in the city and waded through the carnage to pray at the holy sites.

The Muslims weren't impressed, but they didn't get upset until the Christian conquerors decided to levy a tax on Muslim boats sailing by the tiny kingdom. Under Saladin, the Muslims ousted the Christians in 1187.

Modern resolution

The British eventually took over control of the Holy Land from the Turks in 1919 and made Jerusalem the capital of what was then called Palestine.

When Jewish rebels wanted to persuade the British to go home, they knew where to strike. They blew up the King David Hotel in 1946, which housed British officers and was located in the heart of Jerusalem.

The British let the United Nations decide what to do. The U.N. resolved to divide the land into two countries, creating Israel for Jews and Jordan for Arabs. Under this plan, Jerusalem would be an international city, but Jewish and Arab leaders immediately rejected that aspect of the plan.

The division of the land into separate countries didn't appeal to anyone else either. As a result, Arabs and Jews have fought several wars since the UN vote in 1948.

Israel named Jerusalem its capital, but the city hasn't gained complete recognition from other countries. Many don't want to upset Arab nations, which don't accept that Jerusalem is Israel's capital or even acknowledge Israel's existence at all. Many countries retain embassies in Tel Aviv, a modern Israeli city west of Jerusalem.

Today, Jerusalem is a modern city with more than 700,000 residents, according to a 2007 census report. Of those, about 66 percent are Jewish. The city is divided geographically into an old and a new section, and into neighborhoods dominated by different religious sects.

Jerusalem in symbolism

Over time, Jerusalem began to represent more than just a religious Middle Eastern city. It became an ideal. The city was transformed into an image of a heavenly community, far different from its physical reality.

The Crusaders, for example, were positive that they had seen the heavenly version of the city waiting to descend and replaced the small, weather-beaten community they had captured. They also thought Jerusalem was the center of the Earth. They believed the world rotated around it, in the same way the Earth was at the center of the universe.

The prophets understood what Jerusalem truly meant. It was to be the site of the final gathering of people and the beginning of eternal peace:

> "In the last days, the mountain of the house of the Lord will be the most important of the mountains. It will be raised above the hills. All the nations will come to it. Many people will come and say, 'Come, let us go up to the mountain of the Lord, to the house of the God of Jacob. Then He will teach us about His ways, that we may walk in His paths. For the Law will go out from Zion, and the Word of the Lord from Jerusalem.' He will judge between the nations, and will decide for many people. And they will beat their swords into plows, and their spears into knives for cutting vines. Nation will not lift up sword against nation, and they will not learn about war anymore." —Isaiah 2:1–4

The symbolic nature of Jerusalem included the particular emblem worn by the Crusaders and known as the Jerusalem cross. The image has four arms at equal distances, symbolizing the four directions and the belief that Jerusalem was the spiritual center of the earth.

Later scholars suggested that the cross represented the spread of Christ's message through the writings of Mathew, Mark, Luke, and John, who are symbolized by four additional "crosslets."

Sacred Sites of Judaism

Early residents of what is now Israel founded plenty of sacred sites beyond Jerusalem. As members of the oldest monotheistic religion, Jews had a head start in designating holy locations. The many stone *cairns,* or altars, scattered around the landscape testify to their enthusiasm.

Bethel: Home of the law

Bethel was the site where Jacob dreamed of angels walking on a ladder from heaven. Located north of Jerusalem, the city was known as Luz until Jacob snoozed there. Its new name means "House of God."

People probably started living in Bethel about 5,000 years ago, which is at least 2,000 years before Jacob could have wandered by, but the community was destroyed around 1200 BC.

Because of the city's holy sheen, the Ark of the Covenant was housed there (Judges 20:26–28), and Samuel set up a court there to hear disputes (1 Samuel 7:16). The city eventually vanished under the onslaught of the Muslims in the late 600s AD. Today, historians think a small community named Benin is all that remains of this once-sacred town.

Shechem: Future home of the Samaritans

The ancient city of Shechem was first settled possibly 5,000 years ago. Shechem (meaning "shoulder") was a crossroads community that was razed an estimated 22 times before vanishing around AD 200.

Abraham first came to Shechem when he entered Canaan. Jacob settled there and buried his idols in the soil. Joshua held a historic meeting there to declare his affinity for Yahweh.

After Judah and Israel split into separate countries around 900 BC (see Chapter 3), the northern tribes named Shechem their capital. It was later renamed Samaria. The tribes built their temple there because, in Samaritan tradition, the near-sacrifice of Isaac took place on Mount Gerizim near Shechem.

Mount Moriah: Site of the Wailing Wall and the Dome of the Rock

Mount Moriah became famous as the spot where Abraham journeyed to sacrifice his son, Isaac. Later, King Solomon built the First Temple there.

The "mountain" is really a point on an elongated ridge that runs along the southern edge of old Jerusalem. Today, it holds a wall still standing from the Second Temple, called the Wailing Wall, as well as the famed Muslim mosque called the Dome of the Rock.

Historians speculate that the traditional site of Mount Moriah may actually have been miles away in Shechem, where there is a Mount Moreh. Jews and Muslims prefer the traditional site in Jerusalem.

The meaning of the name *Moriah* has puzzled scholars for centuries. Take your choice of meanings:

✔ **The teaching place,** because the Temple was there

✔ **The place of fear,** because the Temple scared pagans

✔ **The place of myrrh,** referring to one of the spices burned on the Temple altar

✔ **Land of worship**

✔ **Vision**

✔ **The land of the Amorites,** named for a tribe that once fought with the Israelites

✔ **The land of the Hamorites,** named for residents of Hamor who supposedly lived in Shechem before the Israelites arrived there

Mount Zion: A conquered fortress

About one-half mile (600 meters) to the west of Mount Moriah is the small peak of Mount Zion on the same southern ridge. *Zion* means "fortress" and was thought to derive from a Jebusite citadel that King David had to overcome. In time, Zion became synonymous with Jerusalem. The Bible sometimes calls Jerusalem Zion or Mount Zion.

Jews who were determined to create a Jewish state in Israel called themselves *Zionists,* a name reflecting their zeal to return to Jerusalem.

Today, Mount Zion houses the traditional tomb of King David as well as the Church of the Dormition and the Institute of Holy Land Studies.

Mount Sinai: God and Moses's chat room

Named for the Babylonian goddess Sin, Mount Sinai is the mountain in the Sinai Desert where Moses reportedly received the Ten Commandments directly from God.

In the Bible, the mountain was described as being shrouded in clouds, but narrow enough to be surrounded by the escaped slaves. No mountain has ever been found that fits that description, but one mountain in the Sinai Desert has been given that historically significant name.

Mount Sinai, which is not the tallest in the area, contains a mosque and a Greek Orthodox chapel. The chapel supposedly includes the quarry where the rock used for the Ten Commandments was located. There's also a cave named for Moses in the side of the mountain.

Some researchers have claimed to have found the missing Ark of the Covenant on Mount Sinai. That may not be true, but in a nearby monastery of St. Catherine, German scholar Constantine Von Tischendorf in the 1860s unearthed the oldest copies of the New Testament Gospels ever discovered.

In Islam, All Roads Lead to Mecca

The Muslim counterpart to Jerusalem has to be Mecca, although the reasons are vastly different. Jerusalem is important to Muslims because that's where Muhammad ascended into heaven. Located in the Arabian Peninsula, Mecca, on the other hand, is the most important city in Islam.

Mecca is the home of Muhammad and the Ka'baa (shown in Figure 12-2), and the religious capital of Islam (Chapter 7 talks more about this). All Muslims are obligated to pilgrimage to Mecca, in Saudi Arabia, at least once in their lifetime. That's one of the five pillars of the faith (see Chapter 8).

Figure 12-2:
The Ka'baa in Mecca is visited by Muslims from all over the world.

(c) Bettmann/Corbis

Non-Muslims today still are not allowed to visit Mecca. Those who try to sneak in face execution under Islamic law.

Sunnis and Shi'ites disagree on many issues, but not on the importance of Mecca. They prohibit hostilities during the annual pilgrimage to the holy city.

Mecca, however, didn't reach the same status in Islam as Jerusalem did in Judaism and Christianity, for several reasons:

✔ Islam didn't create symbols and has rejected most mythology. There's no place for God's home in Mecca.

✔ Muhammad made Mecca his most important city, but didn't invest it with any major centers of worship. The Ka'baa was already there.

✔ Muhammad was not treated as a deity. His home and the places he walked are important, but they weren't given holy designations as the way the sites of Jesus's life were. Moreover, Muhammad supposedly left this earth from Jerusalem, not Mecca.

✔ Some Arab scholars have even argued that Medina is a holier site because Muhammad went there from Mecca when he fled from persecution. When the Prophet conquered Mecca, he transferred his base away from Medina (see Chapter 7 for the details).

Few other cities or locales in the Muslim world are considered sacred, an idea that is outside Islamic teachings.

However, a couple of sites are viewed as important, including:

✔ **Abu El Abbas El Mursi Mosque in Alexandria, Egypt:** Although dating from 1775, it was built by Algerians over the tomb of the 13th century saint Ahmed Abu al-Abbas al-Mursi (Abu'l 'Abbas).

✔ **Al-Masjid al-Nabawi Mosque (Mosque of the Prophet) in Medina:** Reportedly built on the site of Muhammad's home, the mosque houses the tomb of Muhammad as well as early caliphs Abu Bakr and Umar ibn al-Khattab.

✔ **Tomb of Ali in Najaf, Iraq:** This is where Ali, Muhammad's son-in-law and the fourth caliph, is buried. Shi'ites consider this site sacred.

✔ **Imam Reza Mosque in Mashad, Iran:** The tomb of a famed Muslim leader, the site is popular with pilgrims who can't afford to go to Mecca.

Christian Sacred Sites

In the sixth century when Saint Benedict sent his monks into Ireland to convert the residents to Christianity, he ordered that sacred pagan sites be preserved. However, he insisted that the monks build churches on those sites or convert existing buildings into Christian houses of worship. Those weren't unusual instructions. Most sites deemed sacred by Christians were once sites where followers of other religions worshipped.

Today, Roman Catholics recognize at least 50 sacred sites around the world. Protestants never adopted the idea of a sacred location, although they have identified historic sites of religious importance. Naturally, they also recognize locales associated with the story of Jesus as religiously significant. We discuss some of the most prominent Christian sites from ancient times in this section.

Sites may be *shrines* (a site designated as a place of worship) or a physical place, such as a *grotto* in Bethlehem where Jesus was supposedly born.

Shrine of Thomas Becket

Located in Canterbury, the shrine of Thomas Becket honored the murdered English archbishop who was killed by henchmen of King Henry II in the 12th century. Becket, who had been Henry's friend, was *canonized* (declared a saint) almost immediately, and his tomb became the most important shrine in England.

When Becket was martyred, local people came to the church and obtained pieces of cloth soaked in his blood. Rumors soon spread that people who touched the cloth were cured of blindness, epilepsy, and leprosy. Monks at Canterbury Priory began selling small glass bottles of Becket's blood to visitors. The keeper of the shrine also would give pilgrims a metal badge that had been stamped with the shrine's symbol.

The pilgrims in the famous medieval poem *Canterbury Tales* were on their way to this shrine.

When the English became Protestant in the 1500s, the shrine lost its allure and was eventually destroyed during aerial bombings in World War II.

House of the Virgin Mary

Located in Ephesus, Turkey, this shrine still exists. It's supposedly the final home occupied by Jesus's mother, although a place in Jerusalem claims the tomb of Mary.

The small humble stone house on Nightingale Hill is cared for by monks and nuns, and draws a large number of Christian pilgrims and Muslims. Mary is venerated in both faiths. The Koran mentions her more than 30 times. One of the lines of the Koran echoes the Christian teaching that Mary was a virgin whom God handpicked to give birth to his son, Jesus: "Mary, God has chosen thee and purified thee. He has chosen thee above all women." —Sura 3:41

Assisi, home of Saint Francis

Once the home of Saint Francis, perhaps the most beloved of Catholic saints, the small town of Assisi is one of the most popular pilgrimage sites in Italy. Francis founded the Franciscan Order of Monks and is buried in his hometown.

The artwork in various churches around town would be enough to attract visitors there. Included are gorgeous wall paintings by artists in the 1400s, as well as paintings by later artists depicting the saint's life.

The city of Assisi has been sacred for thousands of years. Etruscans, the ancient Italian people who preceded the Romans, thought the springs there were holy. About 100 years before Jesus, a temple was built there to honor Minerva, the Roman goddess of wisdom and war. Later, Christians built a variety of churches in Assisi. The last one, the Basilica of San Francesco, is still there, although it had to be extensively repaired after being damaged by a 1997 earthquake.

Lourdes and its healing waters

The unknown community of Lourdes, France, suddenly became a pilgrimage hot spot after Bernadette Soubirous claimed to have been visited there by the Virgin Mary on February 11, 1858. Eventually, Bernadette described 18 appearances in the next five months.

A small *grotto* (a cavelike shrine) where the apparitions began contains springs whose waters are supposed to heal visitors. The Bureau des Constatations stands near the shrine. There, visitors verify illnesses and receive certificates of cures. Records indicate that 4,000 people claimed to be cured in the first 50 years that the shrine existed.

The Vatican: Small, but holy

The Vatican (see Figure 12-3), the smallest country in the world, is less than a quarter of a square mile in size (less than a half of a square kilometer) and located in downtown Rome. The word comes from the Latin *vates,* which means "tellers of the future." This was the name given to a hillside on the west bank of the Tiber River in Rome because fortunetellers would line up daily to hawk their wares to passersby.

Figure 12-3:
St. Peter's
Square at
the Vatican.

The site was linked to many religions before Christianity arrived. The Phrygian goddess Cybele was worshipped here. So was the risen god of the Greeks, Attis. Roman Emperor Nero had a circus built here (in ancient Rome, a *circus* was an oval-shaped arena used for games or chariot races). That circus was where many Christians were reportedly martyred in revenge for the great fire that decimated Rome in AD 64.

In Christian tradition, Saint Peter was crucified upside down here. Romans supposedly killed him because of his beliefs. He asked to be crucified upside down so that he wouldn't duplicate Jesus's death.

Because the area became a graveyard, the grounds were filled with monuments, mausoleums, tombs, and altars to various gods until Emperor Constantine decided to build a church there.

The Vatican has been the home of the pope since the 1500s and was separated from Italy in the 1920s. (For more about the Vatican and the Catholic Church, see Chapter 6.)

St. Peter's Basilica

Perhaps the holiest site in the Roman Catholic faith, St. Peter's Basilica (a *basilica* is a fancy church where certain ceremonies of the Catholic Church can be performed) was built at the place where Peter, the apostle who is considered the first pope, supposedly was crucified and buried. His tomb reportedly is under the main altar. Other popes are also buried in and below the basilica.

Located in Vatican City, the church was once the largest in the world. It can hold 60,000 people.

In ancient times, it was the site of the Circus of Nero (see the preceding section). It also served as a pagan and Christian burial site. In AD 324, Emperor Constantine broke ground for the basilica.

The basilica was repaired in the 1500s with the artist Michelangelo designing the familiar dome.

Other Catholic sites

There are more than 50 sacred Catholic sites scattered around the globe. Some, like Nazareth where Jesus lived and Bethlehem where he was born, are obvious. Others are not.

Here are a few of the more significant ones.

- On September 14, 1975, Pope John Paul II proclaimed Elizabeth Ann Seton a saint; she was the first American-born citizen to be given this honor by the Catholic Church. Her shrine in Emmitsburg, Maryland, includes a basilica, the original stone house where she established her religious community in 1809, and the white house where she began the Catholic parochial school system in 1810.

- Fatima, Portugal, became a world-famous pilgrimage destination because of reported sightings of the Virgin Mary there in the early 20th century. The place is located in a barren area, but contains the Shrine of Our Lady of Fatima, which is dedicated to the Virgin Mary and the young people who claimed to have seen her.

- The reported visions at Medjugorje, Bosnia-Herzegovina, began on June 24, 1981. Six Croatian children said they saw a beautiful young woman with a child in her arms on a hill. Her messages continued for a decade and focused on peace, the importance of belief, and the efficacy of fasting. Pilgrims usually visit the Shrine of the Queen of Peace, built to commemorate the visions.

  The children who saw the visions didn't seek religious vocations, such as becoming a nun or a priest. Today, several of them are married and have children; one lives part time in Massachusetts.

- A church in Capernaum, Israel, has been built over the traditional site of Saint Peter's home. Evidence collected from one room in what was a series of buildings includes graffiti in the plastered walls, some of which mentions Jesus as Lord and Christ.

  In 1990, the Franciscan monks who tend the once-abandoned site built the Church of the Primacy of St. Peter over the site. The church has a glass floor so visitors can see the original building below.

✔ A statue of the Virgin Mary in Copacabana, Bolivia, is believed to work miracles. Carved in 1576, the *Dark Virgin of the Lake* has become the most important pilgrimage destination in that South American country.

✔ The Cologne Cathedral dedicated to saints Peter and Mary in Cologne, Germany, is believed to hold the three skulls of the Magi who visited the baby Jesus. The building was once the tallest in the world and still claims the world's largest church façade.

No one has explained how the Magi, who came from Persia and, according to the Bible, returned to their home after bringing gifts to the Holy Family, ended up buried in Europe. Nevertheless, the cathedral has been a popular pilgrim destination since being built in the 1200s.

✔ A painting of a the Virgin Mary, which survived a 1600s bakery fire and reportedly confers blessings on those who pray to her, is enshrined in a church in Maria Plain, Austria. Located in a hilltop shrine, Our Lady of Maria Plain has been a popular pilgrimage destination for more than 300 years.

Composer Wolfgang Mozart wrote his *Coronation Mass* inside the sanctuary there, and popes have prayed there.

Chapter 13

Thy Kingdom Come: The Messiah Concept

Maybe you've heard this joke before: A poor Russian man rushes home to his wife. It's the middle of the 1800s, jobs are scarce, and the family has suffered for years trying to make ends meet. The husband is excited. "Honey," he cries, "I got job."

The wife clasps her hands in joy. "That's wonderful," she exclaims. "What are you going to do?"

The man puffs up proudly. "I am to sit by the front gate of the city, and, when the Messiah comes, I get to notify the mayor."

The woman's face falls. "You idiot," she shouts. "That doesn't pay anything."

"Yes," the man admits, "but it's steady work."

Sure, it's an old joke, but it deals with one of the most endearing and enduring ideas in religious life: the Messiah. Born in the turmoil of Jewish history, swept along on the rising tide of Christianity, and engrained in Western religious thinking for centuries, the messianic belief remains as viable today as when it was first developed.

This chapter looks at the origin and history of an idea that has found a home in all three monotheistic faiths.

The Origins of the Messiah Concept

The idea of a *messiah* touches the core of the human soul, reflecting a yearning for contact with God and a desire for a better life. It generates an image of an ideal human who, God-like and serene, enlightens society and rules over a world at peace.

The view of a messiah has changed over the centuries. In early Jewish thought, anyone could be a messiah. To create one, a priest blessed some olive oil, and then poured the holy oil on the head of the selected individual. The honored individual then became an *anointed* king or, in Hebrew, *meshiach.* In Greek, the word is translated as *christ.*

In Jewish tradition, kings weren't the only ones awash in holy oil. Priests were anointed, including Moses's brother Aaron (Exodus 29:7) and the priest Zadok (1 Chronicles 29:22). The high priest was denoted as anointed (Leviticus 4:3, 5 and 16). Even a prophet, Elisha, was to receive a shampoo of holy oil. But when God tells Elijah to anoint Elisha (1 Kings 19:16), Elijah just throws a cloak over him instead.

Christianity expanded the messianic concept greatly. The early Christians believed a messiah would save mankind from sin and reunite believers with God. They created an almost mystical individual who was personified by Jesus. The other monotheistic religions weren't far behind in adopting that viewpoint.

Every Sunday, Christians around the world bow their heads and prayerfully call for the imminent arrival of their Messiah. The great medieval philosopher Moses Maimonides spoke for many Jews when he proclaimed, "Though the Messiah may tarry, yet I still believe."

Today, Reform Jews tend to hope for a messianic era, something like Isaiah's paradise, rather than a person. Other Jews await an individual, the Messiah, sent by God to begin an era of peace and love.

The Muslims, as discussed later in this chapter, also await the *Mahdi,* a divinely guided individual who will bring everyone into the Islamic fold.

Isaiah outlines a role

This vision of an ideal, anointed king was given flesh in the writings of Isaiah, a biblical prophet whose book contains material from at least three authors across several hundred years.

The key passages have been challenged historically because they seem to depict a messiah who dominates the world, a concept from a much later time period than when the first Isaiah lived, around 800 BC.

Taking them as written, Isaiah foresees an individual born of the line of Jesse, David's father (Isaiah 9–11). This regal individual will be wise, brave, and religious. He will also be righteous and faithful, refuse to fight for conquest, turn weapons into plows, and establish justice — sort of an early Boy Scout. The people in this ideal kingdom will be farmers, never will be attacked by others, and will serve as an inspiration to neighbors.

> "For unto us a child is born, unto us a son is given; and the government shall be upon his shoulders; and his name shall be called Wonderful, Counselor, the Mighty God, the Everlasting Father, the Prince of Peace. Of the increase of his government and peace there shall be no end . . ." —Isaiah 9:2–7

Isaiah predicts that a young woman will give birth shortly to this child, who will be called Immanuel (meaning "God is with us") in remembrance of the defeat of invading armies (Isaiah 7:14). That statement about the special birth is repeated in Matthew (1:23) and refers to Jesus, although Isaiah clearly is talking about his time period and not one 700 or so years into the future. After all, young Immanuel was born then but vanishes from history.

Other prophets predict a messiah

Other prophets, such as Jeremiah, Zechariah, and Ezekiel, also refer to the Messiah. Naturally, they are talking about the Jewish version — the anointed king, not a savior of sin.

- ✔ Jeremiah saw the Messiah as the "righteous sprout of David" who will set up a wise government (Jeremiah 23:5, 6). (See the next section to find out how King David fits in with the idea of the Messiah.)

- ✔ Ezekiel said the Messiah will become "a mighty cedar" (Ezekiel 17:23) and predicted that David would return to rule the people: "After the fall of the nation, the Jews of the Exile dreamed of the coming of a second David, who would reestablish them as a glorious nation" (Ezekiel 9:9–10).

- ✔ Zechariah created a peaceful image by having his Messiah ride into Jerusalem on a lonely (and lowly) ass (Zechariah 9:9) instead of in front of an army — an idea later borrowed by Matthew in the New Testament.

The messianic concept takes shape with King David

King David of the Israelites united Israel by first conquering the southern tribes (Judah and Benjamin), and then overcoming the northern tribes (the remaining ten tribes; see Chapter 2 for more on the tribes of Israel). David was succeeded on the throne by his son, Solomon, and, in turn, by Solomon's son, Rehoboam. Rehoboam, David's grandson, failed to hold the realm together, and it split into two independent countries.

The era beginning with David took on a golden hue, which glittered increasingly brighter as years passed and the tribes integrated (as the tribal units disintegrated). But after Israel divided under Rehoboam, the land would never see such unity again.

Southern residents in Judah gazed longingly at the northern realm and dreamed of a time when their monarch again would rule a united kingdom. In the past, their anointed king had only one role — to rule properly in accordance with God's rules. However, after the northerners took their royal crown and went home, the southern tribes underwent a change in thinking.

- ✔ The southern anointed king or "messiah" gained a new assignment: He was not only to rule the southern tribes, but was to reunite Judah with its rebellious northern sister. Because David's dynasty ruled Judah, the Messiah naturally was thought to be an offshoot of the Davidic family.

- ✔ After the Jews were conquered by the Babylonians in the sixth century BC, the messiah was expected to fulfill Moses's role with the exiled Jews. The new Moses would have to lead the Jews is the opposite direction — from Babylon in the east to Israel in the west.

- ✔ Once limited to a known king of Judah, the messianic belief quickly encompassed any unknown member of the Davidic family who would restore the monarchy of a united country.

In time, the concept involved the entire world of the early Jews. The idea was also coupled with the religious belief that if the Jews obeyed God's laws, they would finally be rescued from oppression.

The messiahs disappear

By the time the Jews had endured Assyrian, Babylonian, Persian, and Greek control from around 800 B.C. to when the Romans show up in 63 B.C., however, their views of a messiah had dissolved.

The prophets had predicted the Messiah would

✔ Initiate a total peace

✔ Reunite Judah and Israel

✔ Return the Jews currently in exile

✔ Usher in a new, wonderful, endless era in which everyone obeyed

None of that had happened. As a result, the term "messiah" rarely appears in literature for centuries. When the Jewish kings after 142 BC failed to live up to the ideals of the zealous religious sects, messianic ideas began to flourish again.

New messianic duties surface

A group of conservative Jews, known as *Essenes,* revived the messianic idea. They left society in the first century BC to create their own colony in Qumran to await the end of the world. Although they didn't mention a messiah — they do see a descendant of David arising to destroy their enemies — they talked about their departed Teacher of Righteousness.

The Teacher, who challenged Jewish kings who ruled after the Syrian war ended, apparently wanted a *theocracy* (a religious form of government) built around the sacred laws, and he rejected the combination of the high priest–king that the Jewish authorities were following as sacrilegious.

According to documents found in the Qumran caves, the Teacher was either killed or exiled, and his followers awaited his return and the revival of the holy Jewish state he envisioned. That idea parallels older messianic beliefs.

Some historians initially suggested that Christianity borrowed its messianic claims from the Essenes. That idea has been rejected because of the vast differences between the two ethical teachings. Several scholars have proposed that Jesus may have trained as an Essene. That argument still lingers because there's no way to prove it one way or the other.

The Romans create more fervor

Pompey the Great, the Roman general, strode into Jerusalem in 63 BC and helped spur the messianic concept even more.

Once again, the Jewish state was under foreign control. Once again, only God and his chosen representative could restore Israel to Jewish leadership. Once again, literature of the era was filled with messianic comments. Historians like Josephus, Tacitus, and Suetonius all mentioned the term. So did the great Jewish philosopher Philo, who lived in Alexandria in the first century AD.

Jewish writers look to a messiah

A variety of authors commented on the messianic concept from the second century BC into the first century AD.

✔ *The Vision of the Seventy Shepherds of the Book of Enoch* (*circa* 120 BC) is the first known book in this era to refer to the Messiah. In the text, the Messiah is envisioned as a white bull as the world ends. The creature awes the heathens, who then turn to worship the Jewish god.

✔ *The Testament of Levi*, written around the same time, said the Messiah would come from the tribe of Levi, which Moses set aside to serve the priests.

✔ Around 83 BC, the Sibylline Books describe a messiah as a divinely sent king whose job is to end all war on earth.

✔ *Psalms of Solomon*, written after the Romans showed up, insisted the Messiah was the son of David who would appear whenever God decided he was needed and then get really mean.

✔ The *Apocalypse of Baruch* — which is contemporary to the writing of the four Gospels in the late first century AD — foresees the Messiah destroying the Roman Empire.

✔ One of the strongest sources of the biblical view of a messiah may have come from the *Book of Enoch*. It describes the Messiah as a heavenly creature, "an embodiment of justice and wisdom and the medium of God's relationship with man." His name is "son of man," a term that crops up in the biblical book of Daniel and in the New Testament. This Messiah also judges good and evil in heaven and on earth.

Enoch also contains words that clearly foreshadow the Gospel book of John: "At the beginning of the creation of the world was born the King Messiah, who mounted into God's thoughts before the world was made."

✔ In rabbinic literature of the late first century, the Messiah is identified as a descendant of David. There was a prayer for the coming of the Messiah.

The most famous Jewish sage, Hillel, tried to stem the philosophical cascade. He went so far as to argue that there would be no messiah in Israel's future because such an individual had lived at the time of King Hezekiah in the 8th century BC, according to an account in the Talmud (Sanh. 98b). Ironically, Hillel lived around the time of Jesus. His was a lone voice.

Two messiahs?

Jews couldn't agree whether this anointed king would regain control of Israel through a war that destroyed the enemy or through *piety* (religious acts) that caused God to act. Opinions varied. In time, they began to argue that there would be two messiahs.

One would be a messiah whose prayers brought divine action. He was said to be of the line of Joseph, the biblical patriarch who became a leader in Egypt. The other messiah, naturally belonged to the line of the great warrior king, David.

That idea would become entrenched in Judaism and not disappear until the 17th century AD.

Later messiahs in Judaism

As a result of all this thinking about messiahs, through the centuries, a variety of Jews have popped up and claimed to be the messiah. They include:

✔ Simon Bar Kosiba, who led the Jews in one final attack on the Romans around AD 132. He didn't like the messiah idea and preferred to be known as *nasi* (prince). He also took the name Bar Kochbah (meaning "son of the star") to emphasize his status.

One of the great sages of the day, Akiba, called him the Messiah.

Kosiba launched a bold attempt to take back Israel from Rome. The war started when Emperor Hadrian, once a friend of the Jews, announced a plan to turn Jerusalem into a pagan city-state. The emperor also wanted to build a shrine to the Roman god Jupiter where the Temple stood.

After Kosiba's initial success, the Roman army proved too overwhelming. Kosiba was killed around AD 135, and Jews were banned from living in Jerusalem.

✔ David Alroy, the subject of a book by 12th-century traveler Benjamin of Tudela. Alroy was described as a Jewish scholar who was also versed in alchemy and magic. When taken prisoner, he miraculously escaped and supposedly fled across the Gozan River on his turban.

Thieves took advantage of Alroy's claims that he was the Messiah, and they insisted that Jews wait on their rooftops for golden chariots to whisk them off to Jerusalem. As the Jews vainly watched the night sky, their homes were looted.

✔ Another pseudo-messiah (Abraham Ben Samuel Abulafia) tried to convert the Catholic pope to Judaism in the 12th century; a second (David Reubeni) claimed he was leading an army behind Arab lines and tried to con money from world leaders before being unmasked in the 16th century.

✔ In 448, a self-proclaimed messiah, inspired by the story of Moses crossing the Red Sea, announced he would lead his followers dry-shod from Crete to Israel. He bravely stepped off a cliff with his followers. Several drowned. His fate (and his name) remain unknown.

✔ In 645, another supposed messiah, also unidentified by name, assaulted several Muslim strongholds before being caught and, ironically, crucified.

✔ One would-be messiah in the eighth century took the name Abu Isa (meaning "father of Jesus") and raised an army of 10,000 zealots. The ragtag host decided to take Palestine by force and confronted Caliph Abd al-Malik and his battle-hardened soldiers. The resulting massacre abruptly ended Abu Isa's brief career. His followers, however, said he did not die, but "slipped into a hole in a mountain."

✔ In 1665, Nathan of Gaza, the leading rabbi of the day, declared Sabbatai Sevi, a Turkish mystic, the Messiah. Sevi tried to wrest control of Israel from the sultan, only to be offered a choice of conversion or impalement.

Something of a wimp, Sevi instantly donned the green cap of a Muslim and spent the rest of his life to trying to convert Jews to Islam. After his death, a new religion, called *Donmeh* (meaning "heretic") arose. Followers still exist in Turkey and are waiting for Sevi to return and to complete his messianic mission.

Christians Adopt Jesus as the Messiah

The messianic concept percolating through Jewish society was picked up by the Gospel writers of the New Testament, who assigned the role of the Messiah to Jesus. They had plenty of material in sacred texts to draw on:

✔ God promised David and his descendants an eternal kingdom: "And thine house and thy kingdom shall be established forever before thee." —2 Samuel 7:16

✔ To the early sages, saying the "son of David" was a subtle reference to the messianic figure. Mark knew that: "Jesus, son of David, have mercy on me." —Mark 10:47 So did Matthew: "Hosanna to the son of David." —Matthew 21:9

As the Jews had done before them, Gospel writers searched the sacred texts for clues. They found every reference they could to a messianic figure and transferred the references to Jesus. This kind of research is known as *typology,* from the Greek *typhos,* meaning "model" or "pattern."

Jesus's followers, who were crushed by the death of their master, revised Jewish thinking about the Messiah so Jesus could fulfill the role of the Messiah. The next section compares Jesus as the Messiah to people the Jews believed were messiahs.

Comparing old messiahs to Jesus

The Jews were willing to acknowledge almost anyone who fulfilled the messianic duties as the Messiah. They didn't have to be Jewish.

- ✔ Around 538 BC, Cyrus the Great of Persia, a Zoroastrian, allowed the Jews to return to Israel. The verifying edict issued by Darius, the third Persian king, still stands and is recorded in the canonical book of Ezra (4:12).

  Credited with having accomplished one of the divinely ascribed tasks of returning the Jews to Israel, Cyrus naturally was called a messiah by grateful Jews (Isaiah 45:1–7). The first non-Jewish messiah, he was given the power to secure peace and freedom for God's chosen people. He was God's shepherd (Isaiah 44:28) because Davidic kings had failed. (See the earlier section, "The messianic concept takes shape with King David," for more about the Messiah's relationship to David.)

- ✔ After Cyrus came Zerubbabel, grandson of the last independent king of Judah. He was assigned by Darius to lead Jews from Babylon back to Israel in the generation after Cyrus, and he was immediately called a messiah (Haggai 2:20–23).

- ✔ Alexander the Great was next in line almost 200 years later. His Jewish cohorts were impressed by his achievements and called him the Messiah. They expected him to usher in never-ending peace around the world, which the prophets had envisioned.

The ever-changing messianic concept included Jews and non-Jews in its wide embrace. There are obvious differences between how Christians viewed Jesus as the Messiah and how other, earlier messiahs were seen.

Mortality

Cyrus, Alexander, and Zerubbabel were mortal men: Cyrus died in battle. Zerubbabel disappeared after returning to Jerusalem and may have been executed by the Persians who feared he would be crowned king. Alexander died of fever in 322 BC.

The view that the Messiah is mortal has continued throughout Jewish history. In 2 Baruch and 4 Ezra, two extra-biblical works of the first century AD, for example, the "royal messiah" will have only a temporary reign.

In contrast, Christian theology teaches that Jesus died on the cross; then rose from the dead to eternal life.

Divinity

Messiahs were not believed to be anything other than men, although Greek followers of Alexander certainly thought he had some divine qualities.

Jesus is considered to be God. In the Roman Catholic creed, Jesus, God the Father, and the Holy Spirit form the godhead.

Miracles

The old messiahs performed no miracles, nor were they expected to. They were to accomplish God's work, not demonstrate some special powers.

Jesus is described as having performed a variety of miracles. The idea that a messiah would perform signs, as noted in the Gospel of John (7:31), is not duplicated by any Jewish authors.

Goals and predictions

The old messiahs achieved their goals: Cyrus let the Jews return to Israel; Zerubbabel led them to Jerusalem; Alexander conquered the known world. To be acknowledged as a messiah, a person must bring the promised land of Israel and the Jewish people under Jewish control.

Jesus predicted the end of the world, which hasn't happened yet. He thought the Romans would return Israel to the Jews, but they never did. Jesus's death, in Jewish thinking, ended his messianic claims. Nothing in the Jewish religion acknowledges a dead messiah. Messiahs are to accomplish their assignments while alive.

Impact

The Messiah was to bring a change in an existing situation, not necessarily one that had international impact. Cyrus, whose conquests created the Persian Empire, allowed Jews who wanted to leave Babylon to return to their native land. Zerubbabel simply led them back from Babylon. Alexander's exploits had greater repercussion, because he spread the Hellenistic culture throughout the Near East and into India. He went no farther, however.

In contrast, Jesus is depicted as having been sent to the entire world. His death did not cause an apparent ripple in Roman or Jewish history. Only later, nearly 300 years after his death, did Christians become a formidable force in the Roman world and bring about a new era.

Lineage

The old messiahs were not necessarily of the line of David nor born in Bethlehem. Zerubbabel probably was a kin of David — the connection is alluded to in Psalm 72 — but was born in Babylon. Cyrus and Alexander certainly were not affiliated with David or Israel in any way. Many prophets, but not all, said that the Messiah must come from the line of David. Hosea (3:5) and Jeremiah (30:9) foresaw the new leader not as David returned but a "future ideal ruler from his family, a perfect servant of the Lord." Only Micah suggests that the Messiah would be born in the same city that David was born in (Micah 5:1–3).

Jesus was described in three of the Gospels as descending from David. Matthew lists Jesus's family line from verses 2 to verses 16 in chapter 1 of his book. Luke does the same thing, although names in his genealogy are different, in chapter 3 verses 23 through 38 of his book. In chapter 3 of John's Gospel, he is said not to be related to David.

These early writers saw Jesus as the promised Jewish messiah, but who was even greater than earlier writers had imagined.

The end of the world

Cyrus, Alexander, and Zerubbabel aren't tied to any end of the world concept. Jesus is, heralding a *Kingdom of God,* the era when God will rule and bring current existence to a close.

Other messianic figures around the time of Jesus

Although historians are unclear if Jesus saw himself as the predicted Messiah, they do know that many people in the first century AD certainly felt they deserved that title. Early Christians had to cope with messianic claims by these people:

- ✔ Simon and Athronges arose after the death of Herod in 4 BC. Simon had been a slave of Herod who burned down the royal palace at Jericho and many other stately mansions. Under Simon's leadership, peasant armies attacked Sepphoris and Jericho in hopes of recapturing goods seized by Herodian officials. Athronges, who was a "mere shepherd," Josephus called him, but he gathered followers who proclaimed him king.

  Both Simon and Anthronges were eventually killed by the Romans, who also suppressed a messianic movement by razing Galilee's capital, Sepphoris, in 4 BC. The duo had some success battling the Romans, however. The Romans needed three legions and four regiments to succeed.

- ✔ John the Baptist was trying to purify followers in preparation for *Armageddon* (the final battle between good and evil; see Chapter 14). John's followers continued to believe in him as the Messiah for several hundred years after his death around 34 AD, before they began to follow Christian practices or returned to Judaism.

- ✔ Another unnamed prophet led a movement to rebuild the old Samarian temple on Mount Gerizim. The Northern tribes of Israel had built the temple after they broke away from the Davidic dynasty. Pontius Pilate, who became notorious for his connection to Jesus, crushed that effort and killed the prophet.

- Theudas, who died in about AD 45. Apparently, he was trying to re-create the Exodus, possibly by crossing the Jordan River (see Chapter 3 for an explanation of the Exodus). The Judean governor of the time, Fadus, promptly sent troops who massacred the Theudas and his followers. Theudas's head was then displayed in Jerusalem.

- In AD 56, the Egyptian and his followers approached a high wall in Jerusalem, clearly hoping to imitate Joshua at the battle of Jericho. The governor of the time, Felix, sent his troops to stop them. Many died, but the Egyptian vanished into history.

  Felix also had to contend with a variety of unidentified millennial prophets. "Imposters and deceivers called upon the mob to follow them into the desert. For they said they would show them unmistakable marvels and signs that would be wrought in harmony with God's design," the Jewish historian, Josephus, reported.

- Menachem had an equally brief career. The son (or grandson; the chronology isn't clear) of Judas, a crucified revolutionary messiah from Galilee, he came to Jerusalem to lead the AD 66 revolt against the Romans and the assault on the royal palace. However, Menachem became a tyrant and was eventually tortured and killed by his opponents.

- Simon ben Giora, which means "Simon, son of the proselyte" (a *proselyte* is someone who has been converted from one religion to another), was the most prominent of the militaristic messianic figures of this era. In AD 66, when the Jews revolted against the Romans, he emerged as one of the leaders in the surprising rout of the Roman forces in Jerusalem.

  Simon established his headquarters in Hebron, probably intentionally mimicking David who had been anointed king of Judah in the same city. He then went to Jerusalem and helped lead the unsuccessful attempt to hold off the Roman onslaught, while simultaneously battling with members of dissident groups.

  To emphasize his role, he made a final, grand entrance in front of Roman troops. "Imagining he could cheat the Romans by creating a scare, he dressed himself in white tunics and buckling over them a purple mantle arose out of the ground (a trapdoor) from the very spot where the Temple formerly stood," Josephus reported. Befitting a defeated head of state, he was seized, displayed, *scourged* (whipped), and executed.

- A prophet around AD 62 told his followers they would receive salvation and freedom from their worries if they followed him into the wild, according to Josephus. (Sounds pretty good, doesn't it?) Festus sent his troops, who made short work of the certain imposter and his followers.

- In AD 73, a prophet named Jonathan, a weaver, led Jews into the desert. The Romans found him there and put an end to his dreams of being the Messiah.

Recent messianic figures

Messianic figures (self-proclaimed or otherwise) in the last few hundred years include:

- **Father Divine (1864?–1965):** His followers called him "God." Born in the mid-1800s, George Baker (both his name and date of birth are uncertain) claimed he came to earth on a puff of smoke about the time of Abraham. He died in 1965, worth an estimated $100 million.

- **Aleister Crowley (1875–1947):** Crowley's version of a messiah was predicated on sexual orgies and pagan rites. He was tossed out of France and Italy for his heretical views, one of which was "the only sin is restriction." He died after World War II following a lifetime of drug abuse, including heroin.

- **Rabbi Menachem Mendel Schneerson (1902–1992):** The leader of the ultra-Orthodox Lubavitch movement of Chassidic Judaism, the "Rebbe" rarely set foot outside his neighborhood during his entire leadership, but his influence was felt worldwide. The Rebbe decided the fall of Communism in the late 1980s and the Gulf War in the early 1990s heralded an era of peace and tranquility for all mankind, the time of the Messiah. Many of his followers decided he fulfilled that role, although Schneerson didn't claim the title.

- **Francis Pencovic (?–1958):** He founded WKFL Foundation in 1948 to teach wisdom, knowledge, faith, and love (hence the acronym). He also set up a colony in Ventura County, California, and claimed he was Christ. He changed his appearance to match that of Christ's; he grew a beard and wore flowing robes and a large cross pendant. He said he had arrived on earth in a spaceship 240,000 years earlier. He was assassinated in 1958.

- **Oric Bovar (1917–1977):** He gathered a small flock by the mid-1970s, including a handful of celebrities attracted by his message of no smoking, drinking, drugs, or extramarital sex. His followers were disappointed after he called himself Jesus Christ and shifted Christmas to August 29, his birthday. Bovar eventually made a fatal leap from his apartment.

- **David Koresh (1959–1993):** This former rock musician led a group called Branch Davidians in Waco, Texas, after claiming he was the new messiah. He predicted the end of the world would come in 1993. He lived in anonymity for several years until 1992, when his men killed several government agents who came to the compound to check out reports of illegal firearms. The ambush led to arrival of the FBI, who besieged the compound for more than 70 days that year. Eventually, after receiving reports of child abuse and other crimes, FBI agents moved in with tanks and tear gas. Koresh apparently ordered the compound set on fire or set the blaze himself, which killed 75 children and adults, including him.

- **The Rev. Sun Myung Moon (1920–):** The religious leader proclaimed himself a messiah and founded the Unification Church in the 1950s. The religion is based on Moon's messianic claims with strong ties to Christianity.

- **Vissarion (1961–):** This former Siberian traffic warden found inspiration in the collapse of the Soviet Union and declared himself the Messiah. Apparently, thousands of his compatriots believe him. Once known as Sergei Torop, he has five children and rules from the "City of the Sun" in Krasnoyarsk, Siberia.

Jesus wins out

The followers of Jesus eventually overcame all opposition. He became the true Messiah in Christianity. He is the promised deliverer who saved the people of Israel and was anointed as prophet, priest, and king by God. He will return, they argue, to establish a world kingdom of peace and justice, centered around Israel, as predicted by the prophets.

Islam Develops a Messiah: Madhi

The Jewish-Christian view of a messiah reached into Islam, too. The Sunni and Shi'ite sects have developed their concepts of this figure. As with the other monotheistic faiths, people arose to claim this special title.

In Islam, the messianic figure is called *Mahdi* (meaning "divinely guided one"). He is seen as someone completely obedient to the will of God. He will orchestrate a community lifestyle where Muslims can live according to the principles of Islam.

The term *Mahdi* doesn't appear in the Koran, but seems to have developed in the first few centuries after Islam was founded. The idea may have seeped into the faith from Christian sources as Muslim armies spread throughout the Mediterranean region.

The Shi'ite vision

The Mahdi is central to the Shi'ite belief in Islam. They believed Muhammad bni l-Hanafiya, son of Ali, was the Mahdi.

Muhammad (not to be confused with the prophet Muhammad) appears to have rejected any special designation as the Mahdi, but Shi'ites around that time believed in him. Members expected Muhammad to rise from his grave on Mount Radwa.

Another Shi'ite sect arose and focused on Hussein, the second son of Ali. Hussein and his followers attempted to grab the Caliphate but were massacred in 680. Shi'ites mark the anniversary of the battle with great mourning. Hussein's tomb in Karbala, Iraq, is a sacred place of pilgrimage.

Regardless of who the Mahdi is, the Shi'ites believe he will return to bring justice to the entire world, echoing Christian views of Jesus.

Sunnis disagree

To the Sunnis, a Mahdi is a righteous figure, but not one of worldwide significance. This approach parallels traditional Jewish concepts. The Jewish messiah, after all, was only coming to help the Jews. To the Muslims, the term Mahdi has been associated with various individuals in Islamic history, including:

✔ Ali, Muhammad's son-in-law.

✔ Hassan, Ali's son.

✔ Caliph Umar II (717–720). Despite his short reign — he was poisoned by opponents — he was recognized as a sincere, pious man who helped reform the leadership and build the faith.

Other Mahdis

The term *Mahdi* is sometimes reserved for converts to Islam because they are believed to be guided by Allah toward the truth. In addition, a Mahdi may be a military leader, such as El Mahdi and Ibn Tumart.

✔ Ibn Tumart was an Islamic reformer of Morocco in the 1100s. He declared a holy war against anyone who disagreed with him and proclaimed himself Mahdi. He came up with a genealogy that linked himself to Ali, Muhammad's faithful son-in-law.

A successful general for a time, Tumart had the population of Tin Mal destroyed, massacring 15,000 residents. Eventually, his army was defeated, but after his death, his followers ended the existing dynasty and imposed their own in his name. Tin Mal in Morocco still exists and is the site of pilgrimages.

✔ El Mahdi was a Sudanese leader, who, in 1881, declared himself the Mahdi. He brought the central and southern Sudanese tribes together in a revolt against the Turks.

At one time, he was an incredibly powerful leader who overwhelmed English troops led by General Charles Gordon. Today, Saudi Arabia still follows precepts laid down by El Mahdi. Movements that believe in his teachings exist in many Arab countries, often causing unrest because of their members' strict conservative views in contrast with more liberal ideas of political leaders.

The last Mahdi?

Caliph an-Nasir (1180–1225) was the last great ruler of the Muslim world before the Mongols under Genghis Khan annihilated them, opening the door to Turkish rule. An-Nasir used some devious diplomacy to try to consolidate his power, helping lead to the Mongol invasion.

However, he was known for maintaining peace during his reign and encouraging education. As a result, some Muslims define him as the last Mahdi.

Chapter 14

Holy Catastrophe: End of the World

*I*n 1999, as the clock ticked down toward 2000, millions of Jewish, Christian, and Muslim believers wondered if the world was about to end. A computer glitch was expected to shut down telecommunications at midnight, creating widespread havoc and destroying much of civilization.

Y2K, as it was called, referred to the fact that computers were programmed to move ahead with each new year. As a result, computer experts were sure that when computers automatically updated from 1999 to 2000, they would actually go from 1999 to 1901. Billions of dollars were spent to fix the error.

When the calendar flipped from December 31, 1999, to January 1, 2000, nothing happened. Believers who saw the computer problems as the latest sign the world was ending were disappointed. They thought for sure that this significant event would bring about *Armageddon* (the final battle between good and evil; the word is taken from a plain near the Israeli city of Megiddo where the showdown is supposed to take place). The world's end was predicted even before Jesus lived.

The hope that the world is ending continues to thrive despite repeated disappointment. This chapter looks at a concept that is integral to all three monotheistic religions.

Where Did the Idea of the End of the World Come From?

Logically, the world will end sometime. Physical law demands it. After all, at some point, billions of years from now, the sun will burn out, taking Earth and the entire solar system with it. Of course, ancient peoples didn't have the scientific knowledge we have today, but they still made assumptions about the end of everything.

Many people don't want to wait for science to run its course. They're sure God will blast the sinful world much sooner than that. They collect "signs" of the coming *tribulation* (great sorrow and distress).

For example, believers today see the battles in the Middle East between Israelis and Palestinians as an indication of the coming end. They point to the return of Jews to Israel, corrupt government, and even the giant tsunami that hit Indonesia in 2004 as clear indications that the end is near.

This idea predates Judaism, Christianity, and Islam. Greeks, Romans, and other people believed in cycles of life. Their gods destroyed and then rebuilt the world many times.

The concept of the end of the world became popular among Jewish authors around 160 BC as Jews struggled to understand the ghastly murders associated with the war between Hellenistic Jews and their religious counterparts.

Jewish prophets didn't originate the end of the world concept; they simply tied it to a divine being, a *messiah,* who would initiate the process. (Chapter 13 talks about the idea of the Messiah.)

Scholars have created words to describe writings dealing with this awaited cataclysm: *eschatology* and *apocalypticism.* The words are used synonymously, but do have slightly different meanings:

- ✔ **Eschatology,** from the Greek for "end" or "final," is the scientific term of the study of the end of the world.

- ✔ **Apocalypticism,** from the Greek word for "revelation," refers to the religious aspect. It places less emphasis on individual events and more focus on God's saving power.

Judaism's Belief in the End and Its Influence on Christianity

Although the Old Testament doesn't discuss the end of the world, ancient Jewish writers drew upon the biblical account of Noah for inspiration. According to the account in Genesis, Noah built a large boat (his famous *ark*) and housed his family and animals on it while God sent an enormous flood to wipe out the rest of mankind.

Jewish philosophers wondered: Why couldn't God again obliterate those who oppressed them?

The prophet Joel captured the image of the apocalypse, noting that on that day, the unrighteous and the Gentiles would be annihilated: ". . . let all the inhabitants of the Land tremble: for the day of the Lord cometh, for it is nigh at hand" (Joel 2:1).

Ezekiel, whose writings date from the time of Babylonian exile in the mid-500s BC, said that after the world was destroyed, a prince of the House of David would humble the Gentiles and redeem Israel (Ezekiel 34:23). Jewish sages called the expected intervention of God into man's affairs the *Day of the Lord.*

Jews developed a variety of explanations for why the destruction of the world was necessary:

- ✔ **As the traditional tribes disappeared, Jewish leaders confronted more powerful cultures.** They could see their young people being drawn away and thought that only divine intervention could save the people from assimilation.

- ✔ **Independence seemed to be an idle dream.** The Romans were so powerful that only divine retribution could overcome them and return Israel to the control of the Jews.

- ✔ **All other efforts to build a theocracy had failed.** (A *theocracy* is a government or country ruled by a person or persons who believe themselves divinely guided.) Prophetic hopes turned to bitterness. With such outcries came the only solution — complete destruction of hated enemies.

The predictions of the end of the world were there for anyone to read in the writings of the prophet Zechariah. The Messiah will defeat the Gentile nations (Zechariah 14:10) and restore the kingdom of Israel (Zechariah 14). The Jews in exile will return and rule in an age of spiritual harmony (Zechariah 14:5). God will be recognized as the universal king (Zechariah 14:9), and the idea of an ideal life on earth as foreseen in Isaiah 42:6 will be fulfilled.

The end as predicted in the book of Daniel

Any belief in the concept of the final destruction is directly linked to Jewish writings, in particular the book of Daniel. Produced around 160 BC, the text follows the exploits of an ancient figure — Daniel is mentioned briefly in earlier, non-biblical writings — whose image had been updated to offer courage to Jews battling the hated Syrians in a war destined to end in a Jewish victory in 142 BC.

The Syrians, under the Jewish governor Jason, attempted to force the Jews to disobey Jewish laws and worship their king as god. In the text, the Babylonians also require religious submission. Daniel, a prophet of the Jews who supposedly was held in Babylonian captivity, refuses to obey the laws.

God rewards Daniel by keeping him healthy on a limited diet and protecting him during a visit to a lion's den. Those Babylonians who do obey the hated requirements fall victim to God's punishment instead, a fate the author hoped was reserved for the Syrians.

Toward the end of the book of Daniel, the text shifts from Hebrew to Aramaic (2:4 to 7:8) and captures the mood of its time. The author of Daniel decided that God delayed inaugurating his kingdom because the Jewish sins had not yet abated. The writer then reinterpreted the prophetic writings: The 70 years promised by Jeremiah for the return to the holy state of Israel after the Babylonian conquest really meant 70 weeks of years (Daniel 9:2, 24). That works out to 490 years — or about 100 years after the lifetime of the author, dating from the setting of the book in the Babylonian conquest.

The book also introduced a theory of resurrection (Daniel 12:2) — possibly also mentioned by Isaiah in a late apocalyptic addition to an earlier book (Isaiah 26:19) — and includes the only mention of the word "messiah" (referring to a mythical leader rather than an anointed king) in the Old Testament. Angels, too, make an appearance, possibly borrowed from the Persians.

The book became popular reading after the Romans took control of the Jewish land in 63 BC. As a result, anyone living in Israel around the time of King Herod (37–4 BC) probably believed wholeheartedly that the promised end had finally shown up. They excitedly awaited a messiah to deliver them from that evil leader who was only half-Jewish and who built temples for Roman gods. The enthusiasm is why so many people in this era claimed to be the Messiah. (See Chapter 13 for the brief biographies.)

Other prophesies predict the end

To augment Scripture, Jewish writers developed separate predictions. Forged Roman *oracles* (fortunetellers) claimed that a great man would rise from the East as the world disintegrated: "Near at hand is the end of the world, and the last day, and the judgment of immortal God for such as are both called and chosen . . . a holy king shall come who shall rule over the whole earth for all ages of the course of time."

Those predictions and related prophecies were widespread, carried by Jews and their supporters. An estimated 10 percent of the population was Jewish or *God-Fearers* — individuals who liked everything about Judaism, supported synagogues and holidays, but declined to be circumcised. Other people followed Jewish rules without accepting Judaism.

The death of Augustus

When Emperor Augustus died in AD 14, after ruling since 44 BC, many people felt the world had to end. The long-lived Augustus, after all, was the only emperor many of them had ever known. Moreover, in Roman theology, he was worshipped as a god, both during his lifetime and after his death. To Romans, God had died.

Augustus's death heightened Jewish convictions of the imminent end of the world. When Jesus started preaching amid the cry of other prophets that the final days were upon the inhabitants, the people of Augustus's era, unlike any before this, were ready to greet a messiah.

The destruction of the Temple: A sign for Jews and Christians

When the Temple in Jerusalem was destroyed in AD 70, many people hopped on the bandwagon. The world had to be ending. God had left his house.

The fledgling Christian movement picked up this idea and engrained it in its thinking. All early Christian writers, led by Paul, argued that the world was ending soon.

His epistles are filled with such claims of an immediate end. For example, in 1 Thessalonians, perhaps his oldest letter, Paul wrote that "we who are still alive and remain" will join those already dead "to meet the Lord in the air" (1 Thessalonians 4:17).

The Gospels, written after Paul's death, echoed his thoughts: "Verily I say unto you, there are some standing here, which shall not taste of death, till they see the Son of man coming in his kingdom" (Matthew 16:28, Mark 9:1, and Luke 9:27).

Naturally, this idea caused a problem. Everyone who believed was convinced the world was ending soon.

St. Augustine in the fifth century spoke out against such beliefs, but they have remained an integral part of Christian thinking, particularly among evangelical Protestants. Jesus will return to fulfill his mission, beginning a time when the righteous will be rewarded and nonbelievers punished.

Other predictions of the final year

The world didn't end in AD 70 when the Temple in Jerusalem was destroyed, but the concept of earthly destruction never faded from Jewish thinking either. Jewish scholars buckled down to read the Scripture and eke out the true date.

- ✔ In early Jewish thinking, 1096 was one of the years when the end might come, based on a numerological interpretation of Leviticus 25:24: "Ye shall grant a redemption for the land."

- ✔ Various interpreters suggested that the line in Job 38:7, "When the morning stars sang together," pointed to 1492. That year, however, Jews were expelled from Spain.

In 1492, Duke Don Isaac Abravanel, the leader of the Spanish Jewish community then being forced to leave Spain, predicted the coming of the Messiah and the resulting punishment of Gentiles. He picked the early 1500s as his target date. Author of commentaries on the biblical books of Joshua, Judges, and Chronicles, Abravanel did his own calculations to arrive at the magical date. He hoped publishing his research would encourage disheartened Spanish Jews.

Jews used the letters of their alphabet to better analyze their sacred books. That's because each letter is assigned a number. For example, the Hebrew letters for "end of days" add up to 408. That number in Hebrew corresponds to the year 1648. As a result, 1648 became the focus of enthusiastic hopes. But the year went by without catastrophe, although it was marred by *pogroms* (persecutions and massacres of Jews) in Poland.

Jews lifted hopeful eyes to the next option: 1666. Some scholars foresaw the end in that year based on study of the *Kabala,* a collection of mystical ideas that existed in a Jewish undercurrent beginning in the Middle Ages.

Jews had been prosperous in some communities, but the majority had descended into abject poverty, particularly in Poland, where the largest percentage of the Jewish population lived at that time. The kabalistic teachings took on added meaning among Jews while they struggled amid a hostile Christian society.

Many Christians also saw 1666 as the exact year for the end of the world. They based it on a section of St. John's book of Revelation, the last book in the New Testament. In part of a lengthy and often confusing text, John says the mark of this demonic antichrist is 666:

> "Let him that hath understanding count the number of the beast: for it is the number of a man; and his number is six hundred threescore and six."
> —Revelation 13:18

Predicting Armageddon: Your guess is as good as anyone's

If you're reading this, the world still hasn't ended. Here are some of the dates when people thought the world was going to end:

- Around 300, Bishop Eusebius, the first historian of the Roman Catholic Church, bemoaned the many persecutions of Christians and consoled himself by announcing that the martyrs foreshadowed the end of the world.

- Near the end of the fourth century, Martin of Tours, who was later sainted, insisted the world would end before 400.

- In the 13th century, the pope asked Joachim of Fiore to determine the last days of the earth. The holy monk decided that the final day was due somewhere around the middle of the century. He identified Frederick II, one of the great rulers of history, as the antichrist, but both men died before the projected date of Armageddon.

- In 1284, Pope Innocent III amended Joachim's forecast by deciding the world would end 666 years after Islam was founded. Even the sanctified numbers didn't do the trick.

- In 1524, astrologers busied themselves with a prediction of a massive flood that year to end civilization.

- In the 1830s, Joseph Smith, founder of the Mormon faith, revealed that God told him that he would be 85 when the world ended. He didn't live that long.

- In 1844, many people gathered on a farm in upstate New York, certain that apocalyptic predictions were right.

- Many Mormons still thought 1891, when Smith would have been 85, would be the end.

- The year 1914 was big with Jehovah's Witnesses. World War I began, but not the apocalypse.

- Herbert Armstrong, founder of the Worldwide Church of God, was partial to 1936. When that turned out to be wrong, he pointed to 1975.

- Pat Robertson, a long-time American religious leader in the conservative Christian movement, gave his blessing to 1982.

The predictions continue today, pinpointing years in the future based on the Mayan calendar, world events, or revelations.

Readers decided it referred to the year 666 or 1666. Because 666 had come and gone without destruction, Christians looked eagerly at the next option.

Since then, many other years have also been pinpointed without any success. Christian sects like the Jehovah's Witnesses and Seventh-day Adventists started because of inaccurate end-of-the-world predictions.

The Christian notion of the "antichrist"

Christian religious beliefs have often included the emergence of a terrible foe to battle Jesus. This enemy is identified as the *antichrist* and first showed up in the book of Revelation. There, he is described as a "person, a beast" (Revelation 13:1). Later prophets took a swing at identifying this awful person, including Nostradamus, a Frenchman who lived in the 1500s.

Every now and then, the antichrist shows up in some religious tract or in the media to threaten the population. If someone was sure the antichrist was born, then the countdown to the earth's final years would begin.

Virtually every renowned world leader for centuries has been called the antichrist by an opponent.

Islam's View of the End

Just like Jews and Christians, Muhammad was also convinced the world was going to end soon. The Koran has dozens of predictions about the end of the world. Muhammad envisioned the end as being very close, possibly within a few years after receiving his revelation.

Scholars have suggested that the rapidly approaching end may have spurred Muslim armies in their rapid-fire conquests in the decades after the death of their founder in the seventh century.

Turning to texts for support

Islam writings about the end of the world remain popular. They are derived from three main sources:

- ✔ **The Koran and other sacred books:** In the text, Muhammad describes various scenarios when the world will end. One includes the discovery of a mountain of gold by the Euphrates River in Iraq. The gold will incite fighting and the deaths of mankind.

- ✔ **Anti-Jewish conspiracy theories:** Modern Muslims often interpret lines in the Koran about the Jews as forecasting huge battles leading to Armageddon. Jews are accused of wanting to rule the world and of distorting the Bible for their own purposes.

- ✔ **Protestant claims about the return of Christ and the end of the world:** Christians and Muslims believe that the return of Jesus will inaugurate the final end, but Muslims believe Jesus will accept Islam and reject Christianity.

Is the U.S. the great Satan?

An Egyptian writer's works have given new support for the end of the world ideas in Islam. In 1987, Said Ayyub published a book called *The Anti-Christ.* This text became very popular, although it was banned in some moderate Middle Eastern countries, because it labeled the United States as the "Great Satan."

Ayyub claimed to have interpreted all the events of the modern world as if they were predicted in either the Muslim traditions or the Bible. Since then, believers have tried to add details to his framework, including the war in Iraq in which the U.S. has played a major role.

By the way, American writer Hal Lindsey did the same thing in the 1970s. He wrote a book called *The Late Great Planet Earth,* which has served as something of a textbook for evangelical Protestants awaiting the final days. He said the Soviet Union would attack Israel. Obviously incorrect, he now suggests that only his timing was off, not the reality of Armageddon.

The end is near

To Muslims, the time for Armageddon again seems to be drawing near. They see their faith challenged by Christian missionaries, mass media, and the Internet, and confronted by modern Christian crusaders in the guise of U.S. and coalition soldiers in the Iraq War.

Their views got a kick in the rump with the claim that a red heifer, a reputed sign of the coming apocalypse, was born in Israel. Supposedly, the birth in 1997 (or 2002, as some claim) was the first in Israel in 2,000 years.

The little calf shows up in the book of Numbers: "Speak unto the children of Israel that they bring thee a red heifer without spot, wherein is no blemish, and upon which never came yoke" (Numbers 19:2). Paul then augments the commandment with this in an epistle:

> "For if the blood of bulls and of goats, and the ashes of an heifer sprinkling the unclean, sanctifieth to the purifying of the flesh: How much more shall the blood of Christ, who through the eternal Spirit offered himself without spot to God, purge your conscience from dead works to serve the living God?" —Hebrews 9:13–14

For some people, the heifer came to symbolize when the world would end. That view has seeped into Islam.

Muslims, well aware of biblical prediction about the end of the world, saw the heifer's birth as confirmation of their views that the end is just around the corner. They believed this was the sign of the appearance of the *Dajjal,* the Islamic antichrist figure.

The end of world concept has also invigorated terrorists groups, who sometimes see the American president or the United States as the antichrist. Terrorist literature relies on the predicted end of the world to forecast the demise of Israel and to recruit followers. In the pamphlets, they argue it's time to work for Allah and his purposes rather than their own.

How the End of the World Will Take Place

Although all three faiths are awaiting the end of the world, they don't agree completely on the details.

Signs of the end

Every religion believes it can pinpoint the exact moment by looking at appropriate indications in various natural catastrophes, political events, wars, and special symbols, such as the possibility of building a third Temple in Jerusalem.

The failure of similar signs in the past to accurately forecast the end of the world doesn't seem to bother true believers. They assume the dating was off for some reason and that the next selected time will be correct.

Judaism

According to Jewish religious scholars who studied the Torah to figure out when the world will end, ten signs will accompany the messianic "birth pangs" of the end times:

- The world is either all righteous or guilty.
- Truth is in short supply.
- Inflation will soar.
- Israel begins to be repopulated.
- Wise people will be scarce.
- Jews will despair of redemption.
- The young will despise the old.
- Scholarship will be rejected.
- Piety will be held in disgust.
- Jews will turn against Jews.

Christianity

The actual signs vary according to which denomination is issuing them. Here are some basic ones that have biblical support:

- ✔ Wars between nations (Matthew 24:6–7)
- ✔ Famine and earthquakes (Matthew 24:7)
- ✔ False christs (Matthew 24:5)
- ✔ Reestablishment of Israel (Isaiah 11:11–12)
- ✔ Temple worship restored (Daniel 9:27; Matthew 25:15; 2 Thessalonians 2:4; Revelation 11:1–2)
- ✔ Persecution of the Jews (Matthew 24:9–10, 16–20)
- ✔ Global preaching of the kingdom of God (Matthew 24:14)
- ✔ Celestial disturbances (Matthew 24:29; Revelation 6–19)

Despite the signs, in Christian teachings, no one knows when the end will come. The apostle Paul started out very enthusiastic about the arrival of Armageddon, saying that people reading his epistles would see the end shortly. Later, when nothing happened, he tempered his thoughts by calling on believers to be patient (2 Thessalonians).

Islam

Seven major and minor signs are supposed to reveal that the end times have arrived. These have been derived from sayings in the Koran. Muhammad was often explicit, such as when he described the discovery of gold (see the "Islam's View of the End" section) or offered general concepts:

Major signs:

- ✔ Gross materialism
- ✔ Women outnumber men
- ✔ Muslims defeat Jews in battle; Muslims and Christians battle unbelievers together; then Muslims defeat Christians in battle

Minor signs:

- ✔ Increase in bloodshed and war
- ✔ Contraction of time
- ✔ Religious knowledge decreases
- ✔ Prevalence of the ungodly

How the end will begin, so to speak

The end will be very noisy, according to all three religions.

- The Koran foresees music and the dead rising. "And the trumpet shall be blown, and, lo! they shall speed out of their sepulchers to their Lord." —Sura 36:51

- In Christianity, the trumpets blare, too. "And he will send his angels with a loud trumpet call, and they will gather his elect from the four winds, from one end of the heavens to the other." —Matthew 24:31

- Jews will hear the *shofar* (ram's horn), which is blown annually during High Holiday services.

Jesus gets an encore to limited audiences

In Judaism, Jesus has no place. Jews don't believe a messiah is necessary to initiate the end of the world, and they don't accept Jesus as the Messiah.

In contrast, Christians and Muslims expect him. "And if I go and prepare a place for you, I will come back and take you to be with me that you also may be where I am." —John 14:3

When Jesus returns, as spelled out in the book of Revelation, humans will be overwhelmed with tragedies. Finally, those who have been saved, the true believers, will be lifted to heaven while the rest of humanity will be sent to eternal punishment.

No Christian sect believes the end of the world will be peaceful.

In Islamic teachings, Jesus (or, as he is called in Arabic, *Isa*) will return to overthrow the Devil in the battle of Aqabat Afiq in Syria, or at the Lud gate in Jerusalem. According to another account in the Koran, Jesus will "kill all pigs and break all crosses," confirming Islam as the only true religion.

After 40 years, Jesus will die and be buried next to Muhammad in Medina. In Islamic teaching, Jesus never died on the cross, but has been waiting for just the right moment to return.

Then Allah will destroy all the nations except Islamic ones. At the end of Jesus's and the messianic Imam's rule, the angels will be destroyed and the earth will "spill out its contents."

Rise and shine for the resurrection

All three religions believe that the dead will rise from their graves. Muslims will gather on the Mount of Olives in Jerusalem. Jews and Christians aren't as specific about where the believers will assemble.

Many people insisted on being buried by the gates of Jerusalem, convinced that when the end does come, the Messiah will start in the Holy City. This way, they would be lying close to the action.

In Jewish theology, people who are dead are only sleeping as they wait for Judgment Day.

Standing by during the destruction

In Jewish and Christian thinking, everything on earth gets obliterated except for angels. In Islam, even angels get their wings plucked.

Humans are another matter. True believers always endure. Israel is shielded by God; Muslims by Muhammad; and Christians by Jesus.

Awaiting the final judgment

God will judge the living and dead. The good are *redeemed* (delivered from sin and taken to heaven; see Chapter 16), and the bad are *damned* (sent to hell for punishment for their sins; see Chapter 17). All the religions accept that. Judaism and Christianity stress that God is just. Islam is not so sure about Allah. "Verily God misleadeth whom he will, and guideth whom he will" (Sura 35:8).

Redemption

All three faiths agree that the righteous are saved and are allowed to spend eternity in heaven. The question is, who is righteous?

✔ Deciding who is righteous isn't a simple task in Judaism. Jews faced a problem because the Bible says that Noah was righteous and so he was saved by God from the flood. But he lived prior to Abraham, the first Jew. Therefore, Noah couldn't have followed Jewish law, which didn't appear until Moses. To solve the problem, Jews came up with the *Noahide Laws*. Anyone who followed these rules was considered righteous. The requirements were limited to seven and included eating kosher food, following the Ten Commandments, believing in one God, and the like. Circumcision wasn't on the list (see Chapter 4 for more on this practice). That's why so many non-Jews during the Roman era were accepted into Jewish circles as righteous people.

✔ In Islam, individuals will be judged on the scales of justice that will be hung on a pillared structure on the eastern side of the Temple Mount platform. If the scales show more good works than bad, a Muslim receives eternal life.

✔ In some Christian sects, belief in Jesus is enough to be saved. Others, such as the Roman Catholic Church, demand good deeds to accompany faith. In the Anglican faith, for example, Christians must overcome their sinful nature by following biblical teachings. To Eastern Orthodox, the way to salvation is hard. They reject the idea of being "born again" in a simple ritual.

Judaism and Islam agree that man is basically good, so believers have a decent chance of going to heaven.

On the other hand, Christianity argues that man is evil and had to be redeemed by the death of Jesus. Nonbelievers therefore are condemned. Christian leaders debated whether people who were born before Jesus lived — people who couldn't have been aware they were supposed to believe in him — were also out of luck. The apostle Paul summed up that view:

> "But, because of his great love for us, God, who is rich in mercy, made us alive with Christ even when we were dead in transgressions — it is by grace you have been saved." —Ephesians 2:1

Not all sects accept that idea, of course. In Eastern Orthodox and Church of God, for example, everyone has a chance to be saved, even nonbelievers. It's a matter of free will. Nonbelievers simply must accept Jesus.

Damnation

Those who fail to go to heaven have different destinations, although all of them will cause a bit of perspiration.

✔ In Islam, non-Muslims and infidels go to a lake of fire.

✔ In Judaism, they are burned for eternity in the fires of Gehenna, the one-time garbage pit outside Jerusalem.

✔ In Christianity, they go to hell for endless torment.

We cover hell extensively in Chapter 17.

How about stopping in purgatory?

Jews don't believe in a kind of way station to heaven where people work off their sins before entering heaven. Neither do Protestants, but Muslims and Catholics do.

The Muslim name for the place is *Barzakh* (meaning "partition"). "Before them is Barzakh till the day they are raised up" (Sura 23:100). While there, a Muslim will see what heaven and hell look like. He will be questioned by angels about his belief. The stay in Barzakh will be brief, however.

Catholics and some other Christian denominations recognize two places:

- **Purgatory** (to make clean), where people can work off their sins. It's not a pleasant place, but, eventually, the person will be eligible to be transferred to heaven.

- **Limbo** (meaning "hem" or "rim"), which is a temporary place for souls who missed out on Jesus or who weren't baptized. The idea existed in Jewish thinking prior to Jesus and was seen as a place of happiness for souls awaiting the chance to enter heaven.

  The Roman Catholic Church, according to published reports, is considering eliminating limbo from its theology.

Part IV
Shared Ideas Among the Faiths

The 5th Wave   By Rich Tennant

Religion

The Virtue of Humility

In this part . . .

Similar religious concepts help link the three religions. Judaism, Christianity, and Islam look to a messenger from God, foresee the day when the world ceases, look to forgive sin, and propose ideas of what comes after death.

Unfortunately, sibling rivalries for the minds and hearts of people have led to multiple conflicts. All three religions encourage peace, but each has let loose the dogs of war on more than one occasion.

Chapter 15

Dealing with Sin

· ·

· ·

In the Broadway show *Camelot,* Mordred bedevils his father, King Arthur, with his amoral behavior. Mordred crowns his performance by singing about the "deadly virtues." By doing so, he reverses conventional thinking: Whatever society thinks of as good — such as honesty, charity, fidelity, and humility — he believes is a sin.

As a result of his attitude and behavior, Mordred destroys Arthur's attempts to bring civilization to old England. Mordred's character illustrates sin's effect on society and how the sinner can undermine everything.

This chapter looks at how Judaism, Christianity, and Islam define and deal with sin. This is not a simple topic. All three religions focus on sin as an integral part of their beliefs, yet often disagree on what it is, where it comes from, and how a person can be saved from it.

What Is Sin, and Where Does It Come From?

Let's start with the word *sin,* which has roots in Old English, Old German, and Norse. It appears to be related to the word "to be" or "it is proven." The Hebrew word for God, *Yahweh,* is also connected to the same root concept.

The Greek version of the word *sin,* used in the New Testament, means "to miss the mark." Ancient English archers used the same word in their sport.

Regardless, none of the original definitions of *sin* seems to reflect an action against God or God's law, which is how *sin* is currently defined. We use the term regularly to label the breaking of moral or religious rules.

Sources of sin: The Devil made me do it and other reasons

If God is good and creates everything, where did sin come from? That question has kept philosophers busy for more than 2,000 years.

The prophet Ezekiel suggested that the Devil (also called *Satan* or *adversary*) was responsible for introducing man to sin because he coveted God's status. By doing so, he misled people. Satan became associated with the serpent who talked Eve into giving her husband, Adam, a piece of forbidden fruit, and with every other mishap in the Bible. Stories grew around the Devil, until he became identified with a fallen angel who was sent to Hell for his nefarious misdeeds. The tale became the source of John Milton's great late-1600s poem *Paradise Lost*. Satan has been blamed for most everything that's gone wrong ever since.

According to theologians, other possible sources of sin include

- **Humankind's corrupted heart:** The idea is that all are born in sin. Many Christian sects accept this teaching, although Jews and Muslims do not.

- **Lust:** This particular sin is considered so awful that the Devil must have created it.

- **Life itself:** Some religions have gone so far as to say that God didn't create life, which they believe is so filled with sin, that the Devil must have.

- **Covetousness** (greedily longing for something): The Ten Commandments includes this particular failing on its list of things not to do. Because God doesn't want people to covet their neighbor's possessions, the Devil must have created this particular flaw in human character.

- **Ignorance:** Lack of knowledge of God can only be the result of the Devil throwing blocks.

No religion blames God for sin. Each religion, however, defines sin differently.

Considering human nature

One of the key differences among the faiths arises in the discussion of the nature of man. Each religion views man from a different perspective. As a result, they see sin differently. The view of how people behave helps explain why people sin.

- ✔ **Muslims believe man is basically good** (Sura 7:23–29). People do follow the wrong path, but the Devil may misdirect a good person in accordance with Allah's will.

- ✔ **Christians insist man is inherently bad.** The sinning started with Adam, and the only reason God hasn't obliterated mankind for such heinous behavior is because of Jesus. "But, because of his great love for us, God, who is rich in mercy, made us alive with Christ even when we were dead in transgressions — it is by grace you have been saved" (Ephesians 2:1–5).

- ✔ **Jews once supported what became the Christian view, but argue now that man can be good or bad.** Therefore, a person can choose to sin or to follow God's laws as given in the Old Testament. Sages have educed 613 laws to be obeyed — sometimes daily, sometimes less frequently. These behaviors (called *mitzvoth* or "good deeds") include daily prayers as well as following kosher laws (see Chapter 4 for details on the laws).

Judaism: Sinners defy God's commandments

In the Hebrew Scriptures, sin is viewed as a hatred of God or defiance of his commandments. People are inclined to be evil but can overcome that feeling. In Jewish thinking, everyone sins at some time. "There is no one who does not sin," King Solomon noted.

Being born meant contact with impurity. "Behold, I was brought forth in inequity and in sin did my mother conceive me" (Psalms 51:5).

Judaism recognizes three types of sins:

- ✔ **Intentional sin (*pasha* or *mered*):** Something done in deliberate defiance of God.

- ✔ **Uncontrolled sin (*avon*):** A sin done through lust or uncontrolled emotion. The sinner knows what he is doing, but isn't trying to defy God.

- ✔ **Unintentional sin (*cheit*):** A sin committed in ignorance. The sinner doesn't know he is violating God's law.

God's response to intentional sin can be fierce, according to Bible stories. In some cases, such as the men who accidentally looked into the Ark of the Covenant, they simply were killed by God (1 Samuel 6:19). Others, like Korah, who revolted against Moses, died when the desert sands opened up under his feet (Numbers 16:18–35). In Chapter 17 of Numbers, thousands of others were killed in a plague for murmuring against Moses.

As a result of such inherent danger, Jews devoted a lot of thinking to the subject of sin. The Old Testament contains 50 or so synonyms for *sin;* the words essentially mean "to be found lacking" or "deficient."

The sin, whatever it is, can't be blamed on God. Instead, each person is responsible for his own sin.

Christianity: We're born with sin

In the New Testament, man is definitely born in sin. The idea came from the first book of the Bible. In Genesis, Adam, the first man, disobeyed God and, with his wife, Eve, ate forbidden fruit from the Tree of Knowledge. That, in later Christian thinking, caused the sin that afflicted everyone. In many ways, Adam's behavior led to a legal flaw, a violation of a contract. Paul explains the link to Adam in one of his letters: "By one man's disobedience, many were made sinners" (Romans 5:19). At the time he was writing, around 50 AD, the New Testament didn't exist, so his thinking was based on the books that are now part of the Old Testament.

Christians believe that the only person born without sin is Jesus. In some denominations, his mother, Mary, also falls into the category.

In Roman Catholic theology, Adam and Eve's big oops is called *original sin,* and Catholics believe that all followers of Christ are burdened with this sin. Original sin is different from *actual* or *personal sin,* which refers to evil words, acts, and thoughts. Actual sins can be *venal* (or minor) or *mortal* (major).

Of course, other Christian denominations don't necessarily agree with the Catholic approach. Some sects see other types of sins:

- *Concupiscence* or sexual sin
- *Eternal* or "unforgivable" sin when someone leaves the faith

Evangelical Christians argue that all behaviors not perceived as good are, by definition, sinful. Accidental sins, then, don't exist.

According to Christians, a mortal (or eternal) sin must

✔ Involve a grave matter

✔ Be committed with full knowledge of the sinner

✔ Be committed with deliberate consent of the sinner

Clearly, this kind of sin is not a mistake you stumble into. Traditionally, the seven mortal or "deadly" sins are pride, covetousness, lust, anger, gluttony, envy, and sloth.

The apostle Paul didn't stop at seven deadly sins. In two separate letters in the New Testament, Galatians and 1 Corinthians, he came up with a lengthy list of sins bound to send anyone to eternal punishment. They include

✔ Adultery

✔ Fornication (sexual relations outside marriage)

✔ Uncleanness

✔ Lasciviousness (pornography)

✔ Idolatry

✔ Witchcraft

✔ Hatred

✔ Variance (choosing another religion)

✔ Emulation (following someone down an evil path)

✔ Wrath

✔ Strife

✔ Seditions (leading people astray)

✔ Heresy

✔ Murder

✔ Drunkenness

✔ Reveling

✔ Effeminate behavior

✔ Thievery

✔ Extortion

Paul insisted that anyone who committed one of these behaviors wouldn't "inherit the Kingdom of God."

Islam: Sin comes from straying off the path

In Islam, sin is what happens when people wander off Allah's path, either through their own choice or are misled. Prophets are the guides who bring believers back to the straight and narrow.

Islam, like Judaism and Christianity, recognizes many types of sins. They include

- **Al Dhanb (offense, crime, misdeed):** "Lo, We have given thee (O Muhammad) clear victory that Allah may forgive thee of thy sin (Al Dhanb) which is passed, and that which is to come." —Sura 48 1–2

- **Al Fahsha' (vile deed, crime, adultery):** "Do not draw near to vile deeds, neither that which is seen or that which is hidden." —Sura 6:151

- **Al Wizr (sin as a heavy load, burden, encumbrance):** "Have we not given thee relief, and removed the burden (Al Wizr) which weighed down on thy back?" —Sura 94:1–3

- **Al Dalal (straying, to be lost):** The reference is to apostates.

- **Al Kufr (godlessness, atheism).**

- **Al Zulm (unjust, iniquity, unfairness).**

- **Al Ithm (crime, misdeed, offense):** "Forsake wickedness; both the open practice and the secret intention thereof. Lo! those who practice misdeeds will be awarded according to that which they have committed." — Sura 6:121

- **Al Fudjur (immorality, depravity):** "And lo! The depraved (Al Fudjur) verily will be in hell, and they will not be absent from it, they will burn therein on the Day of Judgment." —Sura 82:14–15

- **Al Khati'a (sin, offense):** "Whoso committeth a sin (Al Khati'a) or misdeed (Al Ithm), then blames it on the innocent, hath burdened himself with slander (Al Buhtan)." —Sura 4:112

- **Al Sharr (evil):** "Whoso doeth ill (Al Sharr) an atom's weight, will see it then." —Sura 99:8

- **Al Sayyi'a (offense, misdeed):** "Whoso bringeth a misdeed (Al Sayyi'a), such will be flung down on their faces in the Fire." —Sura 27:90

- **Al Su' (evil, misfortune):** "He who doeth evil (Al Su') will have the recompense thereof, and cannot find against Allah any protecting friend or helper." —Sura 4:123

The story of Job: Does suffering lead to sin?

One Bible story asks why good people suffer. In the book of Job, God is walking with Satan and pointing proudly at Job as a true believer. Satan says Job is faithful because he has everything he wants. Take away his wealth and happiness, Satan says, and Job will turn on God.

To test that theory, God lets Satan wreak havoc on Job's life, killing his family, destroying his home, and scattering his flocks. Naturally, the beleaguered man has no idea what's happening or why.

Friends drop by. They insist that Job must have done something wrong to have earned such wrath. Job even questions God, who tells him that no human has the right to challenge him.

In the end, Job retains his beliefs and is rewarded with a bigger family, more animals, and bigger homes.

✔ **Al Fasad (corruption):** "When (the hypocrite) turns away (from thee) to corrupt the world, the crops and the people are destroyed and truly Allah does not love corruption." —Sura 2:205

✔ **Al Fisk (viciousness, moral depravity):** "Verily, We have sent down unto thee clear verses and no one other than the depraved consider them a lie." —Sura 2:99

✔ **Al Buhtan (slander, lying):** "It is not for us to speak of this. Praise to Thee (Allah); this is awful slander (Al Buhtan)." —Sura 24:16

Facing Punishment for Sins

Let's assume a person sins. He robs a bank. He did it willfully and planned it. By any definition, this act is not only a crime against society but is also a sin. That's because God gave laws that were written down in the Old Testament. In fact, the third book of the Bible, Leviticus, means "laws." These rules are designed to enable a person to live a good life and so be rejoined with God in heaven after death. The laws ensure that people are accountable for their sins.

In Christian teaching, Jesus died to release mankind from the sin of Adam, but in all three religions, each person is responsible to atone for his or her own sins. Catholics confess their sins, often on a weekly basis. Jews meet annually at Yom Kippur (see Chapter 4) to confess their sins as a congregation.

What happens when a person commits such a grievous sin? Each religion views the situation differently.

Judaism: God gets angry but can forgive

In the Jewish Bible, sin makes God very angry. Really, really angry. Angrier than anyone can imagine. At one point, he became so upset that he wiped out most of mankind with a flood. In another situation, he leveled the cities of Sodom and Gomorrah. The destruction of the First Temple was the result of sin; so was the Babylonian captivity.

In modern times, some Orthodox Jews have blamed the Holocaust on the sins of the European Jews. That has not been a popular explanation because it places the fault with the victims and not on the perpetrators.

Individuals can be punished as well as entire groups. For example, King Saul (1 Samuel) is punished for failing to obey God's orders to massacre enemies. Other times, the Jewish people collectively are punished.

God is also forgiving. Sages outlined 13 attributes of God's mercy. God is

- Merciful before someone sins, because everyone is capable of sinning
- Merciful after a sin has been committed
- Merciful even when a sinner doesn't expect or deserve it
- Compassionate and eases the punishment of the sinner
- Gracious even to the undeserving sinner
- Slow to anger
- Abundant in kindness
- Truthful, so the sinner can depend on the promise of mercy
- Merciful to future generations based on the good deeds of the past
- Forgiving of intentional sins if the sinner repents
- Forgiving of deliberate affronts to him if the sinner repents
- Forgiving of sins committed in error
- Able to wipe away sins of those who repent

Christianity: Salvation is possible

In Christian theology, sin separates man from both God and the Church and sends the perpetrator to hell (for more on this topic, see Chapter 17). That's why reconciliation with both is important. Reconciliation involves obtaining forgiveness for sins. In the Middle Ages, for example, wealthy men with a long list of sins would leave money to religious groups to perform perpetual Masses in hopes of reducing the time needed to get into heaven.

Salvation — when God delivers people from sin and its consequences — is always possible, of course, but eternal damnation is inevitable without it. (See the upcoming "Receiving Redemption" section for more on how God saves sinners.)

To early Christians — and some sects today — professing belief in Jesus was enough to guarantee salvation. Today, most sects expect a bit more proof of belief. You must truly want salvation for God to grant it.

In Christianity, a mortal sin can cause a person to be *excommunicated*. In the Catholic view, that means a person is cut off from the Church and hope for salvation.

To be excommunicated once meant to be cut off from family, friends, and your community. No one wanted that. Henry II of England, for example, submitted to being whipped to seek forgiveness from the pope after being threatened with excommunication in the 1100s. In more recent times, excommunication has been used sparingly and is seen as affecting only religious life and not social status.

Islam: Cleansing by fire

The Koran recognizes Adam's original sin. (See the "Christianity: We're born with sin" section earlier in the chapter for more about original sin.) However, in Islamic teachings, Adam was one of the prophets and was forgiven by God.

All Muslims go to a kind of purgatory after death where they face questions about their past lives. Those who ask forgiveness are then allowed into heaven. The others go to hell. The eternal fires then can cleanse any sinner who has even a modest amount of faith. Also, if someone commits a sin, most Muslims don't believe that person loses his tie to the faith.

Receiving Redemption

Just like parents don't like punishing their children, God doesn't like punishing his people. So God offers his followers a way to get rid of their sins through a process called *redemption*. Sinners achieve redemption from God by making sacrifices. Without redemption, people who sin face divine punishment that could harm innocent bystanders. That's what happened in the Old Testament accounts where thousands died because someone sinned. For example, in Genesis, the towns of Sodom and Gomorrah are completely annihilated, although only few people were actually involved in the sin of attacking visitors.

The three religions have come up with a variety of reasons to explain why their followers need to be redeemed from sin. They include

- ✔ **The need for salvation:** This is seen as part of human nature, reflected in the earliest sacrifices to get rid of sin.

- ✔ **Man's shortcomings versus God's holiness:** In Christian thinking, God is holy, but man is a sinner. Redemption becomes a way for man to achieve God's *grace,* or blessing.

- ✔ **Man needs to be redeemed:** Redemption soothes a troubled conscience, which is naturally aware of the sin.

- ✔ **The law requires it:** Sinners must be punished, according to sacred texts. Otherwise, the Holy Scriptures are wrong. Redemption is the only option.

- ✔ **God demands redemption:** Many passages in the religious texts have God telling people they must atone for their sins.

- ✔ **Morality requires it:** God told his people how to act, and they must behave according to his word. But God supposedly forgives sinners when they break his rules. Therefore, he has to have a method to accomplish that.

All three religions believe that everyone has the right to choose her own path in life. This concept slipped into Judaism from Zoroastrianism (see the next section). Christians and Muslims believe that if someone chooses not to believe in her faith, then she is condemned to hell. Judaism has no such rule, but teaches that people who don't follow God's laws, as encapsulated in the faith, will not be taken into God's protection when the world ends. (See Chapter 17 for more on what happens to sinners when they die.)

When does redemption take place?

All three religions believe in a final day when God weighs the sins of each person and decides whether to redeem that person. The idea dates far back in time.

For example, the Egyptians thought Osiris, the god of the underworld, conducted a judgment after death. The Book of the Dead provided answers to the difficult questions the dead person would face.

Later, Zoroastrianism put forth the belief that the soul of man must pass over the dangerous Bridge of the Requiter. There, all are judged by Ahura Mazda, the faith's highest god. Those who are good and followed "the truth" enter the kingdom of everlasting joy and light. The ones who chose to follow "the lie" are consigned to the regions of horror and darkness. Many of these ideas seep into monotheism.

Judaism: Purification

The day is coming, according to the prophets, when the Jews' sins will be judged by God. The humble and lowly will be purified, and the others will face the consequences of sin.

The signs to look for are the return of Jews to Israel and the rebuilding of the Temple. When that happens, watch out.

Jews do not believe in Hell. So the only consequence of failing to atone for sin is not being reunited with God. To Jews, that is a terrible fate.

Christianity: Resurrection

The Gospels repeatedly warn of a coming resurrection of the dead. The signs vary depending on the sect, but they include great diseases, famine, enormous earthquakes, and other natural upheavals. Then everyone will be judged and punished or rewarded according to her sins and virtues in this life.

The authors didn't fool around. The threat of eternal damnation was bound to capture everyone's attention.

In the book of Revelation in the Bible, John foresaw a series of judgments: seven seals opened, seven trumpets blown, seven bowls poured out. Members of the 12 Jewish tribes will be saved; others will be cast into a fiery pit. (To read more about John's predictions, pick up a copy of *The Book of Revelation For Dummies* by Richard Wagner and Larry R. Helyer [Wiley].)

Islam: Judgment

Muhammad believed the Day of Judgment was coming. Because no one knows when that will be, he identified signs to look for:

> "At length, when the sight is dazed, and the moon is buried in darkness. And the sun and moon are joined together." —Sura 75:6–9

The Koran is loaded with other clues. If you notice any of these things happening, watch out:

- Lewd acts and working to bring about lewd acts
- The cutting off of relationships
- The trusting of deceivers
- Abundance of wealth
- Increasing of ignorance
- Numerous afflictions
- Widespread trading and business

Those are just minor signs. Major signs are

- A landslide in the East and a landslide in the West.
- A landslide in the Arabian Peninsula.
- Smoke.
- Appearance of the Dajjaal, the beast of the earth, and Gog and Magog, who may have been leaders of Jewish opponents. The terms are used throughout the Old Testament in different ways. They have become symbols of opposition to faith.
- Rising of the sun from the West.
- Fire which would appear from the lower part of Aden (Yemen).

When the day gets here, every Muslim will be weighed against his sins, with those who are worthy going to heaven and those who fall short being purified in hell.

How does someone get redeemed?

Getting rid of sin involves everything from ritual cleansing to prayer. All three religions agree that God always forgives *transgressions* (a fancy word for sins).

How a person obtains forgiveness varies depending on the religion. In early times, human sacrifice was used. The chosen person was asked to carry the sins to heaven with him or her. Later, an animal was substituted, symbolically burdened with sins and then driven into the wilderness. That's where we get the word *scapegoat*.

Judaism

Repentance (the Hebrew word is *teshuvah* and means "return to God") has always been a key component of the faith. Even the destruction of the Temple failed to dampen enthusiasm for it. Rabbis taught that *atonement* (something done to make up for one's sins) that once took place at the Temple now occurs at home.

In the days of the Temple, sinners received forgiveness through the priest by sacrificing a pure animal. The ritual would have been accompanied by song, prayer, and other offerings.

Early biblical writings insisted on sacrifice as an atonement for sin. People were expected to atone for two categories of sins:

- ✔ Sins against man
- ✔ Sins against God

Although sacrifices continued as long as the Temple stood, prophets often rejected sacrifice as not being of interest to God, who, they said, would rather see proper behavior and good deeds.

> "For I desire mercy, not sacrifice, and acknowledgement of God rather than burnt offerings." —Hosea 6:6

In time, as ideas changed, biblical rules about a required sacrifice softened. Repentance and prayer sufficed in the books of Esther and Jonah without the death of an animal.

As a result, the sacrifices ended, but redemption went on. These days, Jews gather for the Day of Atonement (also called *Yom Kippur;* see Chapter 4) as prescribed in Leviticus 15.

The day is spent in fasting and confession of sins as a group. In unison, Jews say, "Forgive us, pardon us, grant us atonement," for a litany of general mistakes against God. On the Day of Atonement, Jews are also expected to ask, and be granted, forgiveness for sins against another person.

Christianity

Christians agree that redemption comes through Jesus. His suffering and death were the atonement that overcomes punishment due to man for his sin. It fulfills the demands of divine justice and supports the sinner who believes.

That idea is echoed in one of the most revered lines in the New Testament: "Greater love has no man than this, that a man lay down his life for his friends" (John 15:13).

Different denominations have developed various solutions to the redemption problem. They include

- ✔ **Baptism:** All Christians believe in baptism. Some sects see it as a way to ritualistically wash away past sins.
- ✔ **Confession:** A Catholic may talk to a priest in private to reveal his sins. The priest then assigns certain actions, such as prayers, to erase the sins. A priest is not permitted to discuss what a person told him during a confession.

✔ **Belief:** Profession of belief in Jesus is sufficient to wipe out sins. Some people waited until the last possible moment for such action. Emperor Constantine the Great, who legalized Christianity in the fourth century, was on his deathbed, for example, when he announced his belief in Jesus.

Islam

The Koran covers atonement and forgiveness. They are seen as two separate topics. Atonement refers to human existence; forgiveness, to Allah at the day of final judgment. So people atone during their lives, but they must wait for the end of the world to find out if Allah has forgiven them.

Atonement

People can achieve atonement through a variety of actions:

✔ **Giving alms:** Making charitable donations of money, food, clothing, and so on

✔ **Good deeds:** Helping the needy and supporting the local mosque

✔ **Prayers:** Fulfilling the Islamic requirement (see Chapter 8) of praying daily

✔ **Belief:** Believing fully in the Prophet Mohammad and in the teachings of Islam

Forgiveness

The options for achieving forgiveness and avoiding much unpleasantness on Judgment Day include

✔ **Good works:** The positive actions a person takes are measured against his sins.

✔ **Obedience to Allah:** A Muslim's obedience to the will of Allah is very important.

✔ **Fasting:** Believers must fast for two months to earn forgiveness for murder. Fasting for three days will obtain forgiveness for a lie.

✔ **Pilgrimage:** As noted in Chapter 8, Muslims are required to visit Mecca, the holy city of their faith, at least once in their lifetime.

✔ **Giving alms:** This is one of the pillars of the faith. See Chapter 8 for details.

✔ **Reading the Koran:** The holy text is seen as more than simple a guide. "When the Koran is read, listen to it, that ye may obtain mercy" (Sura 7:204).

✔ **Recitation of the Creed:** Muhammad told followers, "He is saved by saying, 'I testify that there is no god but Allah, and I testify that Muhammad is the prophet of Allah.'"

Unforgivable sins

Unlike Judaism and Christianity, Islam recognizes three heinous acts for which no redemption is possible.

✔ **The attributing of partners to Allah:** "Allah pardons not that partners should be ascribed unto him. He pardons all except that" (Sura 4:116).

This rule developed because Allah, prior to Muhammad, was said to have had two daughters. Muhammad wanted to be sure that only Allah was worshipped. The rule parallels the first commandment that Moses received in the Old Testament: "Thou shall have no other gods before me."

All three religions condemn believers of other gods. However, because Judaism has no formal theology involving heaven and hell, it can only suggest God punishes nonbelievers. Christians and Muslims are sure hell awaits them.

✔ **The killing of a believer:** "Whoso slayeth a believer of set purpose, his reward is hell forever. Allah is wroth with him and hath cursed him and prepared for him an awful doom" (Sura 4:93).

This unforgivable sin caused a problem in wars between Muslim factions, such as Iran and Iraq, because war leads to death. The same concern came with the sixth commandment: "Thou shalt not kill."

Philosophers found a loophole. The word in the commandment that refers to killing means "murder." As a result, because self-defense is permitted, a soldier can go to war and fire away. In Islam, the same logic is followed. Death in war is not deliberate, which is banned, but accidental. Moreover, Muhammad led an army into battle.

✔ **Apostasy:** This sin refers to people who are raised Muslim but choose to leave the faith. They face a sure trip to hell when Allah starts judging everyone. "Lo! those who disbelieve after their profession of belief, and afterward grow in infidelity, their repentance will never be accepted. And such are those who are astray" (Sura 3:90).

Not all Muslims are willing to wait. Someone who leaves Islam for another religion can actually be killed in some Arabic countries. One of the sayings of Muhammad is that it's not permissible to take the life of a Muslim except in one of the three cases: the married adulterer, a life for a life (if the person is Muslim), and the deserter of Islam.

Excommunication: When Redemption Isn't an Option

Excommunication is serious business and has been a very successful tactic for centuries. Jews and Christians have been known to *excommunicate* those who differ from the faith. In the Christian view, excommunication severs a person's link to God and chance for redemption. The Jews see excommunication as separating a person from the Jewish community, not from God. Only God can forgive or punish in Jewish teachings.

Philosopher Bernard Spinoza, for example, was ousted from his synagogue in the 1600s because he promoted religious views unacceptable to the Orthodox leaders. However, excommunication is rare now. Today, with intermarriage extraordinarily high, and Jews increasingly assimilating and leaving the faith, punitive action would be counterproductive.

The Catholic Church still uses excommunication, which was once a formidable weapon in the war between secular and religious leaders.

In the Middle Ages, kings would grovel to avoid being cut off from God after popes threatened their excommunication. Some kings, like Ferdinand the Great, were excommunicated several times. Other Christians were not allowed contact with an excommunicant.

The weapon lost significance during the Great Schism in the Middle Ages when three popes were in office at the same time and spent their days excommunicating each other.

Still, Catholics in modern times have been excommunicated for various reasons. In the 1960s, priests upset by church reforms announced in 1963 and who refused to drop Latin from the Mass were excommunicated. In 1997, Father Tissa Balasuriya, a Sri Lankan priest, was excommunicated after his writings about the ordination of women and original sin were ruled unacceptable by the Roman Catholic hierarchy.

This extreme punishment was never part of other Christian sects. Some do practice *shunning* — refusing to let anyone talk to the offender and forcing him or her either to leave the religion or apologize.

Chapter 16

Good Heavens: Life after Death

There's just something funny about afterlife. Joke books are full of examples. Here's a good one:

> After a preacher died and went to heaven, he noticed that a New York cab driver had been awarded a higher place than he was.
>
> "I don't understand," he complained to God. "I devoted my entire life to my congregation."
>
> "Our policy here in heaven is to reward results," God explained. "Now, was your congregation well attuned to you whenever you gave a sermon?"
>
> "Well," the minister said, "some in the congregation fell asleep from time to time."
>
> "Exactly," said God, "and when people rode in this man's taxi, they not only stayed awake, they even prayed."

There are many more jokes like this. They're built around the idea of an afterlife, the key component of many religions. This chapter examines what Judaism, Christianity, and Islam teach about paradise and its heavenly occupants.

Where Do Ideas about the Afterlife Come From?

Death puzzled early people, so they developed their own answers about what happened to people after they fell into eternal sleep.

Early humans: Always be prepared

Early graves are often found with remnants of hunting equipment and even food, indicating that survivors thought the dead person would be able to use the supplies in the next life.

Graves found in ancient Mesopotamia, for example, contained food either to nourish the deceased on his long journey or as an offering to the gods. In some cases, there were toys, presumably so the individual would have a favorite object alongside. In ancient Greece, horses occasionally were sacrificed so the deceased would have something to ride after death.

Egyptians: Soul men who needed their mummies

Folks along the Nile composed a Book of the Dead, a guide to what questions the dead person's soul (called *ka*) would face through the treacherous waters of the underworld.

Here's a snippet from one of the chapters in the book:

> "Homage to you, Great God, the Lord of the double Ma'at (Truth).
> I have come to you, my Lord,
> I have brought myself here to behold your beauties.
> I know you, and I know your name,
> And I know the names of the two and forty gods,
> Who live with you in the Hall of the Two Truths,
> Who imprison the sinners, and feed upon their blood."

Knowing the names would help the deceased move past this interview with Osiris, the supreme god of the dead.

Egyptians were convinced that a soul could return to the deceased person's body. To make sure that the soul could return to its home, the Egyptians created mummies. They removed the deceased person's organs and wrapped the body to preserve its shape. Because this was an expensive process, usually only the wealthy could afford it. However, the Egyptians mummified sacred animals like cats, bulls, and crocodiles.

Grave robbers, who were often poor, typically destroyed the mummified body. That way they got the loot as well as revenge on the wealthy resident.

By the way, the word *mummy* comes from the resin used to seal the body, which in Egyptian is called "mum."

Greeks: Dead on their feet

Keepers of the most dominant culture in the Middle East, Greeks thought the dead went through a deep abyss into a kind of netherworld called *Hades*. There, unchanged from the time they died, they wandered for eternity. To get to Hades, they had to cross the River Styx with a creepy boatman, Charon, and his multiheaded dog, Cerberus. The fierce canine made a cameo appearance in one of the *Harry Potter* books.

Hades was divided into different regions, including Tartarus, which corresponds to the Christian hell; and the Elysian Fields, which is closer to heaven (see the next section).

Although multiple, conflicting myths existed about the afterworld, Greeks tended to agree that Hades was located below ground and entered somewhere in the far West. Some historians wonder if the Greeks got the idea of a netherworld existing deep in the bowels of the earth from Greek sailors who had visited the Grand Canyon (Greek sailors were famous for traveling the globe).

In addition, Greeks thought mortals could become immortal. Hercules is an example of a mortal raised to the divine. That idea would also influence the later monotheistic religions.

Romans: A-wandering we shall go

The conquerors of the known world borrowed a lot from the Greeks. They also thought the dead wandered aimlessly in the Elysian Fields. According to both Greek and Roman theology, that dead zone could be reached by the living.

Dead people would enter Hades through an opening in the Earth. These entrances could be anywhere — one was thought to be in Rome. Once inside, you faced three judges who asked about your life. Then you drank from the River Lethe, the river of forgetfulness and one of five rivers in the underworld. The water made you forget your previous life. From there, you might go to the Elysian Fields; the Plain of Asphodel, which was akin to heaven; or to Tartarus, where you'd be harassed by the Furies, the flying images of revenge. Eventually, you could be reborn.

Authors borrow from ancient beliefs

Mythology about death from past cultures remains popular today. Homer, the blind poet whose two books served as the Greek Bible in ancient times and are still studied, depicts his heroes visiting Hades and talking to the "shades" of dead warriors.

Virgil, the Roman poet whose description of Rome's founding remains a classic, has his hero, Aeneas, bravely follow a long corridor into the underworld.

In mythology, Hercules braves the underworld to kidnap Charon's multiheaded dog that accompanies him on trips across the River Styx. The seasons are explained because Pluto, the god of the underworld, marries Persephone, who is forced to spend part of her time above ground (spring) and part below (winter). Television shows like *Hercules* and *Xena: Warrior Princess* created plot lines based on these ancient myths.

J.K Rowling, in her popular *Harry Potter* books, used the three-headed dog Cerberus to guard an entrance to a secret chamber.

The Romans also believed that ghosts could return to earth to haunt the living. In the *Superman* comic, newspaper editor Perry White used to exclaim "Great Caesar's ghost" in moments of consternation. The real ghost supposedly walked about after the emperor's death in 44 BC. Shakespeare used that superstition in his play about Julius Caesar.

Zoroastrians: Choosing between good and evil

The Zoroastrian religion was born in Persia around 550 BC and created the concepts of heaven and hell as we know them.

A mystic named Zarathustra (Zoroaster in Greek) developed a religion featuring two competing gods:

- ✔ Ahura Mazda, representing good, was initially a minor god in the Babylonian pantheon.

- ✔ Ahriman, representing evil, was the proponent of "the lie." Anyone who followed an alternative religion was, in Zarathustra's view, a believer in Ahriman.

Humans were asked to join in the battle between the two and tip the balance, presumably toward the good side.

Zarathustra thought people should prefer Ahura Mazda and would be rewarded for that decision by going to a wonderful place after death. Those who followed Ahriman, however, would be punished in an awful hell-like locale.

What Is Heaven?

Heaven is considered God's home, and was introduced to mankind in the Old Testament. From there, it moves into Christian and Muslim theology. In various Old Testament books, heaven is presented as a physical portion of the universe and as God's living quarters when he's not in the Temple.

The texts assign different functions and attributes to heaven:

- **Firmament:** In this role, heaven is perched on pillars and is divided so that half exists above the earth and the other half is below the earth. This heaven has windows and a foundation. The heavenly waters, which eventually flooded the planet, are held there.

  Blessings come through the windows, while the stars, moon, and sun are set like gems in the firmament. (*Firmament* also means sky.)

- **Everything in the sky:** Later writings suggested that heaven includes the firmament as well as storehouses that hold wind, rain, and snow, along with virtues. "Truth sprouts from the earth and justice peers down from heaven." —Psalm 85:11

- **Home of signs:** The early faithful believed that God used signs to communicate with his people. (No, we're not talking about stop signs and billboards.) For example, after the flood, God placed a rainbow in heaven to indicate his promise never to destroy the earth again. Heaven also reveals signs of God's actions to come on earth.

- **House of God:** Before churches or synagogues, people thought God lived in heaven. "Above the circle of the Earth, God looked down upon the Earth, where the people looked like grasshoppers." —Isaiah 40:22

- **Source of sustenance:** When the Jews fled Egypt and were starving in the desert, they were given *manna,* bread that came from heaven. Blessings originate there, too.

Why a firmament?

In the late 1800s, religious historians were stunned to read a newly uncovered Babylonian book called the *Enuma Elish* that was far older than the Bible and yet contained elements of the biblical creation story.

In the Babylonian account, Tiamat (the name means "chaos") was causing the gods all sorts of problems. They finally hired a hero named Marduk to slay her. He filled her with air and split her in half, creating a canopy above and below the earth, just like the firmament.

Moreover, the Bible reports that before the creation of the earth, there was chaos in the universe. The Hebrew word for chaos is based on the Babylonian word "Tiamat."

Who you'll meet in heaven

God has company in heaven. Several individuals in the Old and New Testaments are taken directly into the sky. They include:

- ✔ Angels such as Gabriel, Michael, and Raphael (see the "Angels: God's Helpers" section at the end of the chapter for more on these folks)
- ✔ The prophet Elijah
- ✔ Jesus (see Chapter 5 for the account of how Jesus was taken into heaven)
- ✔ Enoch, an Old Testament patriarch
- ✔ Paul, the apostle who helped establish Christianity
- ✔ John, author of Revelation, who claimed to have taken a tour of heaven
- ✔ Mary, Jesus's mother.

In Islamic teachings, Muhammad enjoys a visit to heaven instead of dying and is taken up whole like Elijah and Mary.

According to an Islamic legend, Muhammad was sleeping in the Ka'baa when two archangels, Jibril and Mikail, opened up his body and purified his heart by removing all traces of error, doubt, idolatry, and paganism. They replaced such negative stuffing with wisdom and belief.

Muhammad then climbed aboard a horselike animal with a human face and rode to the al-Aqsa mosque in Jerusalem, rising to heaven on a shaft of light.

Opening up the gates of heaven to the righteous

Heaven was seen initially as God's residence alone. Gradually, people began to believe that heaven is where the souls of the righteous go after their deaths.

Jesus serves as the prime example of that view. In Christian theology, Jesus's death, resurrection, and ascent into heaven serve as the model for all true believers. (See Chapter 5 for more about the events surrounding Jesus's death.)

Various sects of Christianity offer differing views. Some believe souls go directly to heaven and that human bodies can be discarded. Others believe that bodies of believers will be revived when Jesus returns to earth.

In Islam, only Muhammad goes to heaven (see the preceding section). His followers "sleep" while they await the Day of Judgment. Their souls remain with them until that day. However, those destined for hell begin to suffer; those on their way to heaven begin to enjoy the bliss.

Traditional Jewish teachings contain no concept of heaven. Instead, Jews "sleep" and await union with God at the end of days.

What is heaven like?

Each religion has its own ideas about heaven.

Judaism

Jewish scholars never developed any blueprint for heaven. The idea of heaven, beyond being God's house, didn't make it into writing. Jews believe that people must worry about earth and their lives here, and let God tend to whatever happens next.

They accept that God uses the afterlife to provide ultimate justice and to let the wicked seek some sort of final redemption. In heaven, everyone enjoys the radiance of the divine presence. It's a spiritual space without ego, aggression, and resentment.

Jews don't believe that they alone will inhabit heaven. There's room for righteous Gentiles. Individual ethical behavior is the only criteria for inclusion. Of course, many Jews believe that their religion provides the best guide to leading such an ethical life.

Christianity

Christian views about heaven vary by denomination, but most agree on two points:

- Heaven is a great place with no pain, disease, or other human weaknesses.
- People bask in the presence of Jesus.

Biblical accounts provide a few additional descriptions:

- No marriage
- No rust, moths, or other forms of natural decay and destruction
- No thieves or theft

Believers foresee a lot of worship, fellowship, and good deeds.

Unlike Judaism, Christians were given an image of heaven. John, in the book of Revelation, described his stopover in the sky motel. He saw multiple glorious thrones, incredible beasts, and elderly people with crowns on their heads, among other miraculous sights.

> "And there were seven lamps of fire burning before the throne, which are the seven Sprits of God." —Revelation 4:5

The vivid description helped give Christians a sense of what awaited them. Later writers enhanced the view. For example, Thomas Aquinas, the great philosopher from the Middle Ages, decided in the 1200s that seven celestial bodies — the sun, moon, and five visible planets — corresponded to the seven heavens in John's vision. One was fiery, only in the sky; another was filled with water. The top layer, or seventh heaven, was filled with light and angels. God lived there, too.

You can get the complete picture of heaven in the biblical book of Revelation or by picking up the *Book of Revelation For Dummies* by Richard Wagner and Larry R. Helyer (Wiley).

Islam

Muslims will have a busier time in their heaven. *Mutahsibir* (heaven) offers sensual pleasure, eating, and happiness. Men will particularly enjoy their stay there. They will be feted by young women. If they get thirsty, they can visit either of two gardens that feature fountains along with lots of fresh fruit.

Sages added to the description. A believer will be given

- A large, private garden.
- Gems, either rubies or emeralds.

- A mansion with 70 rooms, and each room with 70 doors.

- A throne for reclining.

- An *houri* (a dancing girl) who is wearing 70 suits of clothes, each of a different color. She will be beautiful, and the clothes are so thin that her "flesh and blood and bones, even bone marrow, will be visible," according to the Koran.

Much like some Christians, Muhammad also envisioned high-rise heavens. He described heaven as having multiple levels, a floor plan initially proposed by Zoroastrians and Gnostics.

In Muslim belief, Muhammad made a one-day visit to heaven before moving there permanently. In the account in the Koran, he was sleeping by the Ka'baa, the sacred building in Mecca, when the miraculous journey took place.

In the first heaven Muhammad met Adam; in the second, John the Baptist and Jesus; in the third, Joseph; in the fourth, Enoch; in the fifth, Aaron; in the sixth, Moses; and in the seventh, Abraham.

Why go to heaven?

Considering the wonderful descriptions of heaven, it's no wonder most people have the place marked on their maps as a final destination. While religions all chart plans for reaching it, including proper behavior and belief, holy books contain detailed accounts of people taken up into heaven without dying. Scholars who study religion have come up with four explanations for their ascension.

- **Absorption:** Scholars call it an "invasion." This would not be a military raid, but rather an intrusion into the unearthly realm. Elijah's removal from earth on a fiery chariot is seen as an example. (See the biblical book of 2 Kings 2:11–12.)

- **Source of revelation:** Just like when your boss calls you into his office and tells you to close the door so he can talk to you about a new procedure or policy, sometimes God called prophets into heaven to give them a message to take back to the people. Moses gets the Ten Commandments after walking up Mount Sinai into heaven. Later, his brother, Aaron, and the elders of the tribes have a similar meeting with God. The prophet Ezekiel describes his visit to heaven as well and the message he received there. Muhammad, too, shares what he learned on his nocturnal adventure.

✔ **Becoming immortal:** When people are taken to heaven physically and don't return, they are believed to have everlasting life. Initially in the Bible, only Elijah and Enoch were granted this special privilege. However, by the second century BC, heaven was being seen in the Zoroastrian light as the final resting place of the righteous.

Drawing on Greek and Zoroastrian theology, Daniel wrote that the righteous dead are resurrected and, "shining like the stars forever and ever," become immortal (Daniel 12:3).

Matthew echoed that idea in the New Testament: "The righteous shall shine like lights in the kingdom of their fathers." —Matthew 13:34

✔ **Providing a taste of the future:** Initially, Jews felt that some people might visit heaven when they died like everyone else, but then went to some kind of holding place *(sheol)* instead of staying in heaven. Isaiah, for example, ascends to heaven, but doesn't stay there or indicate an intent to return.

Later authors in the apocryphal books of Enoch 1 and Enoch 2, written a few years before Jesus lived, describe Isaiah's visit to heaven. God promises that the prophet will return to heaven and live permanently there. This concept then is amplified in Christianity.

Angels: God's Helpers

Heaven has room for more than the righteous dead. God has angels who live with him in heaven. Few religions agree on what these messengers are like. In Judaism, for example, angels are very human without the wings and halos that often enhance their appearance in Christianity. Angels are very active in Christianity and Islam, even interfering with human life, but not in Judaism. In fact, God is very clear in the story of the Jewish Exodus from Egypt that he, not an angel, inflicted the damage on the Egyptians.

Early concepts of angels

Angels have a long history dating back to before any monotheistic religion existed.

Sumerians

The oldest known civilization in the Middle East had plenty of angels. Some 5,000-year-old stone carvings the Sumerians left behind reveal their belief in angels who ferried messages between their gods and mankind.

The Sumerians also introduced the idea of *guardian angels*, those helpful creatures assigned to protect their charges through life. The Sumerians apparently prayed to those angels, much as pious folks call on angels for assistance today.

Stone altars in excavated Sumerian homes appear to have been dedicated to angels, based on the writings and engravings. Temple walls are festooned with painted images of winged people.

Egyptians

Hieroglyphic images of angel-like beings dating back 4,500 years still grace temple walls in Egypt. One cult worshipped Hunmanit, a group of gods that looked like the rays of the sun. One historian described the image "like the Christian representation of the angel choir of the seraphim."

The Hunmanit was charged with protecting the sun. Because the sun was vital to life, the Hunmanit took on the guardian angel role as well.

Semitic tribes

Not to be outdone by their counterparts, nomadic tribesmen created an angelic army about 4,000 years ago. The winged horde was divided into units and answerable to their array of gods. Each deity had its own group of winged messengers. The angels had their own hierarchy, an idea that would find a home in Christianity.

Assyrians

These fierce fighters also believed in guardian angels and left carved statues of winged beings for archaeologists to find.

Babylonians

They believed angels watched their every move. In one inscription, Nabopolassar, father of Nebuchadnezzar, the king who conquered Jerusalem, wrote, "He (Marduk) sent a tutelary deity (cherub) of grace to go at my side; in everything that I did, he made my work to succeed."

Zoroastrians

Zarathustra, the founder of Zoroastrianism, borrowed his angelic figures from the pagan faiths around him. Mithras was an angel who mediated between heaven and earth. Eventually, he would be called judge and preserver of the world. He was adored as the sun and as a friend, a kind of guardian angel.

Zoroastrianism identified six important angels:

- The Archangel of Good Thought
- The Archangel of Right
- The Archangel of Dominion
- The Archangel of Piety
- The Archangel of Prosperity
- The Archangel of Immorality

The population of heavenly hosts also included at least 40 lesser angels called Adorable Ones. They came in both genders and were linked to some quality or attribute. Guardian angels nested on a lower level and were assigned to a particular person to serve as his protector, guide, and conscience.

Angels in monotheism

All that wing beating in early civilizations stirred up interest in angels in Judaism, Christianity, and Islam.

Judaism

Angels flit around the Jewish Bible. The term *angel* is derived from the Greek *angelos,* which means "messenger." In Hebrew, that's *malak.* The name of the prophet Malachi, who has a book ascribed to him in the canon, is derived from that word.

Messengers first appear in the Bible in the story of Abraham. Abraham greets visitors to his tent who tell him that he and his aged wife will bear a son, a laughable matter because Abraham is 100 and Sarah is 90. But the angels don't mislead the couple: Their son is named Isaac, a name derived from the Hebrew word for laughter.

Then later in the book of Genesis, their grandson Jacob dreams of a ladder filled with angels going to and from heaven.

> "When he reached a certain place, Jacob stopped for the night because the sun had set. Taking one of the stones there, he put it under his head and lay down to sleep. He had a dream in which he saw a stairway resting on the earth, with its top reaching to heaven, and the angels of God were ascending and descending on it." —Genesis 28:11–13

You won't recognize biblical angels from their description in Genesis. Modern descriptions always include wings and, usually, *halos,* those circles of lights that illuminate angel hairdos. No angels in the Old Testament are given those assets. In the dream, they are walking up and down the ladder, unable to fly.

Jewish sages decided the angels needed names. Sages identified four areas in which man needed assistance, and then assigned angels to each task. That way, the angels serve as channels for God's actions on earth.

- **Michael** ("like the merciful God") oversees mercy.

- **Gabriel** ("my strength is God") oversees power and judgment.

- **Oriel** ("my light is God") oversees knowledge of the future.

- **Rafael** ("my healer is God") oversees health.

Their roles are reflected in the traditional way they flank God in Jewish philosophy. Michael and Gabriel stand at his sides. Oriel stands in front; Rafael, behind.

In many ways, the angels replace Greek and Roman deities who shared those same attributes. Athena, for example, was the goddess of wisdom; Apollo, the god of knowledge. In time, those attributes passed into Christianity and were assigned to angels.

Christianity

Angels play a significant role in early Christian theology. The angel Gabriel alerts Mary that she is pregnant with Jesus and tells her husband, Joseph, not to be alarmed. Angels hover around the manger where Jesus is born and carry the news of his birth to the heaven and earth.

They are also there at Jesus's resurrection. "As (Mary Magdalene) wept, she bent over to look into the tomb and saw two angels in white, seated where Jesus's body had been, one at the head and the other at the foot." —John 20:12

As with the Zoroastrians, the Christians came up with a hierarchy of angels. Each category involved different roles in heaven and with men. The seven categories are:

- Angels

- Archangels

- Principalities

- Powers

- Virtues

- Dominions

- Thrones

To augment that army, there are cherubim and seraphim. *Cherubim* are in charge of stars and light. *Seraphim* guard God's throne and continually sing his praises. Separately, guardian angels — the kind that have been around for millennia — hover over their charges.

Archangels are the most familiar to Christians. There are supposed to be seven of them, including Michael, Raphael, and Gabriel. Each is assigned a different sphere of influence. Michael, for example, is the traditional protector of Israel and the Roman Catholic Church. Other angels are assigned such areas as business, the military, and politics.

Like Jews, Christians originally didn't believe in graven images of God or his angels. However, after Constantine legalized Christianity, artists began to depict angels. Renaissance painters eventually created the cherubic characters we are familiar with today.

Islam

In Islam, angels are messengers from God. They brought revelations to Muhammad and helped him prepare for his journey to heaven.

Belief in angels is so strong that it is a requirement in Islam. Muslims see angels (literally) in a different light. Their angels are created from light and are invisible to humans.

They have several basic aspects:

- ✔ They don't have *free will,* so they can't act on their own.
- ✔ They carry out all of Allah's laws without question.
- ✔ They endlessly praise and glorify Allah, just as Jewish angels do for Yahweh.
- ✔ They are honest, tireless, and efficient.

No Muslim has tried to count the angels, but they have identified four of them:

- ✔ **Gabriel,** the messenger carrying Allah's messages to human ears.
- ✔ **Israfil,** who will blow the trumpet on the Day of Judgment. In Jewish and Christian writing, Gabriel gets that assignment.
- ✔ **Michael,** who brings rain and food to people.
- ✔ **Izrail,** the angel of death.

In addition, angels called Munkar and Nakir are sent to a person's grave to question him after his death.

Chapter 17

Hell in a Nutshell

. . . .

In This Chapter

▶ Understanding the origins of hell

▶ Appreciating how hell matured in the monotheistic faith

▶ Meeting the Devil and his advocates

. . . .

*B*ecause the chapter on heaven started with a joke, we'll tell one about hell, too.

A highly successful executive woman was tragically hit by a bus and died. She arrived in heaven where she was met by God.

"Welcome to heaven," God said. "Before you get settled in, though, it seems we have a problem. Strangely enough, we've never once had an executive make it this far, and we're not really sure what to do with you."

"No problem, God. Just let me in," the woman said.

God replied, "What we're going to do is let you spend a day in hell and a day in heaven, and then you can choose where you want to spend eternity."

God put the executive in an elevator and it went down to hell. The doors opened, and the executive found herself stepping out onto the putting green of a beautiful golf course.

In the distance was a country club, and standing in front of her were all of her friends — fellow executives whom she had worked with. They were all dressed in evening gowns and cheering for her. They ran up and kissed her on both cheeks, and they talked about old times.

They played an excellent round of golf and, at night, went to the country club where she enjoyed an excellent steak and lobster dinner. She met the Devil, who was actually a really nice guy (kinda cute), and she had a great time telling jokes and dancing.

She was having such a good time that before she knew it, it was time to leave. Everybody shook her hand and waved goodbye as she got on the elevator. The elevator went up to heaven, and she found God waiting for her.

"Now it's time to spend a day in heaven," God said.

So she spent the next 24 hours lounging around on clouds and playing the harp and singing. She had a great time, and, before she knew it, her 24 hours were up.

"So, you've spent a day in hell and you've spent a day in heaven. Now you must choose your eternity," God said.

The woman paused for a second and then replied, "Well, I never thought I'd say this. I mean, heaven has been really great and all, but I think I had a better time in hell."

So God escorted her to the elevator, and again she went down to hell. When the elevator doors opened, she found herself standing in a desolate wasteland covered in garbage and filth. She saw her friends dressed in rags, picking up the garbage and putting it in sacks. The Devil came up to her and put his arm around her.

"I don't understand," stammered the woman. "Yesterday I was here, and there was a golf course and a country club, and we ate lobster and we danced and had a great time. Now all there is a wasteland of garbage, and all of my friends look miserable."

The Devil looked at her and smiled. "Yesterday we were recruiting you; today you're staff."

To the monotheistic religions and its believers, what happens after you die is not comical. Each faith has developed its own answers. This chapter looks at the origin of and concepts about hell, that dismal damnation where sinners suffer.

Starting with the Roots of Hell

The Bible refers to hell many times, but typically uses the word *Gehenna,* which is a Greek word. That's a nod to the Greek underworld *(Hades)* ruled by a deity with the same name. Hades was a brother of the supreme god, Zeus, and chose to rule over the dead by drawing lots.

Hades' realm was dark and gloomy, but not filled with whips, evil demons, or torment. Instead, the dead existed as shadows of themselves, simply walking about in complete boredom.

Hell actually conveys that meaning. It is derived from an Old English or Germanic word meaning "to conceal." There are no fiery furnaces in that definition, only a sense of a place that is covered or hidden away.

Revealing the earliest references

Egyptians believed the dead must survive a labyrinth before achieving eternal rest (see Chapter 16 for more on this). The Babylonians and Assyrians had no doubt that the afterlife was filled with dangerous demons and other horrors. Of course, fire was present to scorch those who deserved it.

Canaanites named Belial as lord of the abyss, an undersea pit. Moloch, a god whom the Israelites detested because he required child sacrifices, was viewed as lord of a subterranean kingdom of flaming lava.

Jews' souls go to Sheol

The Jewish term for Hades is *Sheol* (meaning "grave"), where the dead live in darkness and gloom. The Jewish Bible saw Sheol as a dismal and dusty city with high, impregnable walls and barred gates. That's the Greek view, too. The Jews were overrun by the Greeks (see Chapter 3 for details) and picked up a lot of their culture. However, Sheol was a temporary place where the deceased waited for God to resurrect them, either in body or spirit.

The righteous may receive fresh water, but sinners are not punished in Sheol. In the apocryphal book Ezra IV, dead souls enjoy seven days of freedom to witness the joys awaiting the righteous and the torments for the sinners.

By the time of Jesus, writers built up Sheol with some fires to blister sinners. They also amplified its meaning. Bodies deteriorate in the grave, so Sheol began to represent a state of degradation from any cause, including sin or simple misfortune.

Souls in Gehenna are goners

The concept of hell got a new name, based on the Valley of Hinnom. This area ran south and southwest of old Jerusalem and had an evil reputation. Ancient Jewish kings once sacrificed animals and children to idols there.

When King Josiah reformed the faith in the seventh century BC and converted Judaism to complete monotheism (see Chapter 3), he condemned the most notorious portion of the valley, which became a garbage pit. Onlookers no doubt were sure they were getting a hint of eternal punishment just looking at the place.

In the New Testament, *Gehenna* (the Greek version of the valley's Hebrew name) is often translated as hell. Christians also used the Greek words *Hades* and *Tartarus* to designate hell.

Muslims can find ten synonyms for hell in the Koran. The most common is *Jahannam,* which is derived from the Hebrew *Gehenna.* In fact, the Koran mentions heaven and hell an equal number of times, which, to believers, is a numerical miracle.

Why punishment in hell?

The Greek poet Homer suggested that sinners might get punished in Hades. Later, Greek cults picked up on that idea and added punishment and reward to the events taking place after death.

Roman authors, like Virgil, described some of the punishments of mortals who offended gods. Some of his images remain metaphors in Western civilization:

- ✔ Sisyphus rolls a boulder up a hill endlessly. As he nears the top, the boulder rolls back, and he must start over.
- ✔ Ever-hungry Tantalus tries to reach for fruit, but the branch jerks away; he tries to sip the water that surrounds him, but it invariably recedes.

Jewish writers, immersed in Greek culture, borrowed some of the concepts in their own philosophical musings about afterlife. Instead of just a place for dead souls to mingle, hell turned into a site for punishment for those who sinned.

What Is Hell Like?

What actually happens in hell depends on the perspective. Jonathan Edwards, a fiery American preacher from the 1700s, used to scare his listeners with his vivid descriptions. More recent views are milder, even benign.

Judaism: Hell is distance from God

The Jewish Bible doesn't focus on afterlife, but on a person's behavior during her earthly existence. Hell isn't a permanent destination, but a learning station. Eventually, the soul graduates to be with God.

Bored for eternity

According to an Orthodox Jewish tale, hell can be pretty boring:

A wealthy miser dies and is immediately ushered into a majestic looking palace filed with gold and silver. The angels who accompany him inform him that this is his place for eternity. Whatever his heart desires he gets. One day, he desires a perfect spouse, and the spouse materializes. The next day, he desires white horses with a golden carriage, and that, too, materializes. Each day, he conjures up another fantasy, and, each day, it immediately materializes.

Slowly he begins to run out of things to ask for. What's worse, he begins to become bored with his lot. One day, he asks the supervising angel if he can see what's going on in hell. Blankly, the angel looks at the man and tells him that he's standing in the middle of hell.

Sages debated this issue over centuries. Ideas changed over that time; so did the name of the place. Afterlife was once called *Sheol* (meaning "grave" or "pit"). Then Sheol was split into levels, including one for those who didn't accept God and one for those who did. Finally, as the land became settled, the word used for hell was the familiar *Gehenna*.

Jewish scholars concluded that a person remains in Gehenna for no more than 11 months before being purified and sent to heaven. A person simply has to accept belief in God to be released.

Of course, not all Jews accepted that teaching. In the book of Daniel, the author says that the dead will awake to everlasting life or to eternal shame (Daniel 12:2). That view would creep into Christianity.

In Jewish thinking, the only torment comes because the soul experiences a distance from God. There are no devils sticking pitchforks into anyone, no terrible fires, no eternal punishment. Jews refuse to believe that a loving god would torment anyone for all eternity. Instead, in the Jewish belief, people just "sleep." They can be awakened, as happened in a vision of dried bones who sprang up to become an army in a vision reported by the prophet Ezekiel. Their souls, however, eventually are united with God. (The idea of God's forgiveness is covered in Chapter 15.)

Christianity: Hell's a place of torment

Christians have taken a dramatic view of hell. Initially, Christian leaders described hell the same way as the Jews did: a holding place before God's judgment of the saints and sinners. (See the preceding section for more on this.) They gave it a name, *purgatory*. Today, Roman Catholics are the only major Christian sect to believe that everyone goes to purgatory before being raised to heaven or dropped into hell.

Hell was a fluid idea at first. It even had some mobility: "And I looked, and behold a pale horse; and his name that sat on him was death, and hell followed him" (Revelation: 5:8). It could be tossed around, too: "Death and hell were cast into the lake of fire" (Revelation 20:14).

On the other hand, the New Testament strongly hints that hell isn't a nice place to visit: "Jesus said, 'Anyone who says, "You fool!" will be in danger of the fire of hell'" (Matthew 5:22).

Remaking the image in the early Church

Hell got a makeover in the second century when Church fathers tried to deal with relentless Roman persecutions that forced some Christians to recant their faith. The question was whether they should allow those who recanted their beliefs to return to the religion after the persecutions ended. The debate split the Church.

Christian leaders worried that if they let people simply come back, they would cheapen the deaths of martyrs who died in support of their beliefs and undermine the faith. On the other hand, they had lost a lot of people who went back to pagan gods to save their own skins.

The answer was to ramp up the fires of hell. That way, people would think twice about leaving their beliefs behind. But, if they left anyway and then came back, they would be forgiven — after a certain amount of punishment in the afterlife — and allowed to go to heaven.

Justin Martyr wrote around 160, "Some are sent to be punished unceasingly into judgment and condemnation of fire." About 20 years later, Theophilus added, "To the unbelieving and despisers . . . there will be anger and wrath, tribulation and anguish. At the end, everlasting fire will possess such men."

The final touches on the idea of hell as it exists today appear in the writings of such authors as Dante and artists like Bosch.

Dante Alighieri's influence

Writing between 1308 and his death in 1321, the great Italian poet Dante created what's probably the best-known image of hell. His immortal poem, titled *The Inferno,* leads readers on a tour of hell and purgatory. His words, still studied today, shaped Christian views of hell forever.

Dante assigned sinners to various levels, with punishment increasing as he and his guide, the Roman poet Virgil, descended.

They start at the gates of hell and meet people like Pontius Pilate, the Roman governor who condemned Jesus to the cross. Then carried across the river by Charon, who ferries souls in Greek mythology, Dante toured the nine levels of hell.

1. Housed here are unbaptized but virtuous pagans. Here Dante encountered people like Homer and Roman poet Ovid, along with the famed general of the Arabs, Saladin.

2. Residents are assigned this level after being overcome by lust.

3. Cerberus, the three-headed dog who accompanies Charon, guards gluttons, who lie in mud and are besieged by continuous cold rain and hail on this level.

4. In this circle live people who cared too much about material goods. They are forced to push great weights together forever.

5. The lazy and angry struggle to breathe in a swamp created by the River Styx.

   The next three groups reside inside a dismal city, Dis, guarded by fallen angels. The Furies from Greek mythology and the snake-headed goddess, Medusa, also protect the community.

6. Heretics live in this circle.

7. People who have committed suicide, murderers, and those who deliberately hurt others financially are next. They are immersed in a river of boiling blood; turned into thorn bushes torn apart by the Harpies, flying avengers from Greek myth; or continually attacked by fierce dogs. The Minotaur, half-man, half-bull from Crete mythology, guards the entry to this level.

8. People who defrauded others or were traitors live here. There are ten different units with various awful punishment in this, the most populous of all the rings of hell.

9. The last section of hell holds the worst offenders, including Satan; Judas, the betrayer of Jesus; and Cassius and Brutus, the main conspirators in the murder of Julius Caesar. They are partially frozen among other torments.

Famed Dutch artist Hieronymus Bosch (c. 1450–1516) used Dante's ideas to create images everyone could relate to. He loved to depict the torments of hell. A member of an unreligious sect, Bosch was unrelenting in his paintings of surrealistic horror. Some of his images, which you can see in Figure 17-1, included

- A strange animal forcing a sharp stick through a large ear

- A dog snarling at an old, impoverished man

- Robbers attacking travelers with a gallows waiting nearby

- A creature with a great head that has opened its mouth to show a table with people behind and under it

✔ A man caught in a big hat with one of his legs sprouting roots

✔ People flying through the air and naked bodies tumbling toward hell

In his *Path of Life,* Bosch painted three panels: The first shows Adam's exile from paradise; the middle presents an infinite number of human vices; and the right shows the exile into hell.

When Dante and Bosch were done, hell was revealed in all its modern glory. It has not lost the blood-curdling sheen since.

Figure 17-1:
Bosch's depiction of hell and its punishments.

Photo courtesy of Erich Lessing / Art Resource, NY

Islam: Hell features wild climate extremes

Muhammad talked about hell and described fires that seared those who were punished. The fires of hell are said to be 70 times hotter than fire on earth.

In Islam, not everyone goes to hell. Only one-time Muslims who later deny the faith get broiled as do those Muslims who kill another Muslim. (See Chapter 15 for the complete details.)

Muhammad's view foreshadows later Christian views that sinners are punished. The Muslim hell is divided into sections, similar to what Dante wrote about in his poem *The Inferno* (see the preceding section). Punishment gets more severe based on the level of evil.

- The second lowest level, Zamheerer, has unbearable cold, ice, and snow, a type of punishment repeated by Dante.
- The lowest pit, Hawiyah, is reserved for hypocrites and people who claim to believe in Islam, but don't in their hearts.

Speaking of the Devil

The name of the ruler of this mysterious world depends on whom you ask.

Early concepts of hell's ruler

The Egyptians identified Osiris as god of the underworld. He had the misfortune to be cut to pieces, but was resurrected when his wife, Isis, retrieved most of the missing parts. Osiris wasn't a bad guy, although he posed some hard questions to incoming souls.

In Greek mythology, Hades may not be a great dinner companion or full of laughs, but he's only a god with a job. Like his brother, Neptune, the god of the sea, he has a realm to run. He's not sinister, just gloomy. Pluto is the same guy in Roman myths. That's why the dark, distant, quasi planet in our solar system bears his name.

For Zoroastrians, Ahriman, the evil god, is the archvillian and corresponds to the Devil. He ends up getting confined to the Zoroastrian underworld where he is bound and left in a pit of nauseating liquids. The prophet Zarathustra saw the world as a battle between good and evil, a concept that would later seep into Christianity.

Judaism: Satan is God's adversary

Jews don't acknowledge the existence of one evil being who counters God. The Hebrew word *satan,* which shows up 26 times in the Jewish Bible, means "adversary," and refers to a person or a godlike individual who can mislead humanity.

- ✔ A satan appears unannounced in the biblical book of Job, where he destroys the life of a wealthy man. In doing so, the satan tries to prove that Job will abandon his faith in God when misfortune strikes. In that account, the satan is nothing more than someone who challenges God.

- ✔ In Zechariah, the prophet sees a satan standing at the right hand of Joshua, the high priest, to "slander and accuse" him (Zechariah 3:1). In this case, the satan may be seen as a symbol for a liar.

- ✔ Philistine rulers getting ready to fight the Israelites complain that David is a satan because he's an Israeli — although aligned on their side — and they don't trust him to fight his countrymen. In that account in the book of Samuel, the term defines anyone who might be a traitor.

- ✔ King Solomon was ready to build the First Temple because he no longer had any satan (or adversary). This time, *satan* refers to generic enemies.

In all cases, satan is an adversary, not a proper name. God sometimes sent a satan to test believers' free will and ability to resist temptation. It becomes the snake in the Garden of Eden, the lust that gets King David to fall in love with Bathsheba, and the unknown siren who lures any Jew away from the law.

Still, it is not all powerful. The letters in satan add up to 364, using numerology; so Jewish theologians said that satan was powerless one day of the year. Naturally, that day was Yom Kippur, the Day of Atonement (see Chapter 4).

Christianity: Satan is the deceiver and prince of darkness

In the New Testament, Satan has great powers. He is the prince of this world, god of this world, ruler of the darkness of this age. John insisted that the evil one actually controls this world (1 John 5:19). That view led to sects arguing that the world was evil, and that the real God was in heaven far away from earth. Today, the bulk of Christians believe Satan is a fallen angel who battles with God.

Paging Mr. Satan

Over the centuries, Satan has accumulated lots of alternative names, including

- Beelzebub, who is actually the Philistine god of flies (or filth).

- The wicked one.

- The deceiver.

- Lucifer.

- Prince of Darkness.

- Mephistopheles from the 1500s legend of Faust. He's a German doctor who sells his soul to the Devil.

- Old Nick.

- Beliel. This is spelled many ways, including Belial, and is derived from the Hebrew meaning "without worth."

In the classic American novella, *The Devil and Daniel Webster*, Satan is asked his name and replies that Scratch will do.

Overall, Satan earns 35 mentions in the New Testament, along with another 30-plus for the Greek version of Devil (meaning "accuser").

Satan is definitely a deceiver. "That ancient snake, named Devil and Satan, the deceiver of the whole world, was thrown down to earth." —Revelation 12:9 John was drawing on the serpent account in the Garden of Eden. The Old Testament stories about a satan inspired many of the early Christian writers.

In addition, early Church leaders read old pagan stories that seemed to parallel the accounts of Jesus and claimed that Satan was using the tales to deceive true believers.

Jesus's crucifixion and resurrection represent victory over Satan. However, early Church leaders noted that because the world had not been cleansed of all sin, the battle was not over. Jesus would come back to complete the task. They speculated about when he would return, kicking off the continual debate over when Judgment Day will come. (See Chapter 14 for details on the end of the world.)

Satan is not considered all-powerful. In the Gospel of Mark, Jesus labels Peter as Satan when the disciple denies Jesus's divinity. However, in Christian explanations, the insult actually was to test Peter and let him prove how strong his faith was. That way, Satan was denied control of Peter. As proof, Jesus gives Peter the keys to the kingdom of heaven. That's why Saint Peter is traditionally depicted as the guardian of the pearly gates.

And, according to Revelation, God can bind, release, and even incinerate Satan.

Over the centuries, Satan evolved into a fallen angel who aspired to take God's place, but failed. His story then became the gist of poetry, novels, and artwork. He has also played a leading role in modern movies, often portrayed as bumbling and stupid.

Satan's appearance varies depending on the author, but there are some consistencies: The Devil supposedly has horns, cloven hooves, and a tail. The three characteristics were borrowed from the appearance of the Greek god of the fields, Pan.

Jews were often thought of as devils. So when they first came to the New World, they couldn't disembark at New Amsterdam (now New York) until they were checked by a doctor to be sure they didn't have horns, hooves, and tails.

Islam: Satan encourages wrongdoing

Satan has a place in Islam, too, but not as a fallen angel or even as an adversary of Allah (see the previous two sections for more on these concepts). Instead, *Iblis* is an angel who declined to bow down before Adam. Allah didn't appreciate that and threatened to punish Iblis, but agreed to let the disgraced angel wait until the Day of Judgment.

Iblis uses all the time he has on his hands to be an enemy of man. He can't actually do anything; he can only make suggestions. Because Muslims believe people can choose between good and evil, Iblis's role is to encourage a person to make the wrong decision.

Iblis has an alternative name, *Shaytan* (meaning "distant"), which is similar to Satan. To Muslims, Shaytan was created from smokeless fire.

Watching Out for Devilish Assistants

Satan in any religion doesn't work alone. There's too much sin for one fellow to create it all.

Ancient Greeks feared *daimons,* the source for the word "demon." They were invisible beings who, following dictates of deities, could help men or lead them astray. Similar entities exist in the monotheistic religions.

Judaism: Demons in nature

Outside the Bible, Jewish philosophers came up with a few devilish henchmen whom no one would want to meet in a dark alley.

- Azazel, the demon of the wilderness who swallows up the scapegoat carrying the sins of the people. Initially, Azazel was the name given the poor animal.

- Leviathan, the great, undefined beast who appears in Job. It is also associated with the whale that swallows Jonah. Isaiah said Leviathan's reign of terror will end on the Day of the Lord:

  "In that day the Lord will punish,
  With His great, cruel, mighty sword
  Leviathan the Elusive Serpent—
  Leviathan the Twisting Serpent;
  He will slay the Dragon of the sea." —Isaiah 27:1

- Rahab, a sea demon. In that role, the name is used synonymously to mean "Egypt." In Talmudic writing, the Exodus from Egypt is described as the slaying of Rahab.

  In addition, a woman bearing this name makes multiple appearances in the Old Testament and New Testament in vastly different contexts. Rahab (meaning "large") is a prostitute who helps the invading Jews slip into Jericho and destroy the city in Chapter 2 of the book of Joshua. In Matthew's genealogy of Jesus, Rahab is a distant ancestor.

- Lilith, a female demon of the night who is linked to Adam in Jewish mythology as his first wife. She refuses to obey Adam and is replaced with Eve.

Christianity: The witches will get ya

The handful of demons that Jews identify are overrun by those who inhabit the Christian mindset. Christians blamed everything on demons, including bad dreams, accidents, and illness. In the Gospel of Mark, Jesus drives devils from a suffering Israelite and into a herd of pigs, which promptly jumps off a cliff.

Night demons who come in male and female form are called *incubus* and *succubus,* respectively.

Apparently having little to do, Christian mathematicians in the 1500s decided Satan's assistants numbered 7,405,926.

The attempt to weed out these awful assistants of the Devil culminated in the Middle Ages with the mass murder of so-called witches. These crones supposedly attended a worship service led by the Devil and did his bidding.

Among other accusations, the Devil supposedly held a Black Mass mocking the authentic one, abused the *host* (the wafer of bread used during the service), and caused people to go astray. He was said to hold orgies as well.

Naturally, witches had to go before they caused more illnesses, put hexes on innocent neighbors, or murdered children.

In this case, Catholic venom against the diabolical forces was matched by Lutheran hatred. By the time the mania ended in the 1700s, more than 250,000 people were killed after being charged with witchcraft. Some researchers claim the total could have reached more than 1 million. Millions of people lived in fear of being accused.

A person who was thought to be a witch rarely escaped death: An accused witch could die under torture or, if confessing to evade that, be burned at the stake.

Poor, mistreated peasants seeking revenge against someone in their village most often accused someone of being a witch. But eminent scholars also gave their names to essays that attacked witches and defended the burnings.

Today, witches are mystical figures that appear in popular culture. Shakespeare added witches to his play about Macbeth, whose wife drives him to kill the lawful king. Friendly witches inhabited the television show *Bewitched*. Fairytales that include troublesome witches, including *Hansel and Gretel*, *Snow White and the Seven Dwarves*, and *Sleeping Beauty*, continue to be read. Witches also reappear every year during Halloween to scare children.

Islam: Powerful genies aid Iblis

The Devil is believed to be descended from Jann, who also gave birth to evil genies. Iblis doesn't need any help to sow mischief, but later storytellers gave him some assistants anyway.

The nice genie (*jinn* in Arabic) who helps Aladdin in both the Disney movie of that name and the ancient tale that the movie was based on, usually was portrayed as ugly and evil. (The genie in the movie looked like a blue balloon.) The genie bestowed powers on people who were able to conjure him up.

Jinns lived in the desert, but unlike the Christian version, aren't immortal. They do mislead people. However, they're more likely to punish people who fail to follow one of the many rules after conjuring up a genie.

What Happens to Satan?

Satan may be laughing with delight, as Don McLean sang in his song "American Pie," but he will lose that chuckle when the world ends.

Judaism: God destroys all

In the Jewish view, God will destroy the world and everything in it. Because a satan represents temptations, when the world ends, there is no temptation left either.

Christianity: Satan puts up a fight

In the Christian view, Satan has great power, so he's not going to bow out quickly and easily. Of course, different denominations take alternative views.

Some believe Satan will be imprisoned; others say he'll be destroyed. Others insist that when God destroys the earth, Satan will be exiled here to rule over a pile of rubble.

In the book of Revelation, John described what will happen to Satan.

> "And I saw an angel coming down out of heaven, having the key to the Abyss and holding in his hand a great chain. He seized the dragon, that ancient serpent, who is the Devil, or Satan, and bound him for 1,000 years. He threw him into the Abyss, and locked and sealed it over him, to keep him from deceiving the nations anymore, until the 1,000 years were ended." —Revelation 20:1–3

> "And the Devil that deceiveth them was cast into the lake of fire and brimstone, where the beast and the false prophet are, and shall be tormented day and night for ever and ever.'" —Revelation 20:10

Hell was actually prepared for the Devil and his fallen angels, according to Matthew (Matthew 25:41). In that case, the Devil starts all over again in the same place that the Greeks, Romans, and other ancient people placed him.

Islam: Judgment comes

The Day of Judgment marks the end of the world in Islam. Some people will not be saved, although Muhammad will intercede and Allah is merciful. They will end up in hell.

Although no one says what happens to Iblis under these circumstances, someone will have to hang around to make sure those confined to hell are properly punished. It looks like he'll continue to be very busy.

Chapter 18

War and Peace: Why Can't We All Get Along?

. . . .

In This Chapter

▶ Discovering the roots of religious conflict

▶ Seeing how wars have been waged over 1,400 years

▶ Looking ahead to complex times

. . . .

*I*n today's world, these three monotheistic religions remain a fact of our lives. Judaism, Christianity, and Islam have been around for more than 14 centuries, and Christianity and Islam each have more than a billion followers.

Throughout history, people have fought over various issues, including national sovereignty, political beliefs, and expansion. At the time of this writing, religion remains a driving force behind conflict on the world stage. The United States — which is 82 percent Christian — is at war within Iraq and Afghanistan, both almost totally Muslim nations, and is on the verge of more conflict with Iran, another Muslim country. Israel, predominantly Jewish, continues to battle Muslims along its borders and inside them.

Many Americans may see the current war as a response to terrorism, not as a religious war. A secular person may discredit any religious motives and look at the fighting in the Middle East as a defensive reaction to the destruction of the World Trade Center and the attack on the Pentagon on September 11, 2001, or as a power grab by America because of the stark need for oil and resources in the near future.

For many Muslims, however, religion dominates their point of view. To them, Americans are outsiders of another faith who have taken Muslim land by force. There is no question that for many Muslims, the war is religious at its core.

Osama bin Laden shunned the American presence in the affairs of Saudi Arabia, home to Mecca, Islam's holiest city. He and other leaders of terrorist groups recruit young soldiers on the basis of Islamic ideology. This seems to be the most effective way to motivate young men to risk their lives: for God, even more than for country.

Of course, some American soldiers are fighting Islamic radicals as Christians. And private military organizations exist in the United States that hire and train professional soldiers *(mercenaries)* chosen for their beliefs that they, too, are fighting a religious war.

At certain times in history, people belonging to these three religions actually got along. Jews once served as advisors to Muslim leaders in Spain and the Middle East, working alongside Christians. They were also key officials to kings in Catholic Spain in the early Middle Ages.

At one time, Islamic nations had peace treaties with Christian countries. Sure, countries battled each other, but on an individual level, fighting wasn't the rule. The religious groups coexisted more or less peacefully, with a certain amount of infighting or squabbling — probably similar to how people of all three faiths coexist in the United States today.

It may seem strange now, given all the battles on the world stage, that peaceful coexistence has been possible at times. Even though Christians, Muslims, and Jews believe in the same God and are tied together with a common ancestor, Abraham, they seem more intent on attacking each other than on holding a family reunion. And as we progress through this century, the impact of religion on world events will probably get more intense.

This chapter looks at how these religions took such a violent path, and what the chances are for peace among these monotheists who all believe in the same, one God.

A Shared Heritage

Despite the many conflicts, Judaism, Christianity, and Islam claim Abraham as their father. They also have additional principles in common and share particular values:

- All of them believe in one God. They may have a different name for God, but the concept is the same.

- God is universal. God doesn't dwell in one place, but inhabits everything and everyone.

- ✔ God is associated with light.

- ✔ Each human has a soul.

- ✔ Although the Bible has many names for God, and the Koran calls God by the name of Allah, God does have one name shared by the monotheistic religions: "I am that I am" (Exodus 3:14); "I am" (John 8:58).

- ✔ Happiness is the supreme goal.

- ✔ Moral laws carry divine support. Every religion preaches morality, formulated into the Ten Commandments in the Bible. The Koran admonishes believers to avoid "exceeding the limits" set by God.

- ✔ All three religions believe in a united mankind.

- ✔ They share a common heritage in the Middle East and in Greco-Roman antiquity. Christianity absorbed many of the ideas that circulated around it, including the Roman form of government. Judaism had to change from a Temple-oriented faith to one built around rabbis and the Torah after disastrous battles with the same Romans. Islam was changed, too, adapting itself after contact with the outside world.

- ✔ The original languages of Judaism, Christianity, and Islam are from the same Semitic language group. They used similar words with similar meanings in their holy texts.

The three religions have a tremendous amount in common. Despite relying on different holy texts, rituals, and houses of prayer, the shared aspects far outweigh the differences. They were born from a common soil, literally and figuratively. You could even say that if Judaism, Christianity, and Islam were any more unified in terms of their principles and past, they might even be branches of the same religion. (Don't tell anyone this!)

Belief in one God

Belief in one God can generate problems — problems that all three religions share. If you believe in multiple gods and things go wrong, you can blame an evil deity. You can accuse the god who was supposed to protect you for being misled by another heavenly creature.

That's evidenced in the literature of the ancient world. In the *Iliad* and *Odyssey,* epic Greek poems that served as the "Bible" of antiquity, the supreme god, Zeus, is bamboozled by gods supporting the Greeks or Trojans fighting in a climactic war. Gods involve themselves in battle, rescuing men or helping soldiers kill their enemies.

That's equally true in the great poem about the founding of Rome, the *Aeneid*. Aeneas, the Trojan hero, is the son of a god, and battles with deities to reach the safety of Italy and fulfill his destiny.

However, if there's only one God who is all good, he can't be blamed for any misfortune. That's why Jewish prophets argued that Jews were being punished whenever foreign armies overran them. Any disaster, including natural events like floods, had to be the result of human failure.

That belief is captured in the Bible: God punishes mankind by destroying all but Noah. God kills thousands who oppose Moses, and so on.

To avoid such calamities, Jews carefully studied holy books line by line, determined to prevent their own mistakes from leading to further problems. They were also obligated to punish those who deviated from their God's laws, because the wrong decision could lead to divine retribution.

Christianity and Islam have followed that approach. People who spread *heresies* — alternative beliefs — have been punished severely in those faiths.

- ✔ Catholic armies slaughtered people who held different Christian beliefs and burned many leaders until the Protestant Reformation in the 1500s became too massive for such punitive action.
- ✔ Failing to follow Islam was grounds for execution 1,500 years ago, and now, in certain places.
- ✔ And because Judaism lacked armies, Jews were left with ousting heretics from their congregations. Around the year AD 70, Jews famously killed one another when they disagreed on how to defend Jerusalem and the Second Temple against the attacking Roman legions under Titus.

Shared internal conflicts

Two concepts have driven Islam and Christianity to internal battles:

- ✔ Failure to follow the faith. This guaranteed eternal damnation.
- ✔ Divergent beliefs. This ensured divine punishment.

Catholics versus Protestants

The holy wars between Catholics and Protestants are among the bloodiest in history. Only the rise of governments that insisted on separation of church and state brought the battles to an end. The separated state became a neutral zone, a kind of third-party arbitrator that would enforce peace on religious rivalries.

Vatican II and Catholic tolerance in our time

The Second Ecumenical Council of the Vatican, more commonly called Vatican II, was the 21st Ecumenical Council of the Roman Catholic Church. It opened under Pope John XXIII in 1962 and closed under Pope Paul VI in 1965. It was largely understood as an effort by the council to be more inclusive of others and more tolerant of diverse interpretations of the religion in order to adjust to a rapidly changing world. Traditional Catholics were upset by some of its statements.

Vatican II is best summarized by the opening words of Pope John XXIII. The intentions of the council were ". . . to transmit the doctrine pure and entire, without diminution or distortion." He added, "It is our duty not only to guard this precious treasure, as if interested only in antiquity, but also to devote ourselves readily and fearlessly to the work our age requires. . . . This sure unchangeable doctrine, which must be faithfully respected, has to be studied in depth and presented in a way that fits the requirements of our time."

This attempt at tolerance and inclusion resulted, however, in inner upheaval and a crisis of identity that the church is still undergoing today. Vatican II stirred up a battle between progressives and traditionalists. Some historians see this as a necessary, healthy crisis that could eventually result in growth and a stronger identity.

Pope John Paul II was a believer in this council's ideas for the future of the church and a force for change. He quoted repeatedly that "Man can fully find his true self only in the sincere gift of self." We find our deeper humanity when we are helping others.

John Paul II reached out to other Christian denominations and other religions with the hope of achieving more understanding among different beliefs.

Today, many Christian denominations are trying to work together. There are still disagreements and some short-sighted thinking — some Catholics, for example, refuse to go into a Protestant church and vice versa — but the era of physical wars has ended.

The last intra-Christian war took place in Northern Ireland, where Protestants and Catholics shot and bombed each other. Peace in the 1990s finally ended that long conflict, which had economic, political, and religious causes.

Sunnis versus Shi'ites

In Islam, the wars between the two major sects, Sunni and Shi'ite, continue today. The religion is now part of the government in certain countries like Iran, eliminating the one mechanism (separation) available to bring about religious peace.

Sunnis and Shi'ites share the Koran and the essential principles of the Islamic faith (see Chapter 7), but they have a deep division over who the proper leadership should be in Islam. This rift broadened over time and shows no signs of healing.

Sunni ideology stresses tolerating the current government as long as it upholds the principles of Islamic belief and law. Two of their common attitudes are expressed in these sayings "Whose power prevails must be obeyed," and "The world can live with tyranny, but not with anarchy."

In contrast, Shi'ite belief is that Muhammad's son-in-law should have succeeded the Prophet in the seventh century. Therefore, all rulers after Muhammad have been illegitimate. As a result, Shi'ites are associated with resistance and opposition, both historically and in modern times. They seek to overthrow all illegitimate rulers in Islam.

In older days, the divisions were there, but they weren't as rigid; a Muslim could move carefully between these two groups because they agreed on the essentials of their faith, if not on the particulars.

As a rule, when external pressures heat up — such as political conflict, poverty, lack of resources, population crowding — then religious differences get hot, too.

Differences, Disagreements, and Conflicts

Despite the many shared values discussed in the preceding section, Judaism, Christianity, and Islam strongly disagree in many areas. If you've read Chapter 11, you know that the roles of the religious leaders vary widely: Catholic priests, for example, are seen as God's representatives, while Jewish rabbis are teachers without a divine imprint.

More fundamentally, at the very core of each religion, beliefs exist about how God's laws apply not only to any one religion, but to all mankind. This gets at the very foundation of the conflicts. If Jews aren't following Christian rules, then they are seen by Christians as violating God's laws. The opposite is equally true in the eyes of any one set of believers looking at others outside the system of belief.

Universality versus exclusivity

Followers of each of these three monotheistic religions believe that their religious truths are *universal* and apply to all mankind. This belief is fully shared among them. But only the Jews see their truths as *non-exclusive.* Christians and Muslims see their religious truths as exclusively true, admitting of no others.

If a religion is believed to be *universal,* then all people are included in its laws, prophecies, and revelations. One and all.

Exclusive religions take a more severe approach: *Only* that one religion and its beliefs and laws are thought to apply to everyone. Any other competing doctrine is believed to be false (it can't *also* be true). A faith that says it's exclusively true sees the person of different belief as a problem.

Judaism is universal but not exclusive; a non-Jew can attain salvation, as discussed later in this chapter. Christianity and Islam aren't so open-minded. Both believe they are the only way to God, that their faith is exclusively true, and that no others can be true. The exclusive faith does not admit salvation (salvation is the prize for good faith, the ultimate goal) outside its own belief system. It also believes it has a duty to bring its "one true faith" to all mankind.

Judaism: Noahide Laws include everyone

Judaism recognized early on that not everyone would or could be Jewish. Sages noted that Noah lived before Abraham and, therefore, couldn't be Jewish. However, God had allowed Noah to survive the flood that killed the rest of mankind and had identified him as a righteous person.

The sages pondered this: If Noah was righteous, then there must be a method for other non-Jews to be acceptable to God. As the result, they came up with what are known as the *Noahide Laws:* laws that Noah followed to become righteous. They allow a non-Jewish person who follows them, and who also believes in one God, to attain salvation.

Those laws are basic:

- ✔ Prohibition of slavery.

- ✔ Prohibition of blasphemy drawn from the second commandment ban against the taking the Lord's name in vain.

- ✔ Prohibition of murder. That's another of the Ten Commandments.

✔ Prohibition of theft. Another rule borrowed from Ten Commandments.

✔ Prohibition of illicit relations, taken from the commandment banning "coveting" of a neighbor's wife and property.

✔ Prohibition of eating raw meat. This is from the kosher laws meant to prevent disease. People used to eat meat cut from a living animal. Health rules created by the Jews banned that behavior.

✔ Establishment of rules of justice. Both Noah and Moses are credited with setting up judicial systems.

Each of these laws featured multiple regulations to ensure exact compliance.

Christianity and Islam: Nonbelievers are excluded

Again, Christianity and Islam are exclusive. Instead of admitting a path to salvation for nonbelievers, both condemn them to eternal torment. Because they each claim to be exclusive truths, they *exclude* nonbelievers. It's even permissible in Islam to kill someone who was born Muslim but left the faith.

By creating an exclusive organization, everyone outside it can easily be seen as the "enemy." This mutual belief in exclusive truth has led to endless wars between Christians and Muslims. It has made it doubly difficult for them to share the same homeland, or to share the Mediterranean world they both inhabited.

Judaism offers a solution

In keeping with Noahide Laws, Judaism, at least in theory, is more open than Islam and Christianity in its doctrine. A famous Talmudic dictum states that any person, even a non-Jew, can attain salvation. How? By fulfilling two requirements:

✔ Living rightly and justly

✔ Believing in one god

In other words, Jews believe that a person must be both moral and a monotheist to receive salvation. If the person accepts these two things, it's possible for that person (a non-Jew) to attain a place in paradise.

Early on, Jews were very busy trying to convert people to their faith. That's why an estimated 10 percent of the Roman Empire at the time of Jesus was Jewish or followed Jewish ideals. However, after the rise of Christianity, Jews stopped *proselytizing* (trying to convince nonbelievers to join them) because they thought Christians were spying on them and telling lies to the Roman government.

Today, by Jewish law, a potential convert must be rejected three times before beginning classes.

The policy about converts, as usual, was made blurry by competing claims, and Jewish leniency toward pagans and members of other faiths wasn't perfect. Many Jewish laws inscribed in the Bible limit contact with non-Jews. Jewish leaders said Jews were a tribe of priests who had to remain pure. In the Old Testament book of Ezra, for example, readers are told about a Jewish man and a non-Jewish woman who were killed because they were having an affair. At the same time, the book of Ruth is a plea for approval of such mixed marriages.

Nevertheless, one thing is clear: As Christianity and then Islam overtook Judaism and spread, Jewish tolerance of others faded away.

Christianity closes doors, and Islam follows suit

Jesus was Jewish and spoke to believers throughout Israel. However, as his followers began to see him as God on earth, they also began to argue that the only route to God was through him. Everyone who didn't accept him, therefore, was doomed to eternal torment.

By the fifth century, Christian leaders adopted ancient Jewish ideas banning mixed marriages and other isolationist laws and applied them to Jews. They felt obligated to convert nonbelievers and even launched massive invasions into pagan lands to force the acceptance of their religion.

Missionaries today carry on the same effort. The approaches are both violent and peaceful, depending on the time and place. (For example, Al Qaeda supporters see themselves as crusaders; Mormons view themselves as missionaries.)

Muhammad listened to the Jewish and Christian concepts carried by travelers throughout the Middle East. He saw the multiple gods of his lands and rejected all of them except Allah. When the traveling merchants talked about God in Arabic, they used the word "Allah." That name corresponds to the name of a god worshipped already in the sacred Ka'baa, which predated Islam as a holy shrine.

Muhammad saw himself as a missionary, like the Christian disciple Paul, carrying the message of Allah to his people. Naturally, he wanted everyone to believe what had been revealed to him.

As a result, Islam, like Christianity, demanded that conquered people abandon their pagan faiths. Muslims of old were no less intolerant of Christians and Jews. Muslims piously pitied them for failing to follow Allah, and they offered them a choice: convert, die, or pay a tax for the privilege of living under Islam.

At first, Muslims had no equal to the Christian churches and no political priesthood. But as they progressed, Muslim incorporated these practices:

- ✔ Imans would oversee local regions.
- ✔ Islam split into Shi'ite and Sunni.
- ✔ A ruling hierarchy watched over and enforced worship rituals to ensure that they were being performed correctly. This was modeled after the hierarchy of the Christian church.

The younger the Abrahamic religion, historically speaking, the more violent. The Koran dismissed all other books, religious or otherwise. Today, memorizing the Koran is both prestigious and practiced. And observance and at least the appearance of respect of Islamic law and practices by a foreigner on Islamic soil is mandatory.

War and Not So Much Peace

When Muslims and Christians met at the border of countries, sparks flew. Armies representing Christians and Muslims have attacked and counterattacked one another in the Mediterranean world as both religions have expanded. Both have commanded vast empires.

Muslims conquer for a time

In the short 100-year span of Umayyad rule in Islam (AD 632–730), Muslims conquered all the way to the Indus River Valley in the East, and as far as Spain in the West — moving like greased lightning! The Islamic empire became larger for a time than the earlier Roman Empire or Alexander the Great's conquests in the fourth century BC.

Muslims expanded and conquered in order to "open" the new society to God's one and only truth, which they alone possessed. The Arabic word *futuh* (meaning "to open") was used in much the same way that the United States uses the word "liberate" these days, as in the "liberation" of Kuwait during the Gulf War. That is, Muslim soldiers arrived in the new place with the belief that they were removing an illegitimate ruler and "opening the people" to God's final revelation, as given in the Koran.

Followers of Islam believe that all human beings are born Muslims, but are converted into Jews and Christians by their parents and misguided cultures, so they must be led back. By bringing God on board, Muslim invaders divinely sanctioned their own actions. This view helped them hold onto their conquests and also justified their leadership position to the new people under their domination. Also, newly conquered (or assimilated) people were less likely to follow other invaders pushing their own separate beliefs.

The Muslims had a Jewish model for their behavior. Early Jews carried God into battle inside the Ark of the Covenant, giving a religious patina to any war. Jews also forced conversions. Residents of Galilee, Jesus's home area, were forced to change to Judaism or face death about 100 years before Jesus was born.

Christianity envelops mankind

Christianity took longer than Islam to win territory and hearts, but the religion covers even more of the globe today. After being legalized in the fourth century, the religion began to expand rapidly. Paganism was suppressed. From the 8th through the 15th centuries, Christians took back Spain and other countries in a series of conquests.

They were motivated by the belief that the world was ending soon. Only those who believed in Jesus, they argued, would be saved. Therefore, by forcing people to convert, Christians were rescuing nonbelievers from endless punishment after death.

That belief also led to internal wars. After all, people who broke away from the Catholic faith were endangering their eternal souls.

Of course, just as with Islam, the desire for plunder, power, and land also motivated soldiers. Still, religious tenets served as a valid reason for converting or killing a nonbeliever.

Christianity had great success with this approach. Today, the religion is the largest in the world. Christians exist in virtually every nation, and have made impressive inroads in Asia, Africa, and South America.

Christian missionaries

Christianity has strived to expand itself as a world religion and power. In church doctrine, we find some related instructions in the Gospel of Matthew, where Jesus instructed the apostles to make disciples:

"Go ye therefore, and teach all nations, baptizing them in the name of the Father, and of the Son, and of the Holy Ghost: Teaching them to observe all things whatsoever I have commanded you: and, lo, I am with you always, [even] unto the end of the world. Amen." —Matthew 28:19,20

Called the *Great Commission,* this directive is understood by Christian missionaries as Jesus's mandate to engage in missionary work. Paul, Peter, and James the Just, leaders of the Church after Jesus's death, are the best examples of the earliest Christian missionaries. During the Middle Ages, the monks and their monasteries functioned as the main arms extending the Church outward from the reaches of the old Roman Empire.

Crusaders carried the Christian message directly to the Muslims in a series of wars starting in the 1000s. Much has been written on these wars.

From the early 15th to the 17th centuries, in the Age of Discovery, Christian missionaries (Dominicans, Augustinians, Franciscans, and others) moved around the world with European explorers and encountered people and places never before known to them in what they called the New World. The Portuguese also sent missionaries into Africa around that time. These are some of the most famous missions in history.

Although some of these missions were inevitably associated with imperialism — because good and bad human motives mix throughout history — other missions were well intended and meant to help others rather than aimed at imperialist expansion.

Protestants have also contributed much in the way of missionary activity, which they see as a duty. The conversion of Native Americans in the Massachusetts Bay Colony in the 17th century was one of their earliest efforts. India and the West Indies also were targets for Protestant missionaries during this same time, led by the Danish.

Since the 1900s, and with an especially strong push after Lausanne I: The International Congress on World Evangelization held in Switzerland in 1974, evangelical groups worldwide have sent out missionaries to probably every ethnic group in the world. Many Bibles and other Christian materials have been distributed around the world. However, this effort is not yet finished. Evangelical churches have been established in more remote, less-Christianized areas.

Not all missionary activity has been peaceful, by any measure. On occasion, natives violently rejected missionary efforts. Other times, Christian missionaries used drastic methods to force conversions. As missionary zealots met nonbelievers or pagans, they unleashed burnings and massacres in the name of God. For example, the Catholic Church created the Inquisition in the Middle Ages to ferret out nonbelievers living among them. The nonbelievers were often burned to death.

No monotheistic religion is exempt from violence. Christians were demonstrative because they possessed institutions — the churches and bishops and priests — to punish *wrong belief.* These upper and middle managers allowed the use of the death penalty for nonbelief. Jews remain too small a group and lack such power, but have turned on one another violently at times (see the next section). Early Islam was more violent than later Islam. As a rule, historically speaking: the younger the religion, the more violent.

Not all religions try to become world powers and expand via missionary activity, war, or a combination of the two. Other major religions, such as Hinduism and Confucianism in the East, made no effort to expand into world powers; they remained essentially local and were content to be so. Doctrine can calm or inflame, depending on how it's expressed. Demanding a belief in a certain religion, however, can only end in conflict.

The Jews Struggle

Jews have been largely tolerant of divisions within the faith since the rise of Christianity. Before that, however, Jews didn't hesitate to attack each other. In the first century BC, for example, Jews who supported the Greek ideas seeping into Jewish culture fought with conservative Jews who wanted to maintain the existing ways. The conservative side's victory is celebrated annually in the holiday called Hanukkah (see Chapter 4).

Perhaps the worst civil war took place in AD 70. Jewish extremists had ousted the Roman army four years earlier. The Romans returned, swept across the land, and surrounded Jerusalem, which was crowded with starving refugees from around the country, as well as members of various Jewish sects.

Jews spent as much time killing their religious opponents as they did fighting off the Romans. As a result, the city fell. An estimated 3 million people were killed, forced to flee, or sold into slavery. In addition, the Temple was destroyed, giving steam to the budding Christian belief that the world was coming to an end.

After the Temple was destroyed in that bitter war, Jews were scattered and often became isolated in a hostile world dominated first by Christians and later by Muslims. Because Islam encourages tolerance of other faiths (a condition brought on by its environment as much as anything, because Islam has spanned across Africa, Asia, and Europe and connected with many cultures and different groups of people), Jews and Christians often worked together and held high positions in the courts of Muslim leaders, but that was only for a brief interlude.

No home anywhere

In Christian lands, Jews were often forced to live into *ghettos* — isolated communities — and prohibited from holding positions in society except as tax collectors and money lenders. Often, they were victims of unprovoked attacks, called *pogroms,* or their children were forcibly converted to Christianity. (See Chapter 3 for more background on Jewish survival in the Christian era.)

The hatred of Jews *(anti-Semitism)* reached a horrific peak when Germany came under control of the Nazi Party in the 1930s. Jews were placed in camps and systematically murdered. An estimated 6 million European Jews were killed in what has become known as the Holocaust.

The persecution of the Jews encouraged many to look for a place they could go, a homeland. Naturally, they focused on Israel, the land that in the Bible was promised to Abraham, the first Jew.

The birth of Israel: More strife

Jews began buying up acres in what was called Palestine in the late 1800s. The nomadic Arabs who sold it had little concept of ownership and thought they were conning the buyers.

Instead, Jews began to move into what became Israel, causing immediate conflict with Arabs who had farmed and grazed the same land for centuries. Fighting between them was bloody but sporadic, until, hoping for peace, the United Nations divided the contested territory into an Arab state (Jordan) and a Jewish state (Israel).

The effort to impose peace failed. When Israel declared its existence and independence in April 1948, Arab nations attacked en masse from all sides. To them, this was a *jihad* (holy war). Nonbelievers had taken over soil in the middle of Islam. Fiery speakers fanned the outrage, using the Koran as a source of inspiration for soldiers. Jews looked to their faith for guidance. But both prayed to the same God. This is where we are today in the region, with war flaring up frequently.

Troubles continue inside Israel

The creation of Israel didn't end conflict among Jews. Many Orthodox Jews don't accept Jews who are members of other Jewish sects. They aren't killing each other, as was done in the final days of the Temple, but the animosity remains. However, they are far too busy fending off attacks by Arabs to take up arms against each other.

At the same time, concessions have been made. Secular, less-religious Jews have welcomed — and even sought out — distant believers in Ethiopia, Russia, and other lands.

As a result, Israel today houses Jews of many different denominations without internal warfare (just a lot of arguing!). On the other hand, the conflict with Arabs remains ongoing.

Finding Solutions in Secularism

All the religious fighting through the centuries has sickened many people. In time, some of the deepest thinkers in the 17th century argued that religion had to be separated from government to end the battles between denominations and religions. This was the first instance of the *separation of church and state,* as it's now called.

The idea of rules and practices that disregard any form of religious principles and worship is called *secularism.* In some ways, secularism could be called the fourth belief system alongside these older three traditions.

At one time in history, religious identity dominated everything. Just as you were a Muslim if you were born in Mecca in the 12th century, you were a Christian if you were born in Venetian society then. These days we can shop for a religion if we like, at least in the places where doing so is permissible. So the idea of being born into a religion, just as a person is born into a nationality, is lost to many of us.

But as secularism caught on, people began to identify themselves as residents of a country, rather than as a member of a religion. Today, many of us don't realize that nationalism — and patriotism — developed only recently.

Separation of church and state in the United States

The idea of separation of church and state was etched into the human mind by the American Constitution, which prohibits the government from creating any law regarding religion. For the first time in human history, you could choose any religion, change religions, or create a new religion without interference from the government.

The idea to separate the two life-guiding systems was first introduced into the Virginia constitution. Thomas Jefferson and other founding fathers had seen what had happened in Europe when Catholics and Protestants viciously battled for decades. Jefferson remembered the constant bloody warfare over religious beliefs when Henry VIII created the Anglican Church. State-enforced doctrine allowed for the massacres, burnings, and torture of nonbelievers that ravaged Europe and Christianity before the emergence of secularism there. Religion and state were one and invincible when they worked together.

When Jefferson represented Virginia at the convention that declared the newly formed United States independent of England, he added the idea of separating government and religion to the Declaration of Independence. He wrote in the preamble to the document: "We hold these truths to be self evident, that all men are created equal, that they are endowed by their Creator with certain unalienable rights, that among these are life, liberty and the pursuit of happiness."

Note that the document doesn't mention religion directly, because it establishes a free *state* for religion. When Jefferson wrote it, he *separated* state and religion, and this separation is so important for religious peace. That same concept was then included in the Bill of Rights, the ten amendments to the U.S. Constitution.

That's why the United States is the largest country in the world with uninhibited religious freedom.

In the Islamic world, secularism struggles

The Islamic world watched secularism rise in Europe and America and has reacted. Right now, secularism is struggling to survive in the Middle East. Only Lebanon and Turkey have no state-endorsed religion, among those states with constitutions; but the former has become a war zone, and the latter is returning to Islamic education, and the old distinction of Muslim versus citizen (non-Muslim) has been kept in place. As conflict in the region grinds on, the awareness of religious identity and differences will only escalate.

Israel recognizes a similar distinction, one that separates Jewish and non-Jewish nationals inside the same society. Israel's electoral system also allows the different religious groups strong political influence, because the parties and their votes are divided along religious lines.

In the Islamic Republic of Iran, as it is named, religion has a powerful influence on the state. The clearest example of a political-religious leader is the Ayatollah, whose power straddles the boundaries between state and religion.

Definitions of identity and loyalty, when they are increasingly based on religious beliefs, can erode the separation of church and state. No matter what the religious identity of a person, nowadays they also have a national identity; and national identity has the chance to act as a binding or moderating force among disparate religious identities trying to coexist. And the opposite happens when religious identity dominates increasingly, when everyone inside the same society becomes acutely aware, in daily life, of differences and to which faith the other person belongs. An internal war can break out, and one religious group may emerge dominant. That group can then take over the law making of the country and exclude all nonbelievers. This pattern has been common throughout history.

Saudi Arabia follows Shari'a law, Islamic law, as the basis for its own social laws. It also has *Wahhabism,* an Islamic movement upon which the nation was founded. Wahhabis are conservative and admit to no law outside religion. Their control of the two holy cities of Mecca and Medina gives Wahhabis great influence on Muslim culture and thinking, as well as the Saudi oil fields in the Persian Gulf. Since 1975, those reserves of black gold have given the Wahhabis the power to promote their interpretations of Islam, using billions from their oil revenues. The term *Wahhabi* was first used by the opposition of ibn Abdul Wahhab. It is an unacceptable term for followers, who find it derogatory. Among themselves, they are called *Muwahiddun* (Unitarians).

The extremes of ultraconservative Islam are evident to outsiders: A Western teacher was condemned for allowing her class to name a stuffed bear Muhammad. Author Salman Rushdie was condemned to die for his novel reconstructing words from the Koran supposedly removed by the Prophet. Muslims, from their viewpoint, may see the occupation of Iraq by the United States as an extreme violation.

The situation in Islam won't change until its leaders accept the existence of divergent views without responding with violence. That's happening in a small way in certain places. In the United Arab Emirates, a collection of seven small states in the Arabian Peninsula, a variety of Islamic sects live together peacefully along with Christians and Jews. The leaders there recognize the financial value of peaceful coexistence. Dubai is a city that has taken off recently and has a burgeoning economy.

Where we are today

Periods of relative peace and coexistence between the three Abrahamic religions have some common points:

- ✔ A single, militarily superior state that imposes peace
- ✔ Economic interdependence that one side can't dominate
- ✔ No zealots in any one of the cohabitating religions agitating for holy war against any other

These conditions have been rare and fleeting. So has religious peace.

The Middle East today still houses Jews, Christians, and Muslims. Jerusalem is still a city of the first importance for all three.

As of the writing of this book, the United States is at war there for several reasons: to combat terrorists; to support Israel against countries that seek its destruction; and to avenge the destruction of the World Trade Center in New York and a direct attack on the Pentagon by militant Islamists.

You could also say that Western Christianity and secular politics is also at war in the Mideast — and is on the verge of more war there with Iran, a land where church and state separation is thin at best under the Ayatollah.

Al Qaeda is currently militant-Muslim in belief and inspiration. And, again, they use these unwavering convictions to successfully recruit soldiers. They are a primary enemy of the United States. Both sides see each other as the defined, targeted enemy. But the militancy is not one-sided. Many Christians have joined in this war for religious reasons, either as national soldiers or as soldiers recruited and trained by private security firms.

So separation of church and state — to create a secular neutral zone inside a society — has at least *a chance* to restrain religious violence and act as a mediating force. But this separation isn't doing too well in the Middle East. The balancing act it provides is waning in a world of different religious claims and religious strife.

People who were moderates and secularists on all sides are rediscovering their religious roots, and the effort to pretend to tolerate religious differences is fading as the pressure builds in war zones. The intensity of war invites the intensity of religious identity; indeed, the two seem to go hand in hand. If one or the other side really believes its own truth is exclusive of all other religious truths, then this is doubly dangerous. It provides more motivation for young soldiers recruited to fight and keep the fires of war stoked.

A common accusation is that the current Mideast conflicts are really about oil, but the issue is more complex than that. After the September 11, 2001, attacks, the United States went to Afghanistan first, which isn't an oil-rich country, in search of Al Qaeda strongholds and training bases. Iraq became a target later, and the justification, at least officially, was to fight Iraq's support of terror and its alleged development of weapons of mass destruction.

It's frightening to think about, but the "oil wars" may not have yet begun in earnest. More overt wars in which oil is clearly the only target will probably happen in our lifetimes. Al Qaeda stated that it attacked the United States on September 11 because of the American presence and influence in oil-rich Saudi Arabia, where Mecca is located. Mecca is the most sacred city in Islam.

What does the future hold?

There's no reason to assume fights between these three religions will end. The beliefs remain strong, and the drive among Christians and Muslims to convert others remains strong. All three faiths are convinced that they alone know the truth.

Still, peace doesn't have to be a total mirage. This survey of the three major Western monotheistic religions has demonstrated how dependent they are on each other. Jerome recognized this in the fourth century. Ordered to translate the holy Christian books, he turned to the Jewish Bible and translated it first. Christian ideas of a messiah, he realized, were meaningless without the earlier texts.

To understand Islam, knowledge of the Bible is needed. Muhammad's entire belief rests on the frail back of Ishmael, who is little more than a name in Genesis.

Despite the clear links, members of the three faiths continue to fuss and fight with deadly intent around the world. Yet, as seen throughout this book, beliefs are very similar. Judaism, Christianity, and Islam are built around a love for one another and a belief in a single God; they all talk of peace and long for the day when all mankind will accept the inspired words of God's prophets. The similarities far outweigh the differences. (We keep saying this!)

Perhaps in the coming years, as communication tightens the bonds that unite all of us, adherents will begin to focus on the beliefs that all three religions share and what tremendous impact they have had together on culture, morality, and ethics. Then in the words of Isaiah, a prophet honored in three religions and whose prediction is recorded in a book revered by the same three religions, there will be peace:

"In the last days, the mountain of the house of the Lord will be the most important of the mountains. It will be raised above the hills. All the nations will come to it. Many people will come and say, 'Come, let us go up to the mountain of the Lord, to the house of the God of Jacob. Then He will teach us about His ways, that we may walk in His paths. For the Law will go out from Zion, and the Word of the Lord from Jerusalem.' He will judge between the nations, and will decide for many people. And they will beat their swords into plows, and their spears into knives for cutting vines. Nation will not lift up sword against nation, and they will not learn about war anymore." —Isaiah 2:2–4

Part V
The Part of Tens

The 5th Wave
By Rich Tennant

"It's true, he's a miracle worker. He did our kitchen, basement, and back patio and brought it in under budget and ahead of schedule."

In this part . . .

*W*e discuss the main misconceptions about the three
religions. We also present our favorite religious
films and the top ways that the religions have influenced
the world.

Chapter 19

Ten Misconceptions about Jews, Christians, and Muslims

*I*f you've read most of the book to this point, you probably have a good grasp of the three great monotheistic religions. Nevertheless, lots of people who aren't as informed as you are now have some very strange ideas about Islam, Christianity, and Judaism.

Some of that has been deliberate. There are folks today, for example, arguing that the deaths of 6 million Jews during the Nazi rule in Germany never happened simply because they don't like Jews. They make that claim despite overwhelming evidence of the tragedy on film, in writing, and in testimony from survivors and participants.

Other people have attacked political candidates because of their religious views. During his 1960 presidential campaign, John F. Kennedy, a Roman Catholic, had to defend his right to believe as he wished, even though he lived in a country that enshrined the concept of freedom of religion. Senator Joseph Lieberman, an Orthodox Jew, ran into the same problem in his 2000 vice-presidential campaign. In some countries, only members of the state-supported religion can run for office.

The only way to reduce tension between people is to counter misconceptions. Here are ten to start with.

Judaism Struggles against Anti-Semitism

Isolated in a largely Christian world, Jews have been misunderstood and targeted for centuries. Not until the 1800s were they accorded equal rights in many European countries. *Anti-Semitism* (strong prejudice against Jews) remains a serious problem worldwide, probably because of some of these misconceptions:

Jews belong to a separate race

This *canard* (a lie told to give reason to do harm) fueled the Nazis, who insisted their "race" was superior to all others. Jews simply belong to a religion. Besides, as any geneticist will tell you, there is only one human race. We are 99.9 percent identical.

Recent DNA testing has indicated that all males can be traced back to an individual who lived about 150,000 years ago; all females to a woman who lived about 250,000 years ago. In short, we are all cousins.

Jews want to take over the world

This idiocy became the rage with the publication in the early 1900s of the forged *Protocols of the Elders of Zion* that "showed" how Jews were supposedly plotting world domination.

The text was originally from an 1868 novel, and then copied by the Russian secret police looking to blame someone for the country's problems before the rise of Communism. It got some mileage in the United States until the hoax was exposed.

These days, Jews are having a hard enough time keeping Israel afloat, much less trying to take on the whole world. Besides, they represent less than 1 percent of the world's population.

Jews killed Jesus

Historians can't figure out when Jesus died, but the Gospels do agree on one fact: Jesus was crucified. That means the Jews didn't do it. Crucifixion is not a Jewish method of capital punishment. Romans crucified people; Jews stoned victims to death. (For an explanation of why the Romans wanted Jesus dead, head back to Chapter 5.)

Christianity Focuses on Fundamentals

It's hard to believe, but there are still some misconceptions about Christianity. Even Christians can sometimes get confused. Here are some basic areas of misunderstanding:

Christians think God will solve their problems

No, sorry. God provides help in times of trouble, a guide to a proper path to follow, and a beacon for the future, but no religion offers a panacea.

Only good Christians go to heaven

A basic tenet of Christianity is that sins can be forgiven. Otherwise, heaven would likely be a very forlorn place.

Christians believe the only way through the Pearly Gates is to have your sins forgiven and that Jesus is the only one who can do that.

A person who is "born again" enjoys a miraculous, dramatic feeling

Born again refers to people who, though possibly raised Christian, had no real acceptance of Jesus until later in life. As such, they accepted him more fully on the second try. Maybe some people see doves and hear choirs of angels, but for most people, the process is usually one of slow realization.

Believers would like this one to be true, but, as with Islam and Judaism, people don't always heed the spirit of the faith. Think of those failures to follow Jesus as part of a long journey toward whatever perfection each of us is capable of.

Islam Emerges to Slow Understanding

You'd figure that any religion some 1,400 or so years old would have become pretty well known by now. That's just not the case. Many Westerners probably didn't know much about Islam — outside of history books — until modern technology in the 20th century began to part what had been a dark veil. Islam didn't even become a world religion until then. As a result, many misconceptions about the faith still linger.

Muslims are violent

Peace is a pretty elusive human desire, but the name of the religion, Islam, is derived from a root word meaning "peace." The Koran does endorse fighting to preserve the home, but not to excess.

War is supposed to be the final option and can be waged only under rigorous conditions detailed in the Koran. Politicians and those with a separate agenda have created a distorted view of Islam.

All Muslims are Arabs

Today, about 1.2 billion people from every part of the world consider themselves Muslims. The largest Muslim community is in Indonesia, and most Muslims live east of Pakistan. The United States is home to about 6 million Muslims. Only about 18 percent of Muslims live in the Arab world.

The religion was born among Arabs, but quickly absorbed Persians, Egyptians, Greeks, and people from many more cultures. In time, it lost much of its Arabic nature.

Muslims don't believe in Jesus or other prophets

Muslims consider Jesus one of God's greatest messengers to mankind. They also accept Moses and the prophets of the Old Testament. However, they, like Jews, don't believe Jesus is the final prophet or God incarnate, as Christians do.

Muslims worship a different God

To Muslims, there is only one god — the same God worshipped by Jews and Christians.

Chapter 20

Ten Films Drawn from Biblical Accounts

In This Chapter

▶ Summarizing some movies with religious themes

▶ Considering their box office draws

▶ Revisiting some of the controversies

The Bible has been a rich source of ideas for Hollywood. Starting as early as 1912 with *The Star of Bethlehem,* in which 200 actors retold the birth of Jesus in just 15 minutes, studios have been producing so many films based on biblical stories that no list could be complete.

Few such films are based on Muhammad for several reasons:

✔ Islam rejects any images of Muhammad.

✔ Islam had little place in Hollywood because the studios and performers were virtually all Christian and Jewish.

✔ There were no ready audiences for such films.

Here are some of the best-known films that draw their plots directly from biblical stories. We didn't include stories that used biblical characters, like *Ben-Hur,* because those films don't retell biblical tales. That also eliminated films like *Oh, God* and *Bruce Almighty.* God is a character in both, but neither are biblical stories brought to life.

That means that many films on this list are older. Movie studios these days aren't as interested in retelling biblical tales. Still, all the movies listed here can be seen on television throughout the year.

We chose the films in this chapter based on sales and, well, because we like them.

The Ten Commandments

With a title like *The Ten Commandments*, viewers know they're in for a good Bible story. This 1956 epic starred Charlton Heston as the graying prophet Moses who was determined to force Pharaoh Ramses II (played by Yul Brynner) to let the Jews leave Egypt. Directed by Cecil B. DeMille, the film earned close to $900 million and was the top seller among movies with a religious story until it was surpassed by *The Passion of the Christ* in 2004.

King of Kings

The 1961 movie *King of Kings* was considered a failure and was the only MGM religious film initially to lose money. However, this account of Jesus's life has continued to earn money and has more than returned its original $6 million investment.

Directed by Nicholas Ray, this film contrasts Jesus's work as a preacher and healer with the fiery antics of rebels opposing the Romans.

Faithfully following the biblical account of Jesus's life, the movie includes solemn narration by famed director Orson Welles and features Jeffrey Hunter in the title role. At 33, Hunter was so youthful looking that critics laughed at his appearance.

Director Cecil B. DeMille produced an earlier version in 1927.

The Greatest Story Ever Told

The last great religious epic, this 1965 movie was a grand retelling of the life of Jesus. *The Greatest Story Ever Told* flopped at first, earning only $12 million against a $25 million cost. However, it has gained in popularity ever since and is a Christmas staple.

Charlton Heston plays John the Baptist. Heston was one of an array of actors and actresses to take cameo roles. Western he-man John Wayne, for example, played a Roman centurion. Others who appeared include Telly Savalas, who went on to star as a TV detective; comedian Ed Wynn; Oscar winner Sidney Poitier; and actors Roddy McDowell and Claude Rains.

The film was nominated for five Academy Awards, but didn't win.

Jesus Christ Superstar

Based on the 1970 musical *Jesus Christ Superstar* by composer Andrew Lloyd Webber and lyricist Timothy Rice, this 1973 film retells the final days of Jesus's life. It updated the stage show with new songs and dialogue designed to appease Christian audiences, but failed.

The movie was severely criticized because the plot is told from the viewpoint of Judas, the man accused of selling out Jesus. The story also doesn't deal with Jesus's resurrection and adamantly insists Jesus was nothing more than a man.

The show started as an album before moving onto the stage and screen. At one time, *Jesus Christ Superstar* was the longest-running musical in English stage history.

One interesting side note: The actor who played Peter struggled to find additional roles on the big screen. He finally quit, changed his name, and became a successful actor and director in the pornography business.

The Passion of the Christ

This controversial 2004 film follows the last 12 hours of Jesus's life as depicted in the Gospels and in the writings of a nun who lived around the start of the 19th century. Directed by Mel Gibson, *The Passion of the Christ* was nominated for three Academy Awards. The actors, largely unknown, spoke in Aramaic, Latin, and Hebrew.

Gibson was severely criticized by Christians and Jews alike. Christians, particularly Catholics, objected to his very conservative views; Jews were upset by the perceived anti-Semitism of the production. The director denied any anti-Jewish feelings, but didn't help his cause any when he launched into an anti-Semitic tirade after his arrest for drunken driving a few years later.

The film earned well over $600 million worldwide and was the highest-grossing R-rated film ever made. In addition, the movie's soundtrack was a top seller.

The Prince of Egypt

The 1998 animated film *The Prince of Egypt* follows the story of Moses through his eventful life. Complete with songs, the film won wide acclaim, although it was banned in several Muslim countries because of what was perceived as an anti-Egyptian script. Egyptians have never been fond of the Jewish story of Exodus. (One pharaoh in the third century BC even authorized a historian to write a book refuting the account.)

One of the most expensive animated films ever made, *The Prince of Egypt* featured the speaking talents of some heavyweight actors, including Val Kilmer, Ralph Fiennes, Michelle Pfeiffer, Sandra Bullock, Jeff Goldblum, Danny Glover, Patrick Stewart, Helen Mirren, Steve Martin, and Martin Short.

The Last Temptation of Christ

Perhaps the most controversial of all depictions of Jesus's life, *The Last Temptation of Christ* was released in 1988 and is based on a 1951 book. Author Nikos Kazantzakis wanted to depict how Jesus faced normal human temptations — including sex — and achieved glory by rejecting them.

The sexual aspects outraged believers. Director Martin Scorcese, who was nominated for an Oscar, added a disclaimer that the movie was not intended to be an exact re-creation of the events in the Bible.

David Bowie, better known for his singing, played Pontius Pilate, the man who condemns Jesus to the cross. Willem Dafoe played the title character.

Solomon and Sheba

Solomon and Sheba tells the biblical account of a visiting queen who falls for King Solomon. The story involves an effort by King Solomon's brother to regain the throne. He hopes the seductive queen will open the door for him. The plot is loosely based on a brief mention in the Bible that the Queen of Sheba visited Solomon.

Italian bombshell Gina Lollobrigida played Sheba in this 1959 epic, and Yul Brynner played the king. Tyronne Power originally was cast as the male lead but died on the set from a heart attack while filming a sword fight halfway though production.

David and Bathsheba

The sordid biblical tale of King David lusting after the wife of a neighbor came to life in the 1951 film *David and Bathsheba*. It has never been considered a great film, but continues to make occasional appearances on television.

Gregory Peck played the wayward king who sees Bathsheba (played by Susan Hayward) in her bath, falls in love with her, and has her husband killed. The story is based on the biblical account. In the Bible, Bathsheba and David's son is Solomon, the second king of Israel.

Samson and Delilah

First released in 1949, this movie told the story of the biblical strongman who brought down a Philistine temple after being captured by his wife's treachery.

Samson and Delilah earned great acclaim, mostly because of the beauty of Hedy Lamarr, who played Delilah, and the spectacular scene where the falling temple crushes the unsuspecting Philistines.

Cecil B. DeMille handled the directing chores. He was outraged when Victor Mature, who played Samson, refused to wrestle a tame lion. As a result, those scenes look very fake.

Chapter 21

Ten-Plus Ways Religion Influences the World

For all of us, religion has been a part of our lives from birth. Even in homes that practice no religion, religious ideas inevitably form our outlook on life.

Figures drawn from the Bible and Koran permeate our cultures, providing examples and setting the tone for our behavior. Movies have helped us visualize biblical figures. Although Islam bans the use of images, the religion itself has been an integral part of movies set in the Middle East, such as *Lawrence of Arabia.*

Other religions came up with the idea of souls, gods, and afterlife. Monotheistic faiths gave us such concepts as reward and punishment after death; redemption; a supreme deity who cares for us; and a sense of purpose.

This chapter examines how monotheistic religions have influenced us through culture and created the structure of our societies.

Read All About It: Literature

Authors have long been part of religion's authority. Early people held writing in great reverence, and scribes were integrated into the early religious establishment from the start. Writing itself was a religious function. The letters of the alphabet even carried religious connotations. The respect for writing, especially anything religious, was one reason the first book ever printed in Europe was the Bible. The reverence felt today for sacred texts is a remnant of that view.

Most writing through the centuries, whether in philosophy, science, or other fields, regularly focused on religious themes. This was true in Europe as well as in the Middle East. Writers enhanced religious tales by bringing them to life. While monks dutifully copied holy Scriptures, writers such as Sir Thomas More and Peter Abelard broadcast religious ideas.

Novelists also followed suit, infusing their books with religious concepts. From Chaucer's *Canterbury Tales* and Dante's *Inferno,* to Shakespeare's *The Merchant of Venice* and Marlowe's *The Jew of Malta* through modern times, authors have feverishly mined the rich deposits of religious ideas for their themes and plots. Many of them are still read. For example, Muslim poet Jalalud'din Rumi, who lived in the 1200s, remains extremely popular, especially in the United States.

Music as an Expression of Faith

Perhaps no area of human endeavor has been more enhanced by religion than music has. David, the great king of Israel, is introduced as a musician. Musical notes still exist in the Bible: not "do, re, mi," but the Hebrew versions which depict *staccato* or long, drawn-out sounds.

Early Jewish services featured music, and they still do today. Early Christians borrowed the idea for their services in churches. The Mormon Tabernacle Choir stands as a modern example of a renowned religious choir, as does the Vienna Boys Choir. Gregorian chants continue to reverberate through cathedrals and halls.

Types of music reflect religious ideas. Slaves in America put their laments to music, creating spirituals and gospel music. That music infiltrated all aspects of American music, leading to jazz and the blues.

Today, the Grammy awards include a category for the top composers and singers in the field of religious music. The Gospel Music Association in 1969 began to recognize the spiritual and artistic efforts of Christian musicians with the Dove awards.

It's virtually impossible to travel through much of the United States without finding a radio station playing religious music. Even mainstream artists have picked up on the concept. The Beatles's George Harrison's great hit, for example, was "My Sweet Lord," which asks to be able to see God soon.

On Broadway, *Jesus Christ Superstar* and *Godspell* have been successes, but religious ideas — including prayers to a deity who oversees life and is concerned about each individual — infuse many other musicals.

Politics and Religion: Not Always Easy to Separate

Religion plays a major role in the political life of many countries. In England, for example, only an Anglican could be elected to office through the mid-1800s. Religion often affects success in a campaign. The United States has never elected a Jew or a Muslim to be president or vice-president.

Early presidential campaigns often focused on candidates' religion. Thomas Jefferson, one of the United States' greatest presidents, faced one of his most severe crises when he said that another person's beliefs were of no interest to him.

The link between politics and religion remains strong in the United States country despite a strong belief of separation of church and state. The *Bible Belt,* a stretch of rigidly religious people throughout the southern part of the United States, continues to influence elections. The late Rev. Jerry Falwell led the Silent Majority, a coalition of conservative Christians whose efforts helped elect presidents who backed their views.

Candidates always try to reach religious sects for good reason. Jews, as a group, vote in higher percentages. Studies have shown that African Americans are more likely than other people to take religion into account when deciding who to vote for.

Issues with religious tinges, such as abortion, have dominated political dialogue for much of the nation's history. Slavery was both condemned and supported through the use of biblical text. The American Civil War, which led to the end of slavery, was seen as a moral fight. "The Battle Hymn of the Republic" was the theme song, in which Julia Ward Howe noted, "Our God is marching on."

World War I was heralded as a great Crusade, drawing comparisons of the battles between Christians and Muslims that took place more than 700 years earlier. Indeed, countries at war have always invoked their deities. The claim by conservative Muslims that America represents the Great Satan is countered by America's view that the U.S. is divinely blessed. God, after all, is always fighting on "our" side.

Bringing the Bible to Life through Art

For centuries, art was the willing tool of religion. Greek sculptors created friezes on temples that depicted the stories of the gods. Their statues were of deities in human form.

Although Jews and Muslims shunned images, Christians adopted the age-old concept. Faced with an illiterate audience, Church leaders turned to artists to portray the great events in the Bible.

No nuance was overlooked. For example, halos weren't allowed in early drawings because they had been a pagan symbol. Then, artists were allowed to paint halos as squares to distinguish them from the round ones over pagan heads. Finally, when paganism was discredited, round halos could appear over saints' heads.

Some of the greatest art ever produced is based on religious topics: Michelangelo's statues of David and Moses and his painting of biblical scenes on the Sistine Chapel's ceiling; Leonardo da Vinci's fresco of the Last Supper; and seemingly endless architectural masterpieces.

Virtually all artwork created during the Renaissance was religion related. Religious figures were often the patrons who could pay the artist. Community leaders who wanted to adorn their homes also chose religious topics to underline their piety.

Recording Biblical Stories on Film

Movies are the modern version of paintings. Using a broad canvas with lavish colors, films present images of Abraham, Moses, Jesus, and many more religious figures. The characters are depicted with loving warmth, endorsing the canonical stories.

Even when they don't retell a biblical tale, films often present ideas that endorse monotheistic religious views. Some of the religious ideas that provide movie themes include:

- ✔ **Triumph of good:** The prophets taught that God ultimately will reward those who do good, regardless of setbacks. Many movies end on an uplifting note for this reason.

- ✔ **Existence of evil:** Ultimately, the idea of evil is religious. In Christianity and Islam, evil is personified as the Devil. He resembles Pan, the Greek god of the fields, who came complete with hooves, tail, and horns.

  Without religion, horror films couldn't thrive. After all, Dracula is eventually vanquished by a cross.

- ✔ **Purpose:** Jews, Christians, and Muslims accept God's presence in their lives. History is a function of God's will. Therefore, everything that happens has a reason, whether or not we can fathom what it is. This idea comforts the bereaving and provides an explanation for the unexpected. Films often portray characters trying to discern the purpose behind an action.

- ✔ **Conscience:** God's presence ensures that people feel a twinge of guilt when doing something wrong. Conscience then motivates people to reform their lives or confess their actions. Countless movie plots revolve around the villain reforming his life to quiet his conscience. James Bond, for example, always wiggles out of a difficult situation because someone with a conscience helps him.

- ✔ **Heaven:** Previous ideas of the afterlife, as discussed in Chapter 16, were limited to broad fields and shadowy figures. Monotheistic religions conjured up instead a heaven that movies often portray as a cloud-filled, ethereal place that is home to loved ones.

- ✔ **Hell:** Monotheistic religions didn't invent eternal damnation, but the idea has been played up in multiple films. In the 1990 film *Ghost,* for example, dark figures carry off the villain, as the hero, played by Patrick Swayze, watches.

Movies also reinforce the importance of bringing a spiritual outlook to life. Although the average American sees only about ten hours of movies a year, the movies have created their own religious platform. As technology and science seem to overwhelm people, audiences are drawn to movies like *The Matrix* and *Star Wars,* which offer spiritual solutions.

Spreading the Word through Television

Television has had only 60 or so years to join the religion bandwagon, but it has taken the lead. That's because television needs material 24 hours a day, and programmers are always looking for something to fill the airwaves.

Today, some cable channels are devoted to religious topics all day. You can watch Christian, Jewish, and Muslim programming to your heart's content. Religious events, such as church services, the pope's Christmas Mass, and the like, appear regularly on local network stations.

Television also has been more aggressive in addressing religious concepts such as the brotherhood of men and the idea that we are all God's children. *Bridget Loves Bernie,* for example, was a short-lived 1970s television show that had a Catholic woman married to a Jewish man at a time when such intermarriage was considered unthinkable.

Viewers of *Barney Miller* were jolted when Hal Linden's character commented that he was Jewish, because religion rarely made an appearance on the airwaves. Characters might have Christmas trees, but they'd make no mention of religion in their lives. Linden's comment changed that.

In more recent years, *Touched by an Angel* and *Highway to Heaven* have continued to broadcast religious ideas through dramas. That's true around the world. Shows in Israel portray Jewish ideals, while those in Muslim countries reflect Islamic themes. All these efforts brought forth the religious concepts engrained in the monotheistic faiths.

Seeking Insight into God through Science

Early scientists like Roger Bacon, a monk, were hoping to understand the mind of God when they began their rudimentary experiments in the Middle Ages. That was true for scholars in the Islamic world as well. They were convinced that research would help unravel the mystery and confirm God's involvement in the world.

Religious scientists continued to want to learn more even as their studies began to undermine cherished views. Religion and science collided in the 1500s and have been ramming into each other ever since. For example, Polish astronomer Copernicus demonstrated in the 1530s that the Earth circled the sun, not vice versa. He waited to release his findings until he was dying so he could avoid persecution by Church authorities who disagreed with his findings. Galileo, an Italian astronomer, was silenced by the Church about 80 years later for declaring other planets had moons.

The debates today over evolution versus creation are simply a continuation of the deep-rooted discussion that harkens back to bygone eras. Ironically, today, more-conservative religious groups are determined to stop the march of science that their forerunners initiated.

Education: Wearing a Skullcap and a Thinking Cap

All education at one time was religious. In Western countries, where religion has been separated from government, that's no longer true, but in the Muslim world, the Koran remains the primary textbook in the classroom.

Jews learned to read and write so they could study the holy Scripture. Christians pored over the texts to appreciate God's love.

Early universities always required religion courses. Yale and Harvard, two of the oldest and greatest American universities, were started to train clergy. Not until the 1920s was the curriculum changed to reflect the movement away from education to a more liberal arts curriculum. That forced some religions to create their own schools for higher education. Oral Roberts University and Liberty University are just two examples.

Today, the burgeoning home-schooling movement is fueled by conservative Christians and Jews who believe secular schools are misleading their children. They point to studies that link education and religion. A Harvard University researcher found that youths who frequently attended religious services were five times less likely to skip school, compared with peers who seldom or never attended services.

Some Muslim nations have carried the idea of religious-backed education to the extreme. In Iran, for example, which is led by a conservative Muslim group, Islam rules every aspect of education. Teaching the Koran is compulsory from the first year in primary school. To get into a classroom, teachers must pass a religious exam that covers Islamic rules, prayers, and the Koran. Students are taught that if they don't obey the rules, they'll burn in hell.

Being Holy Improves Your Health and Well-Being

A variety of studies of religion's impact on society have abounded in recent years since the election of a faith-based president. Those studies have found

- ✔ Regular attendance at religious services is linked to healthy, stable family life, strong marriages, and well-behaved children.

- ✔ Religious practice reduces the incidences of domestic abuse, crime, substance abuse, and addiction.

- ✔ Religious practice improves physical and mental health, longevity, and education achievement.

- ✔ Women who are more religious are less likely to experience divorce or separation than their less-religious peers.

- ✔ Marriages in which both spouses frequently attend religious services are 2.4 times less likely to end in divorce than marriages in which neither spouse worships. Those who view their religious beliefs as "very important" are 22 percent less likely to divorce than those for whom religious beliefs are only "somewhat important."

- ✔ Fathers' frequency of religious attendance was a stronger predictor of their involvement in one-on-one activities with their children than were employment and income.

- ✔ Regular attendance at religious services has been linked to fewer incidents of domestic abuse. The more someone attends services, the less likely they are to be abusive.

- ✔ Of course, religion helps determine whether you support abortion rights and birth control, and, in Muslim countries, female circumcisions.

Social Welfare: Doing unto Others

Humans are social creatures, and religion has made it possible for us to live together in something resembling harmony. Judaism, Christianity, and Islam all stress charity. Jews stood out among pagans by lending their support for their fellow believers. Christianity emphasized that even more, developing hospitals and other ways of aiding people. Islam made almsgiving one of the pillars of the faith (see Chapter 8).

Studies have shown that religious respondents were 15 percent more likely to report having tender, concerned feelings for the disadvantaged. Religious individuals were 40 percent more likely than their secular counterparts to give money to charities and more than twice as likely to volunteer.

Religious institutions have long led charitable efforts. A University of Pennsylvania study found that congregations are almost universally involved in charitable outreach. Jews typically are at the forefront of civil rights efforts.

Disagreeing about Environmental Issues

The environment is one significant issue that has split religions. More liberal groups have endorsed efforts to improve the environment, quoting the Bible that the world has been given to mankind to care for.

On the other hand, conservative Christian groups argue that global warming and other potential environmental disasters only hasten the return of Jesus and the end of the world.

In Islam, the same split exists. The holy texts stress *tawhid* (unity), *khilafah* (trusteeship), and *akhirah* (accountability, or, literally, the hereafter), which serve as the pillars of Islam's strong environmental ethic.

However, more-conservative believers argue that environmentalism is another form of Western control, intended to keep Islam from developing and Muslims from realizing their economic potential. They believe that population controls really are aimed at limiting Muslim modernization and keeping technology in Western hands.

As a result, religion is both a driving and a retarding force when it comes to environmental issues.

Part VI
Appendixes

ANCIENT MOSES

MODERN MOSES

In this part . . .

Appendix A provides a timeline so you can get an idea of when events discussed in this book happened. Appendix B attempts to trace Abraham's family tree back to Adam, the first man, and then ahead to Jesus and Muhammad.

Appendix A

Timelines for Religions

• •

*J*udaism, Christianity, and Islam all may have started with Abraham, but they don't follow the same calendar.

- ✔ Jews use a lunar calendar dated from creation, which they think occurred maybe 6,700 or so years ago.

- ✔ Muslims also use a lunar calendar, but they begin in AD 622, the year Muhammad led his ragtag band of followers to Medina to regroup and then conquer.

- ✔ Christians divided time into two parts: before and after the birth of Jesus. The year 2008 represents 2,008 years since Jesus was born. Unfortunately, the monk who came up with this idea forgot the year 0.

Under the circumstances, figuring out when something happened can get very tricky. Fortunately, most of the world has adopted Christianity's approach to telling time. That's the system we use in the timelines in this chapter.

Some of the dates are only guesses. That's because not a lot of records survive long under the pressure of time. Even rocks crumble; walls of religious structures do, too.

Fortunately, modern archaeologists have come up with some techniques for dating objects:

- ✔ **In situ:** Dating is based on location. A piece of ceramic found under a wall probably is as old as the wall or older. It's not likely to be younger. Many objects can be dated around the same time that way.

- ✔ **Carbon dating:** Anything that lives absorbs carbon. Plants and animals are carbon based. Carbon comes in two forms: Carbon 12, with 12 electrons and protons; and Carbon 14, with two extra protons. Carbon 14 is unstable and begins to deteriorate after the living thing dies. About half of the carbon disappears in 6,000 years. That's called a *half-life*.

> After World War II, scientists figured out a mathematical formula for carbon dating; if you know how much carbon is present, and how much there should be, you can figure out how much time has elapsed.
>
> ✔ **Designs:** Every culture had its own way of making and decorating ceramics and clothing. Any object decorated in a specific way must belong to that culture, which existed in a certain time and place.
>
> ✔ **Language:** Terms that we use today may not have the same meaning years from now. As a result, any documents that survive can be checked for word choice, grammar, and other clues to its dating. That's equally true with paintings on walls, like the ones on Egyptians temples.

As a result, with some minor exceptions, most historians agree to a timeline that tracks religions from their origins into modern times.

What follows are timelines for each religion. Some of the dates are estimates, but the sequences provide a reasonably clear view of the paths Judaism, Christianity, and Islam followed to modern times.

All dates before the birth of Jesus (BC) are estimates.

Judaism

BC

1900	Abraham lives in Chaldea.
1850	Isaac heads the family.
1800	Jacob has 12 sons.
1700	Jacob's family living in Egypt.
1600	Israelites enslaved in Egypt.
1300	Moses leads slaves to freedom, receives Ten Commandments.
1250	Joshua leads conquest of Canaan.
1100	Saul is king.
1050	David is king.
1000	Solomon becomes king, builds First Temple.
950	Country split into two kingdoms, Israel and Judah.

722	Assyrians overturn Israel; ten tribes are lost.
597	Babylonians conquer Judah, destroy Temple.
538	Jews return from Babylonian exile.
332	Greeks conquer Israel.
167	Maccabees revolt against Syrians.
142	Independent Jewish state founded.
63	Romans invade Israel.
38	Herod the Great begins reign.

AD

66	Jewish revolt against Rome begins.
70	Jerusalem conquered by Romans; Second Temple destroyed.
130	Bar Kochba launches final Jewish revolt against Rome.
219	Talmud compiled.
1492	Jews expelled from Spain.
1648	Cossacks lead massacres in Eastern Europe.
1654	First Jews arrive in America.
1887	Conservative Movement founded in America.
1897	First Zionist Congress meets.
1917	British take control of Palestine.
1933	Hitler comes to power in Germany.
1948	State of Israel declared.
1956	Egypt and Israel fight war.
1967	Israel wins Six-Day War, unifies Jerusalem.
1964	Palestine Liberation Organization founded.
1973	Yom Kippur War ends in a stalemate.
1977	Egyptian President Anwar Sadat visits Jerusalem, paving the way for peace.
1982	Israel invades Lebanon and attacks PLO bases there.
1987	Palestinians revolt against Israeli control.

Christianity

BC

4	Jesus born.

AD

27	John the Baptist appears.
30–33	Jesus crucified.
50	Paul begins to write epistles.
62	James the Just stoned to death.
70	Gospel of Mark written.
85	Gospels of Matthew and Luke written.
100	Gospel of John written; book of Revelation written.
144	Marcion excommunicated for rejecting Jewish holy books.
313	Emperor Constantine orders official toleration of Christianity.
325	Council of Nicaea summarizes Orthodox belief.
380	Jerome begins work on Old Testament.
1054	Eastern Orthodox and Western Roman Catholic faiths split permanently.
1095	Crusades begin.
1453	Turks take Constantinople, ending the Byzantine era.
1517	Martin Luther initiates Protestant Reformation.
1534	Church of England breaks with papal authority.
1854	Rome establishes the Immaculate Conception dogma.
1870	Papal infallibility becomes Roman dogma.
1948	World Council of Churches formed.
1962	Vatican Council II modernizes the Roman Catholic Church.

Islam

AD

570	Muhammad born in Mecca.
595	Muhammad marries Khadija.
611	Muhammad begins to receive revelations.
622	Muhammad and followers flee to Medina.
630	Muhammad and followers conquer Mecca.
632	Muhammad dies.
634	Islamic soldiers begin to move into Egypt, Syria, and Persia.
650	Text of Koran established.
656	Ali becomes Caliph.
680	Shi'ites separate from Sunnis.
700s	Islam moves into Europe and India.
1095	Christian Crusaders arrive.
1215	Saladin leads reconquest of Jerusalem.
1380	Ottoman Turks take control of Middle East.
1798	Napoleon invades Egypt.
1919	Ottoman Empire divided among European powers.
1928	Muslim Brotherhood founded.
1948	Israel and Jordan created.
1954	Egypt freed of colonial rule.
1979	Iranian revolution creates Muslim state.
1988	Taliban takes control of Afghanistan.
1990	Iraq invades Kuwait.

Appendix B

Genealogies

● ●

*I*n 1976, author Alex Haley published a book called *Roots,* which described his efforts to trace his family history from the present day back through the years of slavery in the American South to its origins in Africa. His fictionalized account, also presented in a television miniseries, was a phenomenal success that inspired millions of people to seek their own family stories.

Haley's tale resonated so well because of the timing: 1976 marked the United States' bicentennial and reminded people of history. Also, his research found no great leaders or famous people perched on his family tree's branches. His ancestors were ordinary people who lived anonymous lives, something that almost everyone could understand.

Despite the public's fascination, Haley's efforts probably drew a yawn from religions. Genealogies are nothing new in religious history. One rabbi in Daytona Beach, Florida, insists he can trace his family back several thousand years. Many Jewish families carefully preserved records of their ancestors. That's true in Christianity, too, where the Church of Jesus Christ of Latter-day Saints is known for its extensive genealogical records stored in Salt Lake City, Utah.

Christianity has a special reason for wanting to know what branches go where. The founder of the faith, Jesus, supposedly has blood lines reaching to Adam, the first man in the Bible. He also is related to King David, which adds strength to religious claims that Jesus is the Messiah, or the anointed King of Israel. Several prophets said the Messiah would come from the line of David.

Islam, too, wants to demonstrate that Muhammad is the direct descendant of Ishmael, Abraham's oldest son. That can only be done by examining records and finding a link through long-gone great-great-great-great-... (you get the idea) grandparents.

This appendix is an attempt to reconstruct Abraham's genealogy, leading to the three religions that call him Dad. We've eliminated lines that don't lead directly to major figures in biblical history. So, you can follow the line started by Adam all the way to Jesus. A separate line shows how Abraham's son Ishmael is the forefather of Muhammad.

Some of the names that appear on both lists are spelled differently. That was particularly true in Muhammad's genealogy where Arabic versions of names appear. For example, the Arabic name for Abraham is *Ibrahim*. To aid in understanding, a few names have been changed to reflect more familiar English versions.

Unfortunately, at this late date, historians have no way of demonstrating the validity of these genealogies. You'll just have to accept them at face value. After all, based on the Jewish calendar, Adam lived around 6,700 years ago. Haley had enough trouble finding his family records back a few hundred years. Imagine if he had to probe even farther back.

These lists are mostly conjecture on the part of pious people who really wanted to find a great person smiling back from the family portrait.

Judaism and Christianity

Adam to Abraham

Adam

Cain

    Enoch

    Irad

    Mehujael

    Methusael

    Lemach

    Jabal

    Jubal

    Tubal-Cain

    Naamah

Abel

   Seth

   Enoch

   Canaan

   Maleleel

   Jared

   Methusalah

   Lemach

   Noah

Children of Noah

Ham

Japheth

Shem

   Elam

   Asshur

   Arphaxad

   Cannan

   Shelah

   Eber

   Peleg

   Reu

   Selug

Nahor

Terach

Abraham

Abraham to David

Isaac

Jacob

    Simeon

    Reuben

    Gad

    Dan

    Asher

    Levi

    Issachar

    Zebulin

    Naphtali

    Joseph

    Benjamin

    Judah

        Judas

        Phares

        Esrom

        Aram

        Aminadab

Naason

Salmon

Boaz

Obed

Jesse

David

David to Jesus (Matthew's version)

Solomon

Rehoboam

Abijah

Asa

Jehoshaphat

Uzziah

Jotham

Ahaz

Hezekiah

Manasseh

Amon

Josiah

Jeconiah

Shealtiel

Zerubbabel

Abiud

Eliakim

Azor

Sadok

Achim

Eliud

Eleazar

Matthan

Jacob

Joseph

Jesus

Islam

Adam to Ishmael

Adam

Seth

Yaanish

Qaynan

Mahlil

Yard

Akhnookh

Mattooshalakh

Lemech

Noah

Shem

Arfakhshadh

Shaalikh

Aybar

Faalikh

Raa'oo

Saaroogh

Nahur

Terach

Abraham

Ishmael

Ishmael to Muhammad

Naabit

Yashjub

Ya'rub

Tayrah

Naahoor

Muqawwam

Udd

'Adnaan

Ma'add

Nizaar

Mudar

Ilyaas

Mudrika

Khuzayma

Kinaana

al-Nadr

Malik

Fihr

Ghaalib

Lu'ayy

Ka'b

Murra

Kilaab

Qusayy

'Abdu-Manaaf

Haashim

'Abdul-Muttalib

'Abdullaah

Muhammad

Index